Routledge Revivals

Health and the International Tourist

The rapid increase in the demand for international tourism has led a growing number of people to seek holidays and travel experiences in both developed and developing countries. Yet little interest has been shown in the interface between tourism and health. *Health and the International Tourist*, first published in 1996, examines key relationships between travel, tourism and health. Particular attention is given to the behaviour and lifestyle of tourists and approaches to reducing the health risks associated with international travel and tourism.

This was the first book to address tourist health in an interdisciplinary manner, with contributions from professionals in medicine, health promotion, the travel and tourism industry and tourism researchers. It will provide a sound basis for further research and the development of health promotion strategies, and will be of interest to students of health and tourism.

Health and the International Tourist

Edited by

Stephen Clift

and

Stephen J. Page

First published in 1996
by Routledge

This edition first published in 2015 by Routledge
2 Park Square, Milton Park, Abingdon, Oxon, OX14 4RN
and by Routledge
711 Third Avenue, New York, NY 10017

Routledge is an imprint of the Taylor & Francis Group, an informa business

© 1996 Stephen Clift and Stephen J. Pages

The rights of Stephen Clift and Stephen J. Page to be identified as editors of this work has been asserted by them in accordance with sections 77 and 78 of the Copyright, Designs and Patents Act 1988.

All rights reserved. No part of this book may be reprinted or reproduced or utilised in any form or by any electronic, mechanical, or other means, now known or hereafter invented, including photocopying and recording, or in any information storage or retrieval system, without permission in writing from the publishers.

Publisher's Note
The publisher has gone to great lengths to ensure the quality of this reprint but points out that some imperfections in the original copies may be apparent.

Disclaimer
The publisher has made every effort to trace copyright holders and welcomes correspondence from those they have been unable to contact.

ISBN 13: 978-1-138-88947-7 (hbk)
ISBN 13: 978-1-315-71286-4 (ebk)
ISBN 13: 978-1-138-88949-1 (pbk)

Health and the international tourist

Edited by
Stephen Clift and Stephen J. Page

London and New York

First published 1996
by Routledge
11 New Fetter Lane, London EC4P 4EE

Simultaneously published in the USA and Canada
by Routledge
29 West 35th Street, New York, NY 10001

© 1996 Stephen Clift and Stephen J. Page
Individual chapters © 1996 the respective authors

Typeset in Times by
Florencetype Ltd., Stoodleigh, Devon

Printed and bound in Great Britain by
T.J. Press (Padstow) Ltd, Padstow, Cornwall

All rights reserved. No part of this book may be reprinted or reproduced or utilized in any form or by any electronic, mechanical, or other means, now known or hereafter invented, including photocopying and recording, or in any information storage or retrieval system, without permission in writing from the publishers.

British Library Cataloguing in Publication Data
A catalogue record for this book is available from the British Library

Library of Congress Cataloging in Publication Data
Health and the international tourist / edited by Stephen Clift and Stephen J. Page
    p.   cm. – (Issues in tourism series)
   Includes bibliographical references and index.
   ISBN 0–415–10282–0
   1. Travel–Health aspects. 2. Tourist trade–Health aspects.
   3. Travelers–Sexual behavior. I. Clift, Stephen, 1952– .
   II. Page, Stephen, 1963– . IV. Series.
   RA783.5.H399   1995
   613.6'8–dc20   95–17568
                                                                 CIP

ISBN 0–415–10282–0

Contents

List of figures	vii
List of tables	ix
Contributors	xi
Foreword	xvii
Preface	xix
Acknowledgements	xxi

1 Introduction: tourism and health   1
  Stephen Clift and Stephen J. Page

Part I Travel and health: medical perspectives

2 Travellers' health: a medical perspective   23
  Jonathan H. Cossar

3 Travellers' diarrhoea   44
  Rodney Cartwright

4 HIV/AIDS and international travel: a global perspective   67
  John D. H. Porter, Gil Lea and Bernadette Carroll

Part II Tourism, tourist behaviour and risks to health

5 Off the beaten track: the health implications of the development of special-interest tourism activities in South-East Asia and the South Pacific   89
  Brenda Rudkin and C. Michael Hall

6 Dimensions of holiday experiences and their health
   implications: a study of British tourists in Malta   108
   Nicola Clark and Stephen Clift

7 Context and culture in HIV prevention:
   the importance of holidays?   134
   Pamela Gillies and Richard Slack

8 Risk and liminality: the HIV-related socio-sexual
   interaction of young tourists   152
   Nicholas Ford and J. Richard Eiser

9 Tourism prostitution: the control and health
   implications of sex tourism in South-East Asia
   and Australia   179
   C. Michael Hall

Part III Tourism and health promotion

10 Health tourism: a business opportunity approach   199
   Eric Laws

11 Travel health promotion: advances and alliances   215
   David Stears

12 Have fun in the sun: protect yourself from skin
   damage   235
   Ros Weston

13 International tourists: a specific target group for AIDS
   prevention programmes   260
   Georg Bröring

14 Interaction to enhance mindfulness: positive strategies
   to increase tourists' awareness of HIV and sexual
   health risks on holiday   279
   Nicholas Ford, Marlene Inman and Elspeth Mathie

   General index   294
   Place index   299

Figures

1.1	The expansion of international tourism, 1950–91.	2
1.2	Sources of, and settings for, health information and services for the international tourist	9
2.1	Reports of illness in Scottish holidaymakers, 1973–85	28
2.2	Sources of pre-travel health advice for tourists	39
3.1	Areas associated with a high rate of travellers' diarrhoea	45
3.2	Subjective travellers' diarrhoea in British package holidaymakers 1984–93	54
3.3	Subjective travellers' diarrhoea in British package holidaymakers May 1991–September 1992	55
3.4	Subjective travellers' diarrhoea in British package holidaymakers showing differing seasonal variations between countries	56
3.5	Incidence of subjective travellers' diarrhoea in British package holidaymakers visiting Salou, Spain, 1986–93	61
4.1	Estimated global distribution of cumulative HIV infections in adults mid-1994	68
4.2	Advice to travellers on reducing the risk of HIV infection	82
4.3	Estimated and projected annual AIDS incidences by 'macro' region, 1980–2000	83
8.1	South-West England: location and the Torbay district	153
8.2	Conceptual framework of the Torbay survey of young tourists' sexual behaviour	160
10.1	Tourism organisation's focus on health	201

10.2 Key factors in improving holiday access for
     disabled people   211
11.1 Health promotion materials produced in the UK
     on risks associated with exposure to sun   228
11.2 Safer sex on holiday leaflet produced by the
     Gloucestershire Department of Health Promotion,
     UK   229
11.3 Department of Health's Travel Safe campaign
     materials produced in the UK in 1993/94   231
13.1 Health education materials promoting safer sex
     in the context of travel from Australia, the United
     Kingdom and Denmark   264
13.2 HIV/AIDS prevention materials produced in
     Santorini in association with the AIDS and
     Mobility Project   267

Tables

2.1 The growth in international travel, 1949–90
(in millions) 25
2.2 Infections imported to the United Kingdom,
1978–88 26
2.3 Age of travellers and reports of illness in studies
undertaken by the Communicable Diseases
(Scotland) Unit, 1973–85 27
2.4 Area visited, season and reports of illness among
Scottish tourists, 1973–85 29
2.5 Travel-associated admissions by sex and ethnic
origin to ID (infectious disease) wards, Ruchill Hospital,
Glasgow (1985) 30
2.6 Profile of travellers at risk emerging from Scottish
research 32
4.1 AIDS awareness among travellers attending the
Travel Clinic at the London Hospital for
Tropical Diseases 76
5.1 Travel-associated illness reported at the Infectious
Diseases Unit, Auckland Hospital, July–December
1989 93
6.1 Sex, age group and holiday companionship in
the sample of British tourists in Malta 115
6.2 Health problems experienced by British tourists
while on holiday in Malta 116
6.3 Responses by British tourists in Malta to items
in the Holiday Experience Questionnaire 118
6.4 Age differences in holiday experiences among
British tourists in Malta 121

6.5	Percentage levels of agreement among British tourists in Malta to three social life/relationship items by age and partnership	123
6.6	Three factors extracted from the Holiday Experience Questionnaire completed by British tourists in Malta	124
7.1	Response to the Nottingham survey on travel and health by age and sex	139
7.2	Characteristics of travellers abroad in the Nottingham survey	141
7.3	Factors emerging from the Nottingham survey associated with sexual intercourse abroad with a new partner	143
8.1	Sexual behaviour among young tourists in Torbay by sex and age group	166
8.2	Sexual propensities and attitudes of young tourists in Torbay by sexual behaviour on holiday	170
10.1	Reasons for not taking a holiday (English Tourist Board Survey 1985)	208
11.1	Main travel issues addressed by District Health Promotion Units in the UK	226
11.2	Resources used in travel health promotion by District Health Promotion Units in the UK	226
11.3	Settings where local travel health promotion has been developed in the UK	226
13.1	Publications in the 'AIDS and Mobility' database by year of publication	263
13.2	'AIDS and Mobility' network members	265

Contributors

Georg Bröring is presently working as a staff member of the European Project 'AIDS and Mobility', based at the National Committee on AIDS Control of the Netherlands. He graduated in Social Work and has a degree in Sociology/Social Anthropology. Previously, he acted as Scientific Staff Member at the Deutsche AIDS-Hilfe in Berlin. He also co-ordinated outreach activities in the framework of the Stop AIDS Project Berlin. His work at the AIDS and Mobility project is focused on AIDS prevention education aimed at mobile populations in Europe.

Bernadette Carroll was appointed as Travel Health Information Co-ordinator at the Public Health Laboratory Service Communicable Disease Surveillance Centre, London, in March 1993. She is a graduate and a registered nurse with experience in travel medicine. Before taking up her present post, she spent four years at the Hospital for Tropical Diseases, London, as a research nurse and health advisor.

Rodney Cartwright is a consultant medical microbiologist, Professor and Director of the Guildford Laboratory of the Public Health Laboratory Service. He qualified in Medicine from Birmingham and after various clinical appointments joined the Public Health Laboratory Service in 1967. For over fourteen years he has been a consultant advisor to the major British tour operators and more recently to the International Federation of Tour Operators. He regularly visits tourist areas at the request of local and national health authorities to advise on the investigation and management of gastrointestinal infections in tourists.

Nicola Clark is a health psychologist and worked as a Research Fellow on the Travel, Lifestyles and Health project formerly based at the Centre for Health Education and Research at Canterbury Christ Church College for the majority of the project. She currently works as a Research Associate in the Postgraduate Medical Centre at the University of Hull, focusing on improving contraception services.

Stephen Clift is Reader in Health Education at the Centre of Health Education and Research, Canterbury Christ Church College. He has worked in the area of HIV/AIDS and sex education for young people for eight years and has published and lectured widely on this subject. He is currently Director of the Travel, Lifestyles and Health project and is undertaking research on the health risks associated with sexual behaviour on holiday and while travelling, and the health-related behaviour of British tourists in The Gambia.

Jonathan H. Cossar is a general practitioner in Glasgow, a Research Associate at the Scottish Centre for Infection and Environmental Health (SCIEH) and an Honorary Clinical Lecturer at the University of Glasgow. He has written and lectured extensively on travel-associated illnesses, co-chaired at the first three Conferences on International Travel Medicine (Zurich, 1988; Atlanta, 1991; Paris, 1993), and is a member of the editorial group of *NewShare*, the quarterly news, views and notices from the International Society of Travel Medicine.

Richard Eiser has been Professor of Psychology at the University of Exeter since 1979. His research interests include attitudes, social cognition and health psychology, including perceptions of personal and environmental risk. His most recent book is *Attitude, Chaos and the Connective Mind*, Oxford, Blackwell, 1994.

Nicholas Ford is Senior Lecturer in the Institute of Population Studies, University of Exeter. His research interests include sexual and reproductive health and behaviour and HIV prevention strategies. As well as his collaborative work with health authorities in the South-West of England, he has been involved in research overseas in South-East Asia, West Africa and Latin America.

Pamela Gillies is a Senior Lecturer in Public Health at the University of Nottingham and a Harkness Fellow of the

Commonwealth Fund of New York. She has worked as a Consultant to the World Health Organisation's Global Programme on AIDS, designing population-based HIV prevention programmes in developing counties. She has produced and evaluated materials on sex and HIV education and facilitated the promotion of sexual health among prostitute women through NGO community development initiatives. Currently she is directing a project to prepare a European Code against discrimination and HIV/AIDS. Her research and teaching interests include cross–cultural perspectives on sexuality and health and community development responses to inequalities in health.

Michael Hall is Associate Professor and Director of the Tourism Programme and Co-Director, Centre for Tourism and Leisure Policy Research, University of Canberra, Australia. He has lectured and published widely in the tourism and recreation area and is currently undertaking research into sex tourism and the health risks associated with tourist behaviour. His most recent book (with John Jenkins) *Tourism Policy: A Public Policy Approach* is also published by Routledge.

Marlene Inman is Health Promotion Advisor/District HIV Prevention Co-ordinator to Plymouth and Torbay Health Authority. As well as working in health promotion, she has a background as surgery theatre sister and health visitor. Ms Inman designed the 'Sea, Sand and Safer Sex' programme and collaborated in the research surveys that preceded it.

Eric Laws is Senior Lecturer in Tourism at Napier University, Edinburgh, Scotland. He is the author of *Tourism Marketing, Service and Quality Management Perspectives*, published by Stanley Thornes, and *Tourist Destination Management, Issues, Analysis and Policies*, published by Routledge. He is the Editor of the *Tourism Educators' Supplement* to the Journal of the Tourism Society, and a member of the organising committee of CIMTIG, the Chartered Institute of Marketing Travel Industry Group.

Gil Lea has practised travel medicine for twenty years at British Airways and now at Trailfinders in London. She is also a Consultant (part-time) at the Public Health Laboratory Service Communicable Disease Surveillance Centre, London.

Elspeth Mathie is a Research Fellow in the Institute of Population Studies, University of Exeter. Her earlier work includes research into young people's socio-sexual behaviour, AIDS/HIV awareness, provision of family planning services and the female condom. More recently, she has been involved in designing and evaluating a number of peer education projects in the South-West of England in collaboration with local health authorities.

Stephen J. Page was formerly Principal Lecturer and Course Director for Tourism Studies, Canterbury Christ Church College. He is currently Senior Lecturer in Tourism Management, Massey University, Albany, New Zealand. He is the author of *Transport for Tourism* and *Urban Tourism*, both published by Routledge. He is also co-editor of *Tourism in the Pacific* and *The Business of Rural Tourism* due to be published by Routledge in 1996. Whilst at Christ Church College, he was Co-director of the Travel, Lifestyles and Health project.

John D. H. Porter is a Consultant Epidemiologist at the Public Health Laboratory Service Communicable Disease Surveillance Centre and a Senior Lecturer at the London School of Hygiene and Tropical Medicine. He trained in paediatrics in the UK and in epidemiology and public health at the Harvard School of Public Health and the Center for Disease Control, Atlanta, USA.

Brenda Rudkin is an independent researcher specialising in the Pacific Islands, indigenous people and development issues in tourism. She is currently based at Massey University, Albany, Auckland, New Zealand where she is completing a Masters thesis on tourism and development issues in the Solomon Islands.

Richard Slack is Senior Lecturer in Microbiology, University of Nottingham Medical School. He is also Consultant for Communicable Disease Control, Nottingham Health Authority and an Honorary Consultant, Public Health Laboratory Service. In addition he chairs the Nottingham District AIDS Advisory Group and is Co-ordinator of district HIV/AIDS services and is on the management teams of sexual voluntary groups for Drugs and HIV/AIDS. Previously he held posts as Lecturer in Pathology, University of Nairobi, Kenya; Clinical Assistant, Nottingham Genito-Urinary Medicine Clinic; Advisor WHO Global Programme on AIDS contributing to National Plans for Nigeria, Turkey and Cyprus.

David Stears is Director of the Centre for Health Education and Research at Canterbury Christ Church College and a Principal Lecturer in Health Education with a background of teaching in all sectors of education. He is currently Director of the MSc in Health Education and Health Promotion programme at the College. Recent research includes co-directorship of the HIV/AIDS Education and Young People project and an investigation of travel health promotion as part of the Travel, Lifestyles and Health project. From 1992–4 he was Co-director of the Health Education Authority's Secondary Schools HIV/AIDS and Sex Education project – a national training project aimed at supporting sex and HIV/AIDS education in schools.

Ros Weston is a Lecturer in Health Education/Health Promotion in the Health Education Unit, School of Education, University of Southampton and was formerly the UK Co-ordinator for the Europe Against Cancer campaign. Her special areas of interest within health promotion are: theory and practice of health education/health promotion; workplace (she is a member of the European Union Steering Group on Workplace Health); cancer, and loss and bereavement. Currently, she is working on a research project for the European Union on evaluation strategies for cancer education and prevention interventions. Publications include journal articles on cancer education; teaching resources for cancer education, and health promotion.

Foreword

Travel has always been part of the unique character of human life, and the need to explore has been a prime motivation through the ages. Technological advancement over the last half century has enabled travel to be treated as a commodity available for all. Society, its attitude, behaviour and infrastructure has similarly changed, but possibly not at the same pace as technology. The traveller at ease in his community, is then rapidly transposed to a new and different environment in a strange culture and away from normal constraints. What problems does this generate and how does the traveller cope? Not only are psychological adjustments necessary, physical hazards and climatic influences will affect health. Duration of visits abroad are often short, allowing little time for climatic and cultural adaptation. Individuals are only one part of a bigger equation. What are the likely impacts of the individual's travel on his or her home community and on the community visited? How should society protect itself from the hazards encountered by its travelling members, and who should be responsible for their health? What sacrifice should host destinations make to attract visitors and at what social cost? Is the health of the individual to be forsaken for the benefit of the income derived to the community?

I pose these real dilemmas knowing that some of the answers can be found in this book, but most of these questions remain unanswered. In the still early days of travel medicine much is to be discovered, but more disconcertingly I find, more questions are raised when trying to answer some of these problems. And while contemplating these issues, exponential increases in numbers of travellers and their problems continue. *Health and the International Tourist* takes the very important first few steps in tackling many of these issues. It contains the very important mix of authors, clinicians, epidemiologists, public health and social scientists, educators, academics and practitioners, each contributing their unique perspective to their chosen problem, providing valuable data and ideas on how to tackle what are often common problems. Changing travellers' behaviour appears to be the commonly shared purpose across all the health interventions. Many ideas and methods are discussed and presented including some very novel and successful suggestions. Behaviour associated with many health issues has yet to be defined, a deficit which can be regularly noticed when reading the book. Although many important topics are covered, there remain many not included. The context to be considered is therefore much wider than that contained within any book or amongst one group of people. Travel health needs to recruit appropriately skilled and motivated readers. I sincerely hope this book acts as the bait to this purpose.

Dr Ron Behrens BSc MB ChB MRCS MRCP MD
Consultant physician in Tropical and Travel Medicine
Hospital for Tropical Diseases, London
Honorary Senior Lecturer, London School
of Hygiene and Tropical Medicine
19 May 1995

Preface

The second half of this century has seen an enormous expansion in international travel and tourism. With this has come the development of academic interest and research in tourism as a social phenomenon of considerable economic, social and cultural significance. While the expansion of tourism has carried substantial benefits, it has not been without its costs and problems. This book explores one such problem area – risks to health associated with international travel. As tourists travel more often and to further-flung destinations – so the health risks posed by exposure to different climatic, ecological and social conditions have increased. Until recently, concern with health issues associated with travel has been the almost exclusive concern of medical practitioners in the field of 'travel medicine'. Increasingly, however, this area has attracted the attention of social scientists and health promotion specialists – not least because of the emergence in the early 1980s of the new threat of AIDS and the recognition that international travel has been central to the global spread of HIV infection.

This book brings together contributions from medical specialists, social scientists and health professionals who share a common interest in travel and health. The book is multidisciplinary in character and aims to facilitate awareness and understanding across disciplinary boundaries. It is our hope that specialists in the field of tourism studies, in particular, will gain from the specific perspectives offered by practitioners in travel medicine and health promotion and that this book will stimulate further health-related research within the tourism field. Equally, the book is concerned to promote intersectoral collaboration – among professionals working in medicine, tourism and health promotion. Practitioners and students in all of these fields will find information and ideas in this book which should contribute positively to their practice, and help towards ensuring the efficient and effective promotion of health and safety among international tourists.

Stephen Clift and Stephen J. Page
January 1995

Acknowledgements

The book was conceived as part of an ongoing programme of research – at Canterbury Christ Church College – the Travel, Lifestyles and Health Project. The research was supported jointly by Canterbury Christ Church College and the South Thames (East) Regional Health Authority. The editors are especially grateful to Dr Gervase Hamilton (Regional Epidemiologist) for his encouragement and support in this work and to all members of the project consultative group for positive contributions to the development of our work. A special word of thanks is owed to Mrs Gillian Shaw, who valiantly and with patient expertise prepared the manuscript for publication.

Thanks are due also to the following: The British Council for permission to reproduce the figure 'Areas associated with a high rate of travellers' diarrhoea' from *British Medical Bulletin*, 94, 2: 351; Fiona Sandell, Department of Health, London, UK for permission to reproduce material from the Department of Health 1993 'Travel Safe' campaign; Steve Bailey, Health Promotion Gloucestershire, UK for permission to reproduce their leaflet on 'Safer Sex on Holiday' (text by Steve Bailey, Health promotion Officer, HIV/AIDS, graphics by Graphics Studio, Health Promotion, Gloucestershire); Sharon Henry, Health Promotion Unit, Eastern Health and Social Services Board, Belfast, Northern Ireland, for permission to reproduce their 'On holiday at home, prevent skin cancer' poster; Chris Owen, Health Education Authority, London for permission to reproduce health education material promoting skin safety ('If you worship the sun' and 'Sun know how' leaflets) and safer sex ('Going far? advertisement); The Australian Commonwealth Department of Health, Housing and Community Services/Australian National Council on AIDS for permission to reproduce a poster from their Travel Safe campaign; National Board of Health, Denmark/European Project AIDS and Mobility for permission to reproduce the 'AIDS never takes the night off' advertisement; National School of Public Health, Athens, Greece/European Project AIDS and Mobility, Amsterdam, for permission to reproduce HIV/AIDS prevention posters from Santorini, Greece.

Thanks are also due to Nicola Clark for editorial assistance in checking and reading some of the chapters, Susan Page for indexing and John Hills for drawing the majority of the diagrams. In addition, data collection for Chapter 6 was generated with the help of Tourism Students at Christ Church College during their Malta field courses in 1993 and 1994. Assistance from B. Beeley, The Open University, is also gratefully acknowledged with the data collection. Lastly, the list of acknowledgements would not be complete without a mention of the help, advice and encouragement provided by Francesca Weaver, Laura Large and Sally Close at Routledge who have handled this manuscript with their usual care and efficiency.

Chapter 1

Introduction: tourism and health

Stephen Clift and Stephen J. Page

THE INTERCONNECTIONS BETWEEN TOURISM AND HEALTH

The scale of international travel and tourism has increased dramatically during the second half of this century. As Figure 1.1 demonstrates, a sharp increase in the volume of international arrivals and tourist receipts from 1950 to 1980 was followed by a relative plateau in the first half of the 1980s and then by a consistent year on year rise during the second half of that decade. Substantial changes have also occurred in the patterns of international tourism with marked increases in the numbers of tourists travelling to and from South-East Asia and Africa. As Mann and Mantel (1991: 1) note:

> The growth of travel, and particularly of tourism, is well documented and spectacular. Since 1950, the officially reported number of international tourist arrivals has increased almost 17-fold; by 1987, international tourist arrivals in Africa increased to nearly 9 million, and arrivals from Asia and the Pacific leaped an astounding 137-fold to over 32 million. International tourism is now estimated to account for 6% of total world exports and at least 25% of world trade in services.

This remarkable development has led, in academic circles, to increased theoretical and research interest in the economic, sociocultural and psychological dimensions and consequences for the tourism industry. Increasingly too, the health dimensions of travel and tourism are attracting both study and practical interventions to promote healthy and safer experiences of tourism. The renewed vigour of the traditional perspective of 'travel medicine', with its

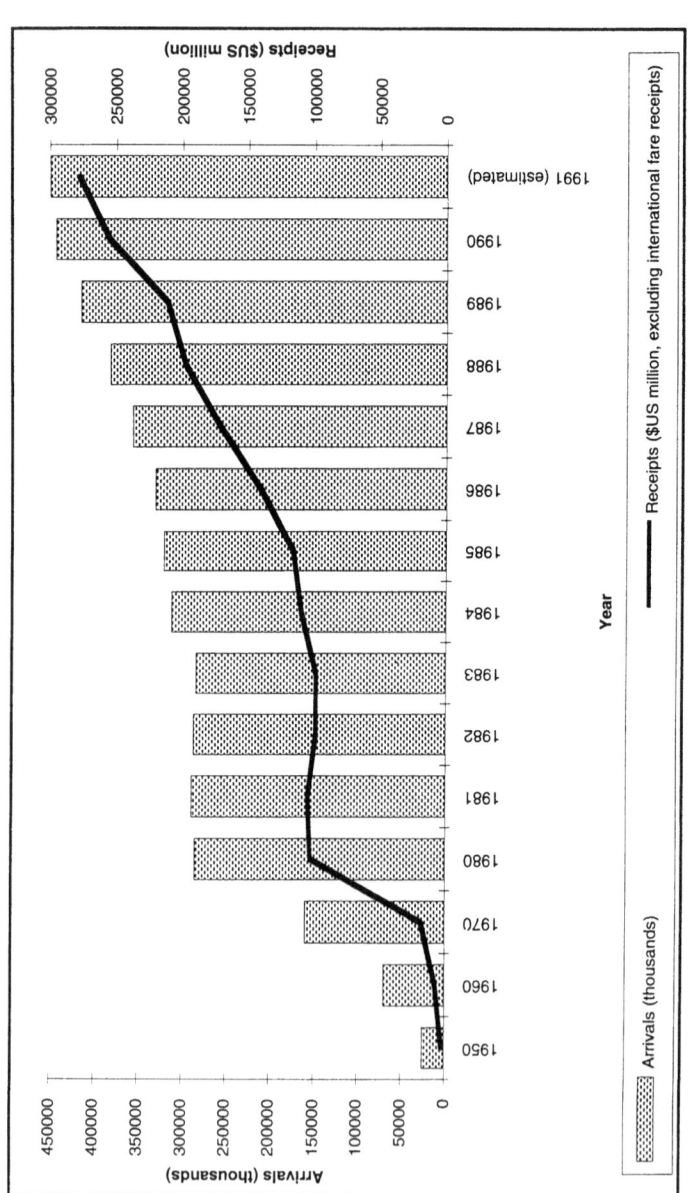

Figure 1.1 The expansion of international tourism, 1950–91

emphasis on epidemiological studies and provision of health protection via immunisation and chemoprophylaxis, is reflected in the formation in 1991 of a new International Travel Medicine Association (ITMS), the launch in 1994 of a new journal (the *Journal of Travel Health*), and the publication of significant reviews of the literature (e.g. Behrens and McAdam 1993; Mårdh 1994). Purely medical solutions to certain health risks, however, either are not available (as in the case of HIV infection), or show evidence of becoming less effective over time (as in the case of certain forms of malaria prophylaxis), or are difficult to justify for the mass of travellers (as in the use of antibiotics to prevent and treat travellers' diarrhoea). As the social and behavioural dimensions of health risks in the context of travel, and the need to encourage patterns of behaviour to reduce such risks, have become more apparent (e.g. practising 'safer sex', and avoiding mosquito bites), interest in the interconnections between health and tourism has also developed in the fields of tourism studies and health promotion. It is clear that relevant research in the field of travel and health requires an interdisciplinary approach drawing on the perspectives and techniques of epidemiology and the social sciences – and that effective interventions to reduce diverse potential risks to health associated with international tourism, requires a co-ordinated strategy of intersectoral collaboration embracing epidemiology, primary health care, the travel industry and agencies of health promotion.

The impact of health threats on tourism

There is no doubt that potential health threats to tourists affect the business of travel and tourism itself, especially when health problems in the relatively new destinations of Africa and South-East Asia assume 'epidemic' proportions. The headline – 'Tours cancelled by holiday giant' (*Daily Mail*, 1 October 1994) – announced the fact that Britain's largest tour operator, Thomson (a division of the International Thomson Group), had cancelled touring holidays in India for two weeks, in response to an outbreak of pneumonic plague. This action by Thomson (which was not followed by all tour operators to India), was only one aspect of the global alarm which escalated in meteoric fashion during late September 1994 as the numbers of suspected plague cases in India increased daily. As the *Daily Mail* reported two days earlier, under the headline 'MPs demand airport checks as fear grows over plague':

> The Government was under increasing pressure last night to introduce tough health checks on visitors from plague hit India. As fears grew over the deadly pneumonic plague, MPs called for Britain to line up with other European countries and take strict measures to prevent an outbreak in this country. Yesterday, Italy and Switzerland, joined France and Germany in imposing rigorous airport checks before allowing visitors from the sub-continent to enter. But the 1,700 who flew into Heathrow alone from India were allowed into Britain with no more than a visual check from immigration officers untrained in medicine.
>
> (*Daily Mail*, 29 September 1994)

For several weeks, aircraft arriving from India at international airports throughout the world were sprayed and passengers given health checks. It was even reported that the German airline Lufthansa 'is putting doctors on flights from New Delhi and Bombay to cut risks of the disease spreading' (*Daily Mail*, 29 September 1994).

It is generally acknowledged, however, that the risks of imported plague were always extremely low, as were the risks to tourists visiting India during this period. Even so, while many airlines and tour operators did not take the measures adopted by Lufthansa and Thomson, the immediate economic consequences for the tourism industry in India were dramatic, with a fall of 70 per cent in foreign visitors in response to the damaging publicity and restrictions imposed on travel.

The 'panic' over the Indian plague outbreak is a phenomenon which deserves fuller examination for the lessons it could provide on the interrelationships between health issues and tourism. Such a case study would be of interest in terms of how the health issues were monitored and communicated in medical circles; represented through the media for popular consumption, and responded to internationally and nationally by governmental and medical authorities. It would also serve to highlight the economic and social impacts which the outbreak had on:

- the Indian economy;
- the local communities which depend on tourism;
- the tourist industry;

- the medical infrastructure which provides advice to travellers;
- and of course, tourists themselves.

The economic, social and health issues raised by such a case are clearly manifold and complex, and yet, the Indian plague incident is only one example of epidemics of infectious diseases which have occurred in different parts of the world in recent years. And ironically, in view of its tragic consequences for the people directly affected by it and its economic impact on India, the plague outbreak was of relatively minor significance as a travel-mediated health threat to other countries and more directly to tourists visiting India, when compared to other health risks. As the *Daily Telegraph* reported at the end of October under the headline, 'Indian plague masks other disease risks': 'The hysteria surrounding India's recent plague outbreak, now officially declared over by the Indian authorities and the World Health Organisation (WHO), has overshadowed recent outbreaks of other diseases which are potentially far more hazardous to travellers' (*Daily Telegraph*, 29 October 1994).

Not least among such health hazards faced by tourists to tropical regions is the threat of malaria. Indeed, at the same time as world attention was focused on the outbreak of plague, a malaria epidemic had developed in India in the western state of Rajasthan, where according to the Indian Red Cross, approximately 4,000 people died, compared with only sixty-two plague deaths. Ron Behrens, Consultant in Tropical and Travel Medicine at the Hospital of Tropical Diseases in London, stated that: 'The plague was never a risk to travellers. But malaria is a disease which potentially affects most travellers (to India and other tropical areas) and kills many' (*Daily Telegraph*, 29 October 1994). In 1991, for example, 2,332 people returned to Britain from overseas travel in malarious areas and developed the disease and twelve of these died as a result. Eleven of these deaths were due to *Plasmodium falciparum* infection contracted in Kenya or West Africa (Bradley and Warhurst 1993).

The implications of international tourism for health

Health issues have commercial significance for tour operators, insurance companies and carriers, and for the economies of tourist destinations. But equally, the business of tourism itself carries health implications on many different levels. Development of the infrastructure needed to support tourism in developing regions can have substantial ecological consequences, which in turn may create health threats for local communities (Ryan 1991; Lovel and Feuerstein 1992). Tourism development can create changes in patterns of employment in local communities and place substantial strains on traditional cultural patterns of life (e.g. Brown 1992). Tourism can also expose unsuspecting and inadequately prepared tourists to new and dangerous threats to their health, which are not present in their home environment. These threats are not static as the Indian plague outbreak illustrates. More significantly, continuous processes of biological mutation and adaptation have led to the emergence of new drug-resistant strains of micro-biological pathogens (as is true for certain strains of malaria), while ecological and environmental changes in certain regions have resulted in the physical environment in some regions of the world becoming potentially more dangerous (for example, the impact of ozone depletion on levels of ultraviolet radiation and increased risks of sunburn and skin cancers in the southern hemisphere – see Dickinson and Pizzala 1993; Bentham 1994).

It is also the case that in certain areas of the world, recent social changes have undermined previously effective programmes of public health measures which had controlled and even eradicated life-threatening diseases. As the *Daily Telegraph* reported in late 1993:

> The health risk to tourists travelling in the former Soviet Union and its satellites appears to have increased since August, when a Belgian tourist died of diphtheria in Moscow. Outbreaks of diseases all but eradicated in Western societies – such as typhoid, cholera, anthrax, bubonic plague and dysentery – have been reported from Siberia to Poland and Estonia to Afghanistan. MASTA (Medical Advisory Service for Travellers Abroad) says that the diseases may always have been present and that the West may only be learning about them now because of greater openness. However, Dr Peter Barrett, its senior medical officer, believes there are other, more important factors. 'Following the collapse of the USSR, public health services, such as clean water supplies, have collapsed and there is also a growing number of refugees crossing borders,' he said.

Drinking water polluted with sewage is blamed for the appearance of cholera and typhoid.

(*Daily Telegraph*, 6 November 1993)

During 1993–4, reports in the British press frequently reflected the varied risks to health and safety faced by international tourists – drawing on research evidence and medical opinion and presenting individual case histories (Woodman 1993 on infectious diseases and Ryan 1994 on malaria, being particularly good examples of well-researched accounts in the press). Such reports are of interest, not only for the information they provide on the circumstances and experiences of individual travellers, but also as evidence of a growing popular consciousness of the range of health problems associated with travel and a concern with the means of avoiding or at least reducing risks. In considering the catalogue of potential health problems associated with travel and tourism, it is easy to understand the exaggeration in Liz Hunt's headline: 'Holidays used to mean sun, surf and sand. Now it's skin cancer, sewage and salmonella' (*Independent*, 3 August 1994). Indeed, some recent accounts of individual traveller's experiences are quite alarming and would scarcely encourage others to follow in their footsteps. The misfortunes which befell Ben West are surely extreme – he contracted three tropical diseases: typhoid, *plasmodium falciparum* malaria and filariasis during a trip to Cameroon – but his experience carries lessons which all travellers to tropical climates clearly need to learn:

> Symptoms to accompany these three illnesses did not appear until after my return to Britain. Because my GP diagnosed influenza – despite me informing her that I'd just been to West Africa, had regular fevers of 105° and was violently shivery – treatment for malaria did not begin for a week which led to the development of a fourth tropical disease, blackwater fever.
>
> (*Sunday Telegraph*, 20 February 1994)

There are lessons, evidently, that medical practitioners also need to learn, and this is further reinforced by the case of Lindsay Purves who also visited West Africa in 1994, and was not so fortunate.

> A young Scots girl has died of malaria after a holiday in Africa. And her sister is in hospital suffering from the disease. Lindsay

Purves (12) contracted malaria on a 'dream trip' to the West African country of Gambia with her mum Christine and sister Kelly (14). ... Doctors believed the two Johnstone girls were suffering from food poisoning or a stomach upset, on their return last week. But as Lindsay's condition worsened, she was rushed to Paisley's Royal Alexandra Hospital on Wednesday. Despite frantic efforts to save her, she died two hours later.

(*Glasgow Evening News*, 4 November 1994)

Health advice, promotion and services for tourists

The international tourist may seek advice about health matters prior to travelling, and advice and services may be needed while abroad and on return if health problems arise. In addition, proactive attempts may be made by health authorities and commercial companies to alert travellers to potential health risks and provide advice on avoiding them. Figure 1.2 provides a schematic account of potential sources of health information and services available to the international tourist and the settings within which active attempts at health promotion targeted at tourists could be undertaken. These sources and settings are organised from left to right in the diagram to show their connection with four main phases involved in tourism:

- deciding on a destination;
- making the necessary arrangements;
- the trip itself (including travel to and from the chosen destination(s));
- the post-travel period.

The decision-making process may well be influenced to a greater or lesser degree by health and safety considerations. Potential tourists may hold a variety of assumptions regarding different areas of the world which lead them to be considered either 'safe' or 'dangerous' with respect to health (Carter 1994). Yet research by Roehl and Fesenmaier (1992) also indicates that certain groups of tourists are prepared to take risks when selecting holiday experiences that promise adventure, excitement and new challenges. Such assumptions will be based on a variety of sources including media reports of the kind discussed above, personal experience, reports from friends and acquaintances, and

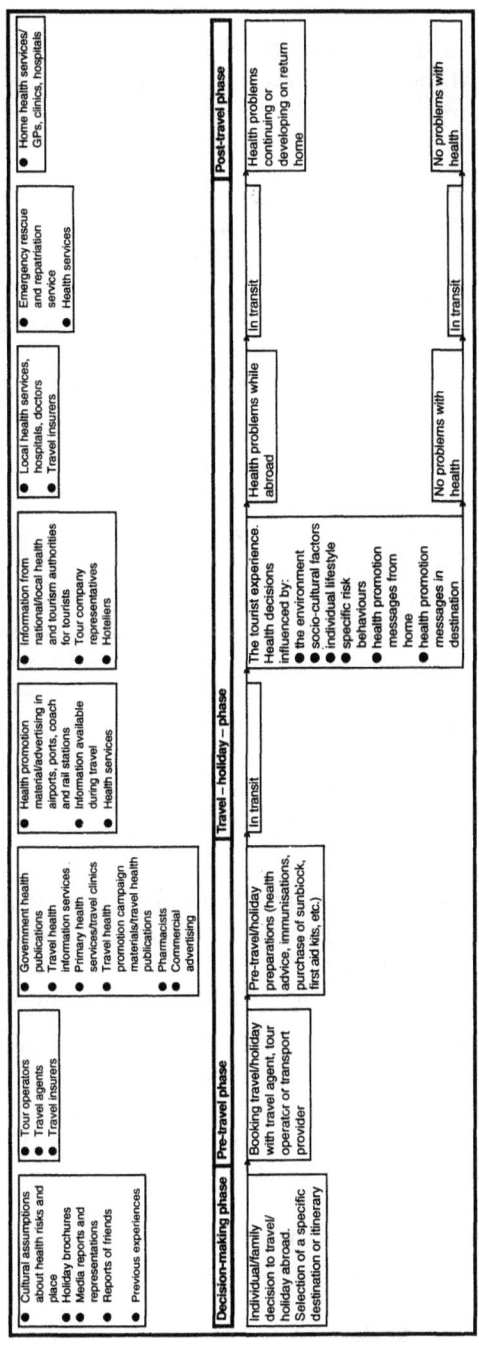

Figure 1.2 Sources of, and settings for, health information and services for the international tourist

information contained in holiday brochures (Cossar, McEachran and Reid 1993). At the time a booking is made and in the period leading up to a trip, advice may be sought from a variety of sources. These may include:-

- travel agents and tour operators;
- commercially published guides to travel and health (e.g. Turner 1991; McPherson and MacFarlane 1992);
- telephone and electronic information services (e.g. MASTA – Medical Advice and Services for Travellers Abroad, and CEEFAX);
- nationally and locally produced travel health promotion literature (e.g. the UK Department of Health 'Travelsafe' leaflet).

Particularly important for a large proportion of travellers at this stage – especially those travelling to less-developed regions – will be a consultation with their general practitioner or a specialist travel clinic, to receive advice on immunisations and sensible health precautions. In these settings it may also be possible for health practitioners to undertake relevant health education on health risks which cannot effectively be avoided by specifically medical means (e.g. accidents, exposure to water and sun, and sexually tranmitted diseases) (Page and Meyer forthcoming: Sloan 1993). In the case of malaria, provision of anti-malarials should ideally be supplemented with education on:

- the need to follow the prescribed regime very carefully (e.g. ensuring that anti-malarials are taken after return home);
- the advisability of avoiding mosquito bites where possible;
- the symptoms of malaria; and
- the need to seek treatment immediately if symptoms appear.

In the course of travel, there may be valuable opportunities for health promotion – information inserted into tickets; advertising at points of exit from the country; and information included in in-flight magazines on aircraft, for example. Health information may also be provided in the holiday destination itself, highlighting particular risks specific to the location and means of avoiding them (e.g. accident risks when skiing; what to avoid when snorkelling; the need for condoms during sexual activity with new partners; and the significance of sunburn in the resort). Finally, if a tourist is unfortunate enough to develop a health problem while abroad, or after returning home, treatment may be needed from appropriate medical services. In some cases problems may emerge during the trip and in others they may not become apparent until after the return home. There is growing evidence (Sanford 1992) that many travellers are reluctant to seek medical advice in developing countries, preferring to rely on their home area or a self-help strategy in the absence of high-quality medical facilities.

While efforts to promote health in the context of travel are generally to be applauded, there are also some drawbacks and problems with such efforts which should be acknowledged. Many newspapers and magazines, for example, offer the traveller information on recent developments and innovations in health protection and these sources may exert a substantial influence on the demand for medical services which are not necessarily justified by the scale of risks involved and the cost effectiveness of prevention. A good case in point is provided by the availability of vaccination against hepatitis A. According to Dr Thomas Stuttaford: 'Before travelling patients may talk to their doctor about typhoid, or even cholera, but they won't mention hepatitis A, although they are a hundred times more likely to catch it when on holiday than typhoid' (*The Times*, 28 June 1994). But fortunately, he goes on to explain:

> The excuse that by the time the holiday was planned it was too late to receive vaccination against hepatitis A has now gone. When Havrix, the world's first vaccine against hepatitis A, was introduced by Smith Kline Beecham in 1992 it had the disadvantage that it needed a course of injections; this month the preparation has been modified and now one shot of the new Havrix monodose given two to four weeks before travel will provide protection for a year; a booster dose given six to twelve months later will extend immunity for up to ten years.
>
> (ibid.)

However, promoting awareness among travellers of vaccination against hepatitis A, and thus, presumably, a demand for it, has been questioned by a recent study showing that such vaccination is not an efficient use of health service resources (Behrens and Roberts 1994). The authors of this study estimate the current annual cost to the National Health Service of giving typhoid and hepatitis immunisation to travellers to be £25.8 million. This compares to an estimated cost of £1.03 million of treating the cases which would arise in the absence of vaccination. In contrast, malaria and its associated mortality results in substantial health care costs which would greatly exceed the cost of chemoprophylaxis. Provision of anti-malarials on prescription is thus clearly warranted on purely economic grounds.

A second issue is that the quantity and range of information and advice available for the traveller on a wide spectrum of health and safety issues can seem overwhelming. The traveller may be faced with the problem of deciding what is really important and what is less so. The burden which concerns about health might pose to the health-conscious traveller is clearly indicated by a fairly typical travel health article which appeared in *Essentials* magazine in August 1994. Somewhat ironically entitled 'Happy, carefree holidays', the feature begins by telling its readers: 'Don't risk spoiling your well-earned holiday – take our emergency pull-out-and-keep guide to help you avoid the avoidable and enjoy a healthy, trouble-free time.' The advice given is generally sensible, but the amount and scope of it is very striking. Before going away, for example, travellers should: visit their doctor for immunisations, prescribed medicines and advice if pregnant; see their dentist to have 'that occasional twinge' sorted out; and ensure that they have adequate travel insurance. A well-stocked first aid kit should be taken, together with British kite-marked condoms 'if a holiday romance is a possibility'. Advice is also offered on how to avoid a rather strange mixture of sicknesses and accidents on arrival in the (unspecified) holiday destination, with no acknowledgement of their relative risks, nor of their potential seriousness. Thus, the list includes heat exhaustion, prickly heat, diarrhoea, malaria, stings from jellyfish and urchins, rabies and AIDS – with equal space given to 'jellyfish and urchins' and the risks of AIDS! Tourists are also advised to check safety standards in their holiday accommodation, to take care in and near water, and to be sensible when driving (since traffic accidents 'cause most deaths among travellers'). The extent to which tourists consume, understand and act on the health advice available to them is an area that certainly deserves further research attention.

THE ISSUES ADDRESSED IN THIS BOOK

As should be apparent from the foregoing sections, the issues raised by the intersections of health and tourism are both complex and diverse. In order to examine this complexity in a rigorous and scientific manner, and to address the social and personal problems involved effectively on a practical level, requires the perspectives of several disciplines and the collaboration of professionals in the fields of medicine, health promotion and the travel/tourism industry. This book aims to stimulate the development of an interdisciplinary perspective and encourage intersectoral collaboration, by bringing together contributions on health and tourism from specialists in travel medicine, the social sciences, tourism studies and health promotion. Existing texts in travel medicine and social science perspectives on tourism provide a valuable supporting context in which to view the issues raised in the chapters that follow (e.g. Behrens and McAdam 1993; Ryan 1991). It may help the reader, however, if certain themes in the book are drawn out in the remainder of this introduction and significant features of each contribution are highlighted.

Travel medicine

Part I includes contributions from specialists in travel medicine. Cossar draws on a wealth of research experience in the area and professional expertise as a general practitioner, to provide a general perspective on travellers' health. Epidemiological and serological studies of travellers are reviewed before the specific risks posed to travellers by a wide range of factors – the stresses of travelling, contact with contaminated water, exposure to harsh climatic conditions, accidents, insect bites and sexual behaviour – are examined.

The chapters that follow focus on two specific health issues – diarrhoeal illness and HIV/AIDS – and together they provide an instructive illustration of the diversity and complexity of the interconnections between travel and health. Travellers' diarrhoea, as its name suggests, refers to a complaint having a specific connection with travel to a new destination and the exposure that brings to enteropathogens not normally encountered in the home environment. As Cartwright points out, travellers' diarrhoea is the commonest travel-associated illness. It can be caused by a wide variety of bacterial and parasitic agents present in the environment and if infection occurs, the symptoms appear rapidly and are very obvious. In principle, the risks of succumbing to travellers' diarrhoea can be reduced by taking care over water intake, food consumption and personal hygiene but, in practice, it may be difficult for individual travellers to avoid and is best addressed by classic public health measures. Finally, while travellers' diarrhoea may be distressing and inconvenient for short periods, it is generally short-lived and responds readily to medical treatment. Cartwright's contribution also demonstrates the responsible stance taken by one of the largest tour operators in the United Kingdom, systematically collecting information on their clients' experiences of health problems and in taking action to help tackle such problems when and where they become apparent.

Porter, Lea and Carroll show that HIV infection has certainly spread internationally as a consequence of travel, and it may well present a greater risk to the traveller in some destinations compared with others as a function of geographic variations in population infection rates. Nevertheless, risk of HIV infection depends entirely on specific patterns of behaviour (sexual intercourse and sharing of drug injection equipment) and the risks can be avoided by not engaging in such behaviours, or substantially reduced by taking well-known preventative measures. Unlike travellers' diarrhoea, infection with HIV remains latent for a considerable period, gives rise to a wide variety of serious and ultimately life-threatening illnesses, and cannot be cleared by simple medical treatments. The fact that HIV infection is, with time, almost invariably fatal, but is also entirely preventable through adoption of clearly defined behaviours, has resulted in an extraordinary increase in social and behavioural research focused on sexual and drug-taking behaviour and considerable investments in HIV/AIDS education and prevention activities. Some of the research that explores the behaviour of travellers and tourists and their risks of HIV infection is explored in Chapter 4.

Social science research

Part II moves the concern away from epidemiological and medical perspectives on travel and health, to the contributions made by social scientists working in the context of public health, the sociology of tourism and the social psychology of tourist behaviour. If the social and psychological factors affecting health in the context of travel and tourism are to be documented and understood, then the perspectives and expertise of social and behavioural scientists are needed to complement the medical perspective. In Chapter 5, Rudkin and Hall examine a variety of health issues – in particular malaria, dengue fever, cholera, diarrhoea and poisoning by fish – which are raised by the development of 'special-interest tourism' in South-East Asia and the South Pacific. In doing so, they place the examination of health in the context of recent developments in the tourism industry in the Pacific Rim – stimulated by commercial interests on the one hand, and the personal motivations of tourists on the other. A further important issue they raise concerns the wider ecological dimensions of tourism development in the Less Developed World and the implications such changes have for the economic growth and performance of such countries and the health and well-being of host communities. The costs to local communities associated with the development of tourism are not necessarily compensated for by the economic gains.

In Chapter 6, the focus shifts from tropical and developing areas, to the more established tourist destination of Malta. Clark and Clift highlight that tourists holidaying for a week or two in the Mediterranean generally have few health problems to contend with and only small minorities experience difficulties with health which seriously interfere with their vacation. Accordingly, they examine aspects of tourist holiday behaviour and experience and explore their longer-term implications not only for health risks – but also for health in a positive sense, including the enhancement of personal development and well-being. Historically, the acceptance of rights to paid holidays and the separation of leisure from work, was justified not only on economic grounds, but also in terms of the health and well-being of individuals and communities. As Urry (1990) notes, holidays and 'going away' are not only 'a matter of status in modern societies', but are also widely assumed to be 'necessary to health'. Nevertheless, the positive health implications of holidays and tourism have rarely been the focus of research. In Clark and Clift's study three dimensions of holiday experience are identified and factors influencing these dimensions are described. The first dimension – 'Sun, Sex and Sangria' – clearly encapsulates a constellation of behaviours which may carry sexual health risks, while the second and third dimensions point towards the more positive, health-promoting aspects of holidays. The circumstances and procedures employed in the research conducted in Malta made explicit and specific questioning about sexual behaviour on holiday impossible – but two significant

British studies described in the chapters that follow have explored these issues among tourists in some detail.

In Chapter 7 Gillies and Slack present findings from what is still the only general population survey of travellers' health so far conducted in England. Some interesting data were collected on issues such as sunburn, accidents and insect bites on holiday abroad – but the main focus of the work was on the sexual behaviour of tourists. Overall, only very small percentages of tourists holidaying abroad reported involvement in romantic and sexual relationships with new partners abroad, but the incidence was substantially greater among younger, unattached men. Increased alcohol use was implicated in sexual activity abroad and the most worrying finding related to the failure by a substantial proportion of sexually active tourists to use condoms consistently or at all. The picture drawn by the work of Gillies and Slack is further reinforced by the findings from the survey undertaken by Ford and Eiser in Torbay in Chapter 8. This study is primarily concerned with the sexual behaviour of young, unaccompanied, domestic tourists in a holiday resort area in South-West England – but its findings have clear relevance to a consideration of cross-border tourism and sexual behaviour. The particular value of Ford and Eiser's contribution lies not only in the detailed information collected on the extent and character of young people's sexual behaviour on holiday – but also in their elaboration of a conceptual framework to help make sense of the data collected. The results serve to characterise the socio-sexual culture among young people on holiday in an English resort, which visitors enter into and help create. It would be both fascinating and of considerable practical significance if the findings from the Torbay study were to be replicated at different tourist sites attracting large numbers of young people, across Europe.

Finally, in Part II the discussion returns to the Pacific region to consider the interrelationships between tourism and the developed commercial sex industries found in several countries in South-East Asia. From the work of Gillies and Slack and Ford and Eiser it is easy to draw the conclusion that sexual activity on holiday is primarily a matter of personal motivation and relaxed inhibitions induced by the holiday atmosphere and increased alcohol consumption. In Chapter 9, Hall makes it clear, however, that socio-economic structures and cultural context are significant factors in understanding the sexual behaviour of tourists in certain

South-East Asian countries. Furthermore, the interconnections between sex industries and international tourism raise important health issues not simply or primarily with respect to tourists, but more importantly in relation to the sexual, mental and social wellbeing of members of the host community involved in sex work. This is especially the case where the human rights of individuals are violated through coercion and where sex tourism encourages the sexual exploitation and abuse of children (see Ireland 1993). Under such circumstances, efforts at influencing behaviour through health education and health promotion need to be superseded by the development of national and international legislation, effective policing, adequate punitive measures and appropriate therapeutic programmes.

Health promotion

The contributions to Part III explore the interconnections between tourism, health (as opposed to illness) and health promotion. In Chapter 10, Laws discusses 'health' as an aspect of the business and marketing of tourism for clients seeking specific treatments or health-related facilities and services. Health dimensions of tourism to Hawaii and Israel in particular are discussed and attention is given to the business dimensions of making tourist destinations more accessible for the elderly and disabled. Stears, in Chapter 11, provides a broad perspective on travel health promotion, drawing on current models of health promotion. This provides a valuable set of guiding principles for the development and implementation of health promotion initiatives in respect to travel and tourism – emphasising the crucial importance of adequate epidemiology, clear aims, effective intersectoral collaboration, relevant resources and systematic evaluation. Evidence is also presented from two surveys of local travel health promotion activities organised at District Health Authority level in the United Kingdom, highlighting the topics, settings and resources which have characterised local health promotion initiatives in this area. What emerges very clearly is that health promotion professionals in the UK have taken their lead from the targets set by the *Health of the Nation* white paper (Department of Health 1992) and focused on 'safety in the sun' and 'sexual health' in relation to travel and holidays. In Chapter 12, Weston discusses the risks of excessive exposure to sunlight, both with respect to skin damage and increased skin cancer risk, and highlights the challenges faced by health promoters in attempting to modify behaviour that people not only enjoy but believe helps them to feel good and look more attractive. Holidays are an important context to consider in relation to the health of the skin, especially in the case of fairer-skinned northern Europeans travelling to much hotter Mediterranean or tropical climates in search of a golden tan. Reinforcing the views expressed by Stears, Weston highlights the need to utilise a systematic model of health promotion to guide the planning, implementation and evaluation of practical initiatives.

The second major travel health promotion topic identified by Stears – sexual health – is the subject of the two final chapters. International tourism by definition involves travel across national boundaries; however, infectious diseases, in particular, show no respect for such boundaries. If efforts to control and prevent the international spread of infections are to be effective, then international networks of communication and collaboration need to be created and to operate effectively. The realisation of this principle is particularly relevant and urgent with respect to HIV infection. In Chapter 13 Bröring provides an account of the work of the European Project 'AIDS and Mobility', which was specifically set up to support and facilitate practical HIV prevention programmes for migrants and tourists within Europe. Bröring focuses in particular on the need for HIV prevention work aimed at tourists and elaborates upon the principles that should guide such activities. Finally, in Chapter 14, Ford, Inman and Mathie provide a description of one such prevention initiative aimed at young tourists on holiday in Torbay. The project provides an excellent model for sexual health promotion aimed at young tourists – grounded in local research and attuned to the needs and culture of young people, it employs outreach workers to engage young people in a participative and enjoyable way, and is systematically evaluated. If such initiatives fail to encourage greater awareness of risks and the adoption of safer-sex practice among those sexually active on holiday, it is difficult to imagine what more could be done.

CONCLUSION

Health and tourism interconnect in many diverse ways. Health issues are of commercial concern to tour companies, travel insurers and tourist destinations, as the development of threats to the health of tourists can have serious economic implications. Given the enormous range of issues involved in a joint consideration of health and tourism, this book can do no more than present a sample of contributions from a fascinating and expanding area of study. It is hoped that this collection will raise awareness of the importance of health issues among researchers and practitioners in the tourism field, and provide a valuable stimulus to the future development of interdisciplinary research and practical collaboration on travel and health. Without greater intersectoral collaboration and greater co-operation between the tourism industry and researchers, unnecessary incidents and experiences may continue to mar the tourist experience on holiday, thereby affecting their perception and overall satisfaction of their visit. Thus, with the global tourism industry operating in a decade of the consumer, there is even greater pressure on finding ways to avoid potential health problems commonly associated with some forms of international tourism.

REFERENCES

Behrens, R. H. and McAdam, K. P. W. J. (eds) (1993) *Travel Medicine*, London: Churchill Livingstone.
Behrens, R. H. and Roberts, J. A. (1994) 'Is travel prophylaxis worthwhile? Economic appraisal of prophylactic measures against malaria, hepatitis A, and typhoid in travellers', *British Medical Journal* 309: 918–22.
Bentham G. (1994) 'Global environmental change and health', in D. R. Phillips and Y. Verhasselt (eds) *Health and Development*, London: Routledge.
Bradley, D. J. and Warhurst, D. C. (1993) 'Malaria imported into the United Kingdom during 1991', *Communicable Disease Report* 3, 2: R25–31.
Brown, N. (1992) 'Beachboys as culture brokers in Bakau, The Gambia', *Community Development Journal* 27: 361–70.
Carter, S. (1994) 'Places of danger and places of safety: travellers' social construction of risky locations in relation to HIV/AIDS', paper presented at 'AIDS in Europe: Behavioural Aspects', Berlin 26–29 September 1994.
Cossar, J. H., McEachran, J. and Reid, D. (1993) 'Holiday companies improve their health advice', *British Medical Journal* 306: 1069–70.
Department of Health (1992) *The Health of the Nation: a Strategy for Health in England*, London: HMSO.
Dickinson, L. and Pizzala, D. (eds) (1993) *Safe in the Sun*, Tunbridge Wells: South East Thames Regional Health Authority.

Ireland, K. (1993) 'Sexual exploitation of children and international travel and tourism', *Child Abuse Review* 2, 4: 263–70.

Lovel, H. and Feuerstein, M.-T. (1992) 'After the carnival: tourism and community development', *Community Development Journal* 27: 335–51.

McPherson, A. and MacFarlane, A. (1992) *The Virgin Now Boarding: a Globetrotter's Guide to Health, Sex and Survival*, London: Arrow Books.

Mann, J. M. and Mantel, C. F. (1991) 'Travel and health: a global agenda' in H. O. Lobel, R. Steffen and P. E. Kozansky (eds) *Travel Medicine 2, Proceedings of the Second Conference on International Travel Medicine*, Atlanta: ISTM.

Mårdh, P.-A. (ed.) (1994) *Travel Medicine*, Scandinavian Association for Travel Medicine and Health.

Page, S. and Meyer, D. (forthcoming) 'Tourist accidents and injuries in Australasia: scale, magnitude and solutions' in S. Clift and P. Grabowski (eds) *Health and Tourism: Risk, Research and Responses*, London: Cassell.

Roehl, W. S. and Fesenmaier, D. R. (1992) 'Risk perceptions and pleasure travel', *Journal of Travel Research* 30, 4: 17–26.

Ryan, C. (1991) *Recreational Tourism: a Social Science Perspective*, London: Routledge.

Ryan, R. (1994) 'Once bitten', *Sunday Times*, 26 August.

Sanford, J. (1992) 'Self-help for the traveller who becomes ill', *Infectious Disease Clinics of North America* 6, 2: 405–12.

Sloan, D. S. G. (1993) 'Travel medicine and general practice: a suitable case for audit?', *British Medical Journal* 307: 615–17.

Turner, A. C. (1991) *The Traveller's Health Guide*, Brentford: Roger Lascelles.

Urry, J. (1990) *The Tourist Gaze: Leisure and Travel in Contemporary Societies*, London: Sage.

Woodman, A. (1993) 'Notes for an invalid abroad', *The Independent on Sunday Magazine*, 12 September: 52–3.

Part I

Travel and health: medical perspectives

Chapter 2

Travellers' health: a medical perspective

Jonathan H. Cossar

INTRODUCTION

Although there have been notable medical advances throughout the twentieth century, the contemporary traveller is still vulnerable to health hazards on account of the very nature of travel itself. Travel exposes the individual to new, cultural, psychological, physical, physiological, emotional, environmental and micro-biological experiences and challenges. The traveller's ability to adapt to, cope with, and survive these challenges is affected by many variables which include his pre-existing physical, mental, immunological and medical status. This in turn is modified by personality, experience and behaviour and differs according to age, gender, culture, race, social status and education. The final aspect of this challenge relates specifically to the unfamiliar environmental exposure which encompasses climate, altitude, sunlight, hygiene and disease prevalence. For these reasons it is not surprising that health problems affecting the traveller have been recognised throughout history.

HISTORICAL ASPECTS

There are many historical examples of health hazards affecting travellers and, indeed, influencing history. For example, in the twelfth and thirteenth centuries the authorities in Venice noted that there was a problem with regular outbreaks of plague affecting the city's inhabitants, which occurred shortly after the arrival of ships from the East. As a result, Venice and Rhodes introduced the first regulations governing the arrival of ships in 1377, whereby they were detained at a distance, complete with passengers, cargo and crew for forty days (*quaranto giorni*), before being allowed to proceed to their final destination (Bruce-Chwatt 1973). This measure is generally accepted as the origin of the concept of quarantine and other cities and countries followed this example until some form of sanitary regulation became commonplace in many countries during the next five centuries.

Further travel hazards were noted in later times – the ill-fated Darien Expedition of the 1690s was a disastrous attempt to establish a Scottish colony on the isthmus of Panama. Some 2,000 Scots died as a result of appalling local conditions where malaria and yellow fever were rife (Steel 1984: 133).

At the turn of the century, considerable numbers of UK citizens were engaged in work abroad. Africa presented notable health risks; for example, the missionaries Mungo Park, David Livingstone and Mary Slessor all died in Africa, succumbing respectively to trauma (drowned while under attack by hostile natives), dysentery with internal haemorrhage, and 'exhaustion'.

More detailed study of 1,427 Scottish Presbyterian missionaries who worked abroad between 1873 and 1929 revealed that 25 per cent had to return prematurely owing to personal or family ill-health, and a further 11 per cent died in service (Cossar 1987). In addition it was noted that the numbers affected by adverse health were greater for those appointed in the earlier years, when less was known about tropical diseases, and the problems were more severe for those appointed to the most climatically rigorous areas, e.g. Western Africa.

Interestingly, missionaries with a medical background experienced fewer problems, probably because of their knowledge of illness and its prevention. The effect of local climate and environment, and a background knowledge about disease, continue to be very relevant to the health experience of the contemporary traveller.

THE GROWTH OF TRAVEL

In 1949, 26 million international tourists were recorded (Table 2.1) whereas by 1990 the figure had risen to 429 million (World Tourism Organisation 1990) (a 17-fold increase), 30 per cent destined for the Mediterranean area. If the number of domestic tourists is added, it has been estimated by the World Tourism Organisation that the world total of arrivals at all destinations is

Table 2.1 The growth in international travel, 1949–90 (in millions)

	1949	1960	1970	1980	1990
Global air travellers	31.0	106.0	386.0	748.0	1160.0
International tourists	26.0	69.0	160.0	285.0	429.0
Visits abroad by UK residents	1.7	6.0	11.8	17.5	31.2

now approximately 4,150 million. Since 1949 there has also been a 37-fold increase in scheduled air travellers (International Civil Aviation Organisation 1990), and an 18-fold rise in United Kingdom residents travelling abroad, with the proportion of those travelling beyond Europe increasing 48-fold (Business Statistics Office 1990). Thus those exposed to the wider extremes of climate and culture are showing the most accelerated growth rate.

Groups contributing to this growth in travel include tourists, political representatives, businessmen, technical experts, pilgrims, migrant workers, students, refugees, immigrants, military personnel, sporting participants and followers, and the hotel and travel support services. Owing to the speed, capacity and frequency of modern travel, moreover, numerous travellers are now more likely than previously to return within the incubation period of many infections; for example between 1948 and the present, the fastest passenger-aircraft cruising speed has risen from 340 to 1,356 miles per hour (Supersonic travel), and the maximum capacity from 40 to over 400 passengers (jumbo jet). The long return sea journey enabling illnesses acquired abroad to be recognised before return is now relatively rare, and therefore both traveller and doctor have to be more alert to this possibility.

HEALTH IMPLICATIONS OF TRAVEL

This contemporary travel phenomenon not only has economic, environmental, cultural and social repercussions but also medical, epidemiological and medico-legal consequences. Some illnesses may be induced by the travel itself such as motion sickness and upsets to the circadian rhythms; unaccustomed exercise or the effects of altitude may exacerbate pre-existing cardiovascular or respiratory pathology. The effects of exposure to unfamiliar infectious agents and the stress of altered climate, environment

Table 2.2 Infections imported to the United Kingdom, 1978–88

AIDS	Leishmaniasis
Amoebiasis	Leptospirosis
Brucellosis	Malaria
Campylobacteriosis	Poliomyelitis
Cholera	Rabies
Cytomegalovirus mononucleosis	Salmonellosis
Diphtheria	Schistosomiasis
Dysentery	Sexually transmitted diseases
Giardiasis	Shigellosis
Helminths	Trypanosomiasis
Hepatitis A and B	Tuberculosis
Lassa fever	Typhoid/paratyphoid
Legionnaires' Disease	

and culture may also cause problems for the unwary traveller, which are compounded by differing medical practices encountered overseas. Headlines may be made by 'newsworthy' imported infections such as the 2,332 malaria notifications recorded for the UK in 1991 (Communicable Diseases (Scotland) Unit 1992) (54 per cent due to *P. falciparum*) or the 79 per cent of heterosexually acquired Acquired Immune Deficiency Syndrome (AIDS) cases (total number to 31 January 1993, 675) (CD(S)U 1993) which were contracted abroad (the same pattern as seen for HIV infection). However, it is only by epidemiological studies that the true perspective of diseases associated with travel can be defined – for example, cases have been recorded of all the infections shown in Table 2.2 (Cossar and Reid 1989).

EPIDEMIOLOGICAL STUDIES OF TRAVELLERS

In 1973 an outbreak of pneumonia with three fatalities in a group of package holidaymakers returning from Benidorm, Spain to Glasgow, Scotland, was subsequently attributed to Legionnaires' disease (Lawson *et al.* 1977). This example of travellers returning with a previously unknown disease, which presented diagnostic difficulties and delay in the home country, motivated the development of a collaborative study of illnesses associated with travel. This was conducted by the Communicable Diseases (Scotland) Unit (CD(S)U), the University of Glasgow Department of Infectious Diseases, and the Department of Laboratory Medicine and the Regional Virus Laboratory, both at Ruchill Hospital,

Table 2.3 Age of travellers and reports of illness in studies undertaken by the Communicable Diseases (Scotland) Unit, 1973–85

Age group	Total respondents	% unwell
0–9	550	33
10–19	1,974	41
20–29	3,033	48
30–39	2,028	38
40–49	2,297	32
50–59	2,381	28
60+	1,239	20
not known	725	32
Total	14,227	37

Glasgow. Over the past fifteen years the CD(S)U has established a system to monitor the health experiences of returning Scottish travellers and also to make specific enquiries into groups of travellers identified as being 'at risk', following an alert about a possible health problem. This epidemiological overview is based on the findings from the research programme.

Analysis was carried out on the information provided by travellers using a twenty-item standard questionnaire (Cossar *et al.* 1990) asking for personal and travel data, with a pre-paid reply envelope addressed to the CD(S)U. Out of a total of 14,227 respondents, 37 per cent gave a history of illness with response rates ranging from 21 per cent (Dewar *et al.* 1983) to 77 per cent (Cossar *et al.* 1984) amongst the component study groups. The attack rates ranged from a low of 19 per cent amongst summer visitors to Scotland in 1980 (Dewar *et al.* 1983) and 20 per cent amongst holidaymakers on winter package tours (Cossar *et al.* 1988a), to 75 per cent amongst those on summer package tours to Romania in 1981 (Grist *et al.* 1985) and 78 per cent amongst 375 tourists returning from Spain who selected themselves for study by writing or telephoning to the CD(S)U (Cossar *et al.* 1982). This followed media publicity on legionellosis and travel in 1977.

Taking the distribution of travellers by age group and illness (Table 2.3), the results show that the highest attack rates were recorded by the under-40 age groups, with 41 per cent of the

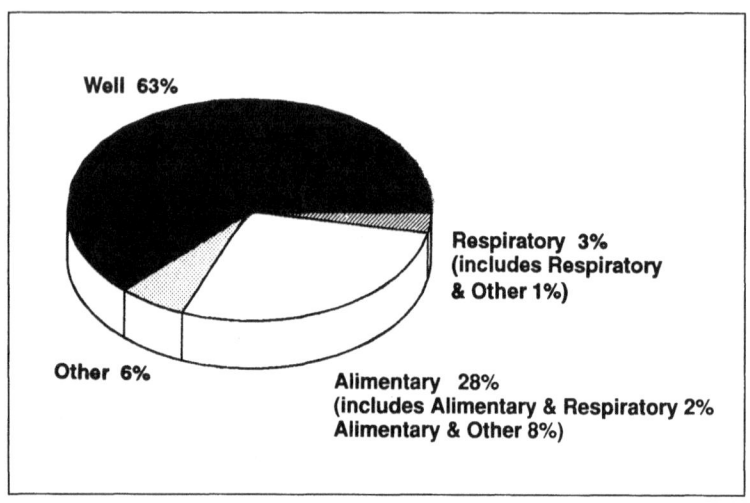

Figure 2.1 Reports of illness in Scottish holidaymakers, 1973–85
Note: n = 14,227

10–19 age group reporting illness and 48 per cent of the 20–29 age group. Thereafter attack rates show a progressive diminution with increasing age.

Eighteen per cent of the travellers reported alimentary symptoms, predominantly diarrhoea and vomiting (Figure 2.1). Taking all the symptom complexes which include alimentary symptoms, this figure rises to 28 per cent of the total number of travellers and to 76 per cent of all those who reported illness.

Comparing the attack rates with the countries visited by the travellers mentioned earlier, there is a general trend that the further south, and to some extent the further east, the travel, the higher the rate for UK residents (Table 2.4). This remains generally true both in summer and in winter. Examples in support of this trend were the 77 per cent attack rate reported by tourists to Northern Africa in the summer and the 57 per cent rate for those travelling to Eastern Europe, and also the 32 per cent attack rate reported by winter tourists to Northern Africa. In addition, attack rates were substantially lower in the winter than in the summer; the mean attack rate for winter travellers being 20 per cent (Cossar *et al.* 1988a) compared with 37 per cent for summer travellers.

Table 2.4 Area visited, season, and reports of illness among Scottish tourists, 1973–85

Area visited	Summer attack rate %	Winter attack rate %
Europe (North)	19	20
Europe (East)	57	12
Mediterranean (Southern Europe)	34	19
Mediterranean (North Africa)	77	32
Average attack rates	77	20

Cossar et al. 1990

Mortality in travellers

A review of 952 persons who died while abroad (Paixao et al. 1991) between 1973 and 1988 revealed that, whilst infection now accounts for only a small proportion (4 per cent) of the mortality, cardiovascular disease was the most frequently recorded cause of death (69 per cent), followed by accidents and injuries (21 per cent). Most deaths occurred in the 50–69 year age range (50 per cent), with the highest cardiovascular mortality (34 per cent) in the 60–69 year age range, and the highest death rate from accidents and injuries (32 per cent) in the 20–29 year age group (with the effect of alcohol as a frequent contributing factor). This highlights the risks of a strenuous holiday in a warm climate for those with a pre-existing cardiovascular problem; and also demonstrates the potential for prevention of deaths in younger travellers by improving awareness of hazards such as road accidents and swimming.

Further evidence that lifestyle has a bearing on travellers' problems emerging from the Glasgow studies is that 37 per cent of 2,784 smokers reported illness, compared with 32 per cent of 7,294 non-smokers – a statistically significant difference. No significant correlation was noted between travellers reporting illness and either the reason for travel, the type of accommodation used, the traveller's socio-economic status, or the length of stay abroad, although the highest attack rates were recorded in those who were unskilled or unemployed, and those who set off with pre-existing ill-health (Cossar 1987).

Table 2.5 Travel-associated admissions by sex and ethnic origin to ID (infectious disease) wards, Ruchill Hospital, Glasgow (1985)

Sex	Ethnic origin	N	%
M: 44	Asian	25	35
(62%)	Caucasian	17	24
	African	2	2
F: 27	Asian	14	20
(38%)	Caucasian	10	14
	African	3	4

Hospital admissions

In attempting to define further the perspective of travel-related illnesses, inpatient data (1985) were analysed from the infectious diseases (ID) wards at Ruchill Hospital, which is the major infectious diseases facility for the Greater Glasgow area (Table 2.5), covering approximately 15 per cent of the Scottish population, 750,000 people.

Out of a total of 1,265 admissions, 71 (6 per cent) were travel-associated, and Asian males accounted for more than one-third of this group; the 20–29 year age group was the most represented (25 per cent). Travel to Southern Asia was associated with 60 per cent of these admissions, correlating with the higher attack rate seen in holidaymakers travelling further south and east; 14 per cent were associated with travel to Spain, probably reflecting the volume of British holidaymakers to that country (5.6 million in 1985) (Central Statistical Office 1985).

Costs

From information supplied by 3,049 travellers from the UK who became unwell whilst abroad, 1 per cent required hospital admission on their return and 14 per cent consulted a doctor. The cost per travel-associated admission in the UK in 1985 was given as approximately £550. If the survey figures for Scottish travellers mentioned earlier are used as a basis for calculating the cost of admission to hospital for all ill travellers, it is estimated that over

£11 million were spent in 1986 in the UK. This amount, as well as requiring uprating for inflation, does not take into account the considerable additional costs involved with primary care consultations, laboratory investigations, specialist consultations, drug prescriptions, loss of working days and loss of vacation time due to such illness, and of course the considerable expense incurred by travellers and their insurance companies from medical treatment obtained abroad (Cossar 1989).

Laboratory information

Analysis of laboratory isolates of pathogens in travellers collated at the CD(S)U reveals that between 1975 and 1986, there had been a five-fold increase in the annual total of reports and a proportionate rise from 62 to 90 per cent in the reports relating to holidaymakers (Sharp 1976; Campbell 1987). Improved reporting may also be a contributory factor to this increase.

Comparing the area visited by these travellers, the isolates in those visiting Southern Europe now comprise 45 per cent of the total, compared with 26 per cent in 1975; there is less proportionate change for those visiting other areas. Cumulative review of the pathogens isolated shows that infections associated with inadequate food handling and poor water supply or sanitation account for 87 per cent of these reports (total number 4,921). This figure only represents the small proportion of travellers who were sufficiently unwell to justify further investigation, but the preponderance of isolates associated with gastro-intestinal illness mirrors the reports of illness found in the questionnaire survey.

Other studies

Review of published surveys from other researchers shows that in a study of travellers' diarrhoea in 16,568 randomly selected Swiss travellers, there was a 28 per cent attack rate (Steffen et al. 1983), and the attack rates in other studies ranged from 18 per cent of 2,665 Finnish travellers (Peltola et al. 1983) to 41 per cent of 2,184 Scottish holidaymakers (McEwan and Jackson 1987). All the studies that specified the most affected age group were in agreement (Steffen et al. 1983; McEwan and Jackson 1987) (i.e. 20–29 years), and similarly where the area was specified, travel to

Table 2.6 Profile of travellers at risk emerging from Scottish research

Package holidaymakers	versus	Other travellers
Inexperienced travellers	versus	Other travellers
Travellers further south, particularly Northern Africa	versus	Other travellers
Summer travellers	versus	Winter travellers
Younger age groups specifically 20–29 years)	versus	Older travellers
Smokers	versus	Non-smokers

Northern Africa (Steffen *et al.* 1983; Peltola *et al.* 1983) or Eastern Europe (McEwan and Jackson 1987) produced the highest attack rates.

The broad correlation of these various findings lends credibility to attempts at detecting patterns of illness derived from the travellers studied, and the use of largely identical methodologies encourages a comparative analysis of relative risk of illness to the travellers, as shown in Table 2.6.

SEROLOGICAL STUDIES ON TRAVELLERS

Different areas of the world have different hazards for the traveller and relevant medical advice specific to the destination country depends upon the pre-existing health status and the immunity to infection of the individual traveller, in addition to the exposure risk which is affected by lifestyle. Some diseases less common in one country are more prevalent in another, which may lead to problems when travellers become complacent about immunisation before travelling to countries where the disease is more common. For example, a traveller from the UK staying in a slum area in Calcutta, without a recent (within 5–10 years) booster dose against poliomyelitis, and unaware that this disease (spread by faecal/oral transmission) is still prevalent in that area, would be at risk of infection (22,416 cases of paralytic poliomyelitis were reported to the World Health Organisation (WHO) in 1989 (WHO 1991)). Again, as a consequence of the recent social catharsis in the former USSR, the collapse of the public health infrastructure which previously delivered a highly efficient immunisation programme, allied to consumer suspicion of the efficacy of the vaccines and safety of the needles used, now means that herd immunity has fallen below protective levels for some common pathogens. It is therefore not surprising that in 1992 an outbreak of diphtheria was reported in Russia with 4,000 cases (Conradi 1993). Thus a disease, previously eradicated, has now returned to present a threat to those of the native population and visitors from abroad with inadequate immunity. It is also causing difficulties for vaccine manufacturers in meeting the demand.

During the period 1979–82, studies on 470 returning travellers from the West of Scotland (Cossar 1991) indicated that 20 per cent had incomplete immunity to poliomyelitis; 64 per cent of those tested (511 travellers) had antibodies to hepatitis A (ranging from 30 per cent for the 10–19 year age group, and rising progressively with increasing age to 89 per cent, for the age group over 60 years); 87 per cent (288 tested) had adequate levels of tetanus antitoxin; and 40 per cent of the 225 travellers tested had adequate levels of diphtheria antitoxin.

These results show inadequate protection to poliomyelitis, hepatitis A, tetanus and diphtheria, putting one in five, one in three, one in eight, and two in three at risk respectively. These data provide a basis for guiding immunisation programmes aimed at the international traveller; for example, the seropositivity profile for hepatitis A supports the cost effectiveness of selective screening in the UK before giving immunoglobulin to older travellers at risk from exposure (Cossar and Reid 1987). The cost of the active hepatitis A vaccine either to the individual traveller, or on the prescriber's budget, also justifies pre-travel screening. Adequate immunisation will provide maximum protection for the traveller exposed to these pathogens, and will also protect the community by reducing the risk of local transmission of infection following importation of such pathogens.

PROTECTING THE TRAVELLER

Whilst it is important that the traveller is advised about the vaccinations appropriate to his destination, it should be emphasised that immunisation and medication can at best only protect against a small proportion (about 5 per cent) of the health hazards to which travellers are exposed. This leaves a vast potential for effective pre-travel health education. The following brief general résumé of some of the commoner topics outlines the range and methods to be encompassed.

Preparation for travel

Good insurance cover is to be strongly recommended. It is a false economy to ignore this issue as the costs of medical care abroad can be financially crippling and due to variability in the standard of local medical care it may be in the best interests of the traveller to be speedily repatriated, which is also facilitated by adequate medical insurance.

In terms of specifying the risk, it is worth bearing in mind that insurance statistics from the USA suggest that three persons in twenty can expect to develop an illness (whether of minor or major significance) every two weeks, irrespective of travel. This is of greater significance in those setting out with a pre-existing illness, who are more vulnerable to develop a health problem, as indeed are the young, the elderly and the pregnant traveller.

It is important that the intending traveller consults for medical advice regarding immunisations in good time (at least 4–6 weeks in advance) to ensure that there is adequate time to complete any complex immunisation schedules. A recent dental check-up will minimise the risk of a painful, expensive experience abroad, as well as anxiety while abroad about the safety of needle and instrument sterilisation.

The journey

The enforced immobility of a long plane journey encourages pooling of fluid in the dependent legs which, in turn, predisposes to the development of ankle swelling and deep venous thrombosis. Travellers with venous insufficiency problems, the elderly and the obese are more at risk, and are to be recommended to try and walk about for about five minutes during every hour of travel as well as to wear appropriate support hose.

Those on daily medications should carry adequate supplies in their hand luggage, otherwise lost baggage can lead to medical complications in addition to frustration.

The modern passenger jet is pressurised to the equivalent of an altitude of 5,000–7,000 feet. This rarely presents a problem for the fit traveller, but the reduced oxygen saturation may present difficulties for those with impaired oxygen-carrying capacity (e.g. severe bronchitics) or those requiring good oxygen saturation (e.g. recent heart attack) which is aggravated in the presence of cigarette smoking.

Due to the system of air circulation within the aircraft, dehydration can be a problem unless adequate fluids are regularly consumed during a long journey.

Finally, it should be borne in mind that an unexpected stopover may occur, exposing the traveller to an unprepared disease risk such as malaria.

Safe water

Water, being a prerequisite for life, can also present particular health hazards for the traveller. Direct ingestion of contaminated water as well as indirect from food consumption of, for example fish, are the most obvious sources of problems. Diseases caused by such ingestion include diarrhoeal diseases, typhoid, cholera, poliomyelitis, hepatitis A and worm infections.

Some simple avoidance strategies include drinking only 'brand name' carbonated bottled waters; boiling which kills all infective agents including amoebic cysts; use of commercially available filters; and chemical disinfection (e.g. 4 drops of 2 per cent iodine to 1 litre of water and allow to stand for 20–30 minutes). Such water should also be used for brushing the teeth!

Similarly, fresh locally obtained food should be regarded as contaminated. Fruit and vegetables are best consumed after thorough washing in treated water or (for salad foods) soaking (12 drops of 2 per cent tincture of iodine to 1 litre water and allowed to stand), before peeling. Raw vegetables and cold food prepared by others is best avoided. Seafood, fish and meat should be consumed well cooked, and unpasteurised milk avoided or boiled.

There are also problems caused by the lack of adequate hygiene and sanitary facilities which predispose to skin and other infections. A further water-related aspect is bites/penetration by water-breeding insects causing disease, e.g. malaria, schistosomiasis.

Sea

Apart from the obvious hazards from recreational pursuits in unsuitable maritime environments, there can now be additional risks as a consequence of modern industrial/agricultural practices. Specifically, chemical contamination of recreational water can give rise to illness such as gastro-enteric upset, although the risk from ingestion of affected seafood is the likelier source of trouble. Also the intensive use of nitrogen-based fertilisers means that the cumulative effect from this being washed off the land predisposes to the development of algal blooms. These have the potential to have an irritant effect on skin and respiratory tissues with the added complication of secondary infection. For these reasons prolonged exposure to contaminated air from such areas or bathing is inadvisable. Any clothing exposed to algae from water-sport activities should be thoroughly hosed down after use.

Clearly, in areas where there is venomous sealife, appropriate precautions should be taken.

Sun

Awareness of the sun's ability to cause not only short-term discomfort from burning but also long-term risks should be fully appreciated. Excessive exposure predisposes to premature skin ageing, skin cancer and cataract development. It is now realised that even a single episode of sunburning in a child carries a disproportionate risk of future skin cancer compared with an adult. Sunlight is also synergistic to fungal skin infections.

Appreciation of these facts by those with high photosensitivity as well as the amplification of the power of sunlight by the effects of water, snow, sand, altitude, latitude and medication will promote a sensible approach in terms of protective clothing, gradual exposure and the use of appropriate sunscreens.

Sex

On account of the sensitive personal nature of this topic, it is one that many advice sources prefer to avoid. However, it has long been recognised that travel is directly associated with making new sexual contact(s), and therefore by definition is in itself a 'risk' factor. Once this is accepted then some of the sensitivities can be put aside. At the same time it seems unfair not to inform the traveller that most of the countries likely to be visited have a higher prevalence rate of HIV than the UK; that almost 80 per cent of the cumulative total of heterosexually contracted AIDS reported in the UK to date were acquired abroad, or that women are 2–4 times more susceptible than men of contracting HIV from unprotected intercourse.

Thereafter specific risk-enhancing factors – such as the greater the number of partners the greater the risk; the higher the frequency of sexual contact the higher the risk; and the choice of a high-risk partner (a prostitute, drug abuser, male homosexual/bisexual) – can be more fully appreciated. The message to be propagated is abstinence; sexual intercourse with one, faithful, lifetime partner; or always carry and use condoms. However, this is an area where much remains to be done in appropriate targeting with suitable material before there can be any realistic hope of modifying travellers' sexual behaviour.

Malaria

The important message about malaria is that no current anti-malarial measures can guarantee absolute protection, although if all mosquito bites can be avoided, then infection will not occur. Even newer anti-malarials, such as mefloquine, have limitations as well as recommendations (Bradley 1993). Therefore, as well as taking the appropriate anti-malarial for 5–7 days prior to entering a malarious area and continuing until four weeks following departure from same, the traveller should take every precaution to minimise mosquito bites.

These precautions include covering exposed skin from dusk onwards and applying an insect repellant containing diethyl toluamide ('DEET') to both the skin and clothing. The use of impregnated wrist and ankle bands is additional protection for vulnerable areas. This is then complemented by the use of permethrin-impregnated mosquito nets over the bed, employing a 'knock-down' spray (pyrethroids) to the room prior to retiring, and a vapona/burning a coil during sleep, which are effective against mosquitoes in *sealed* rooms.

A further more recent concept is the use of 'stand-by' medication provided by the doctor prior to travel for those at risk from resistant malaria in remote locations where rapid access to diagnostic facilities is not possible. The medication is commenced at the onset of typical symptomatology (temperature, fever, chills) whilst locating the nearest medical facility for further help.

Any traveller returning from a malarious area presenting with a 'flu-like' illness should be regarded as suffering from malaria until proved otherwise.

Accidents

Accidents are the second commonest cause of death overall, as well as the premier cause of death in younger travellers. Of the 952 deaths in travellers reviewed by Paixao *et al.* (1991), 197 (21 per cent) were caused by trauma and within this group 78 (40 per cent) were accounted for by the 10–29 year age group. With better insight through pre-travel health education it should be possible to reduce this tragic annual toll of avoidable deaths.

Simple raised awareness of the consequences of a moment's inattention/carelessness, such as diving into unfamiliar swimming pools, not wearing seat belts/crash helmets, failure to remember the contra-traffic direction to the home country, appreciation of differing environmental safety standards (e.g. balcony barrier heights), bites from poorly domesticated animals (perhaps rabid), and exposure to risk of assault by straying from the recognised tourist areas, can minimise preventable accidents. Deaths from assault received a high-press profile with nine such tourist deaths in Florida during the first nine months of 1993. Much can be done by travel agents/tour operators/travel couriers to alert the unwary tourist to 'unsafe/no-go areas and to injudicious conduct'.

All of the above hazards are potentiated by the injudicious use of alcohol, and the natural adventurousness, energy and disinhibitions of youth clearly highlight the prime 'at risk' group.

SOURCES OF INFORMATION AND ADVICE

An inevitable accompaniment to the growth in international travel is that general practitioners and other primary care workers are increasingly contacted by patients seeking advice both prior to travel and following their return, and the intending traveller is faced with a plethora of sources of advice (Figure 2.2).

Although the travel agent may be the most commonly consulted advice source (Cossar *et al.* 1990), there is concern about

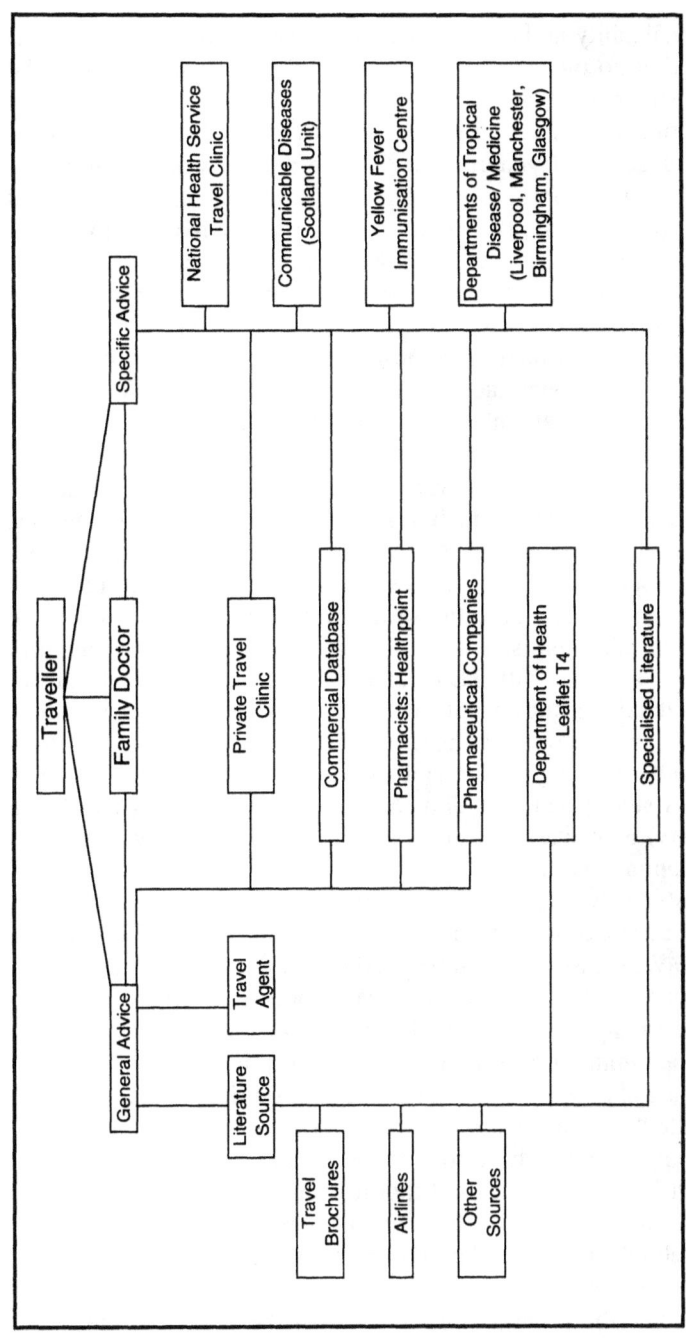

Figure 2.2 Sources of pre-travel health advice for tourists

the availability and quality of that advice (Reid et al. 1986). It is clear that no one source can address all the diverse needs of the traveller, rather a case of 'horses for courses', but that the general practitioner occupies a pivotal role in this field. There are studies that suggest that general practitioners may encounter problems about giving appropriate advice (Usherwood and Usherwood 1989), that general practice may not be the best location for provision of travel advice (Jeffries 1989), but that general practitioners have a medico-legal responsibility to provide accurate advice (Holden 1989).

In recognition of the responsibilities and difficulties which the general practitioner faces in addressing this need, the CD(S)U commenced a telephone advice service for the primary care sector in 1975; in addition a computerised health information database (Travax) (Cossar et al. 1988b) was established in 1982. This nationally accessible database includes recommendations on vaccinations for individual countries, malaria prevention advice, and information about particular vaccines to help in making a balanced judgement when indications are not clear-cut. Details about administration and schedules, interactions between vaccines, and advice for those with HIV infection are included, and current notes detailing known outbreaks, changes in vaccine availability, etc. A recent development is the installation of a UK-wide telephone networking system enabling access by local telephone call from a suitable modem linked to a screen display. This service (Travax) is available to both National Health Service personnel and commercial users.

A study by Arnold in 1990 involving 899 departing UK travellers at Heathrow airport showed a 65 per cent preference for pre-travel health advice to be provided by the general practitioner. This is logical, as the general practitioner is uniquely placed to advise having access to the relevant past medical history, including previous immunisations, allergic reactions, long-term medication and past illnesses, as well as information on the patient/traveller's lifestyle. Such information is essential for the provision of accurate, appropriate advice for the individual traveller. At the same time it has to be recognised that it is impractical for all travellers to attend the family doctor prior to departure and indeed there is much information to be disseminated apart from immunisation advice. Such advice may even be better presented by professionals other than the general practitioner. It is therefore important that every opportunity for the dissemination of appropriate pre-travel health advice be taken whenever the consumer interfaces with the travel 'scene' – be this the travel agent, airline, currency supplier, visa/government agent, in addition to specifically dedicated medical facilities.

CONCLUSION

The growth of travel and the numbers affected by travel-related illnesses, some of a serious nature, means that this subject will increasingly demand recognition by the medical profession, health promotion specialists, the travel trade and travellers. Provision of appropriate advice for the traveller, which is already available, is a shared responsibility and is best channelled through all the agencies that interact with travellers.

Continued monitoring of illness in travellers and provision of information systems about this problem and its prevention, utilising traditional communication channels as well as modern computer technology, with ready access for medical and related workers, is fully justified.

Increased collaboration on travel illness between medical workers, health educators and those involved in the travel trade, will be a very positive and efficacious contribution to reducing illness in, and discomfort for, travellers, and the associated expense that this brings to the health services.

REFERENCES

Arnold, W. S. J. (1990) 'Vaccine information and the practice nurse', paper presented at the Third International Conference on Tourist Health, Venice.
Bradley, D. (1993) 'Prophylaxis against malaria for travellers from the United Kingdom', *British Medical Journal* 306: 1247–52.
Bruce-Chwatt, L. (1973) 'Global problems of imported disease', *Advances in Parasitology* 11: 75–114.
Business Statistics Office (1990) *Business Monitor Annual Statistics* 17, 'Overseas travel and tourism' (MQ 6), Table 8A, London.
Campbell, D. M. (1987) 'Imported infections into Scotland, 1986', *Communicable Diseases Scotland*, Weekly Report 87/47: 7–8.
Central Statistical Office (1985) *Social Trends* 15, Table 10.13, London.
Communicable Diseases (Scotland) Unit (1992) 'Current notes "imported malaria" ', *Communicable Diseases and Environmental Health in Scotland* Weekly Report 92/93: 1.

— (1993) ANSWER (AIDS News Supplement), *Communicable Diseases Scotland*, Weekly Report A.286: 3.
Conradi, P. (1993) 'Russia's diphtheria outbreak worsens', *British Medical Journal* 306: 417.
Cossar, J. H. (1987) 'Studies on illnesses associated with travel', unpublished MD thesis, Glasgow, University of Glasgow.
— (1989) 'A review of travel-associated illness', in *Travel Medicine* (Proceedings of the First Conference on International Travel Medicine, Zurich 1988), Berlin: Springer-Verlag, 50–4.
— (1991) 'An immune profile of Scots travellers: a basis for immunization' (Proceedings of the Second Conference on International Travel Medicine, Atlanta 1991), Atlanta: International Society of Travel Medicine, 298.
Cossar, J. H. and Reid, D. (1987) 'Not all travellers need immunoglobulin for hepatitis A', *British Medical Journal* 294: 1503.
Cossar, J. H. and Reid, D. (1989) 'Health hazards of international travel', *World Health Statistics Quarterly* 42, 2: 27–42.
Cossar, J. H., Dewar, R. D., Fallon, R. J., Grist, N. R. and Reid, D. (1982) '*Legionella pneumophila* in tourists', *Practitioner* 226: 1543–8.
Cossar, J. H., Dewar, R. D., Fallon, R. J., Reid, D., Bell, E. J., Riding, M. H. and Grist, N. R. (1984) 'Rapid response health surveillance of Scottish tourists', *Travel and Traffic Medicine International* 2, 1: 23–7.
Cossar, J. H., Dewar, R. D., Reid, D. and Grist, N. R. (1988a) 'Travel and health: illness associated with winter package holidays', *The Journal of the Royal College of General Practitioners* 33: 642–5.
Cossar, J. H., Walker, E., Reid, D. and Dewar, R. D. (1988b) 'Computerised advice on malaria prevention and immunisation', *British Medical Journal* 296: 358.
Cossar, J. H., Reid, D., Fallon, R. J., Bell, E. J., Riding, M. H., Follett, E. A. C., Dow, B. C., Mitchell, S. and Grist, N. R. (1990) 'A cumulative review of studies on travellers, their experience of illness and the implications of these findings', *Journal of Infection* 21: 27–42.
Dewar, R. D., Cossar, J. H., Reid, D. and Grist, N. R. (1983) 'Illness amongst travellers to Scotland: a pilot study', *Health Bulletin (Edinburgh)* 41/3: 155–62.
Grist, N. R., Cossar, J. H., Reid, D., Dewar, R. D., Fallon, R. J., Riding, M. H. and Bell, E. J. (1985) 'Illness associated with a package holiday in Romania', *Scottish Medical Journal* 30: 156–60.
Holden, J. D. (1989) 'General practitioners and vaccination for foreign travel', *Journal of the Medical Defence Union*, Spring: 6–7.
International Civil Aviation Organisation (1990) *Development of World Schedule Revenue Traffic, 1945–1990 Statistics*, Montreal: ICAO.
Jeffries, M. (1989) 'Booster for GP travel vaccine clinics', *Monitor* 2, 31: 10–11.
Lawson, J. H., Grist, N. R., Reid, D. and Wilson, T. S. (1977) 'Legionnaires' disease', *Lancet* ii: 108.
McEwan, A. and Jackson, M. H. (1987) 'Illness among Scots holidaymakers who had travelled abroad, summer 1983', *Communicable Diseases Scotland*, Weekly Report 87/16: 7–9.

Paixao, M. T. D.'A., Dewar, R. D., Cossar, J. H., Covell, R. G. and Reid, D. (1991) 'What do Scots die of when abroad?', *Scottish Medical Journal* 36: 114–16.
Peltola, H., Kyronseppa, H. and Holsa, P. (1983) 'Trips to the South – a health hazard', *Scandinavian Journal of Infectious Diseases* 15: 375–81.
Reid, D., Cossar, J. H., Ako, T. I. and Dewar, R. D. (1986) 'Do travel brochures give adequate advice on avoiding illness?', *British Medical Journal* 293: 1472.
Sharp, J. C. M. (1976) 'Imported infections into Scotland, 1975', *Communicable Diseases Scotland*, Weekly Report 76/26: v–vi.
Steel, T. (1984) *Scotland's Story*, London: Collins.
Steffen, R., van der Linde, F., Syr, K. and Schar, M. (1983) 'Epidemiology of diarrhoea in travellers', *Journal of the American Medical Association* 249: 1176–80.
Usherwood, V. and Usherwood, T. P. (1989) 'Survey of general practitioners' advice for travellers to Turkey', *Journal of the Royal College of General Practitioners* 39: 148–50.
World Health Organisation (1991) 'Poliomyelitis in 1987, 1988 and 1989 – Part I', *Weekly Epidemiological Record* 66: 49.
World Tourism Organisation (1990) *World Tourism Statistics*, Madrid: World Tourism Organization.

Chapter 3

Travellers' diarrhoea

Rodney Cartwright

INTRODUCTION

The commonest travel-associated illness is travellers' diarrhoea. The incidence among travellers varies not only from country to country but also within countries and from season to season (Figure 3.1). Travellers' diarrhoea, which may only be a mild disturbance of bowel function or at the other extreme may cause severe fluid loss and prostration, has been well recognised throughout the ages. In spite of this, there remains a major lack of detailed knowledge of the epidemiology and micro-biological routes of spread, both of which are important factors necessary for the development of effective control measures. This does not, however, imply a total lack of knowledge or absence of control measures, although the ongoing high incidence of travellers' diarrhoea in some popular tourist areas indicates the need for further studies.

Travellers' diarrhoea is a syndrome associated with travel to developing countries predominantly in tropical and subtropical regions and to holiday resorts elsewhere with impure water supplies and inadequate sewage disposal systems. Attack rates may exceed 50 per cent in tourists to some destinations.

Although not usually a severe illness, the nuisance value of travellers' diarrhoea can be high and may discourage travellers from visiting countries or resorts with a recognised high incidence. The resulting economic impact may be substantial for both the receiving countries and the tourism industry. Travellers returning to their home country with persisting symptoms may require medical attention and may also pose a public health hazard. Outbreaks of gastro-intestinal infection such as *Shigella sonnei*

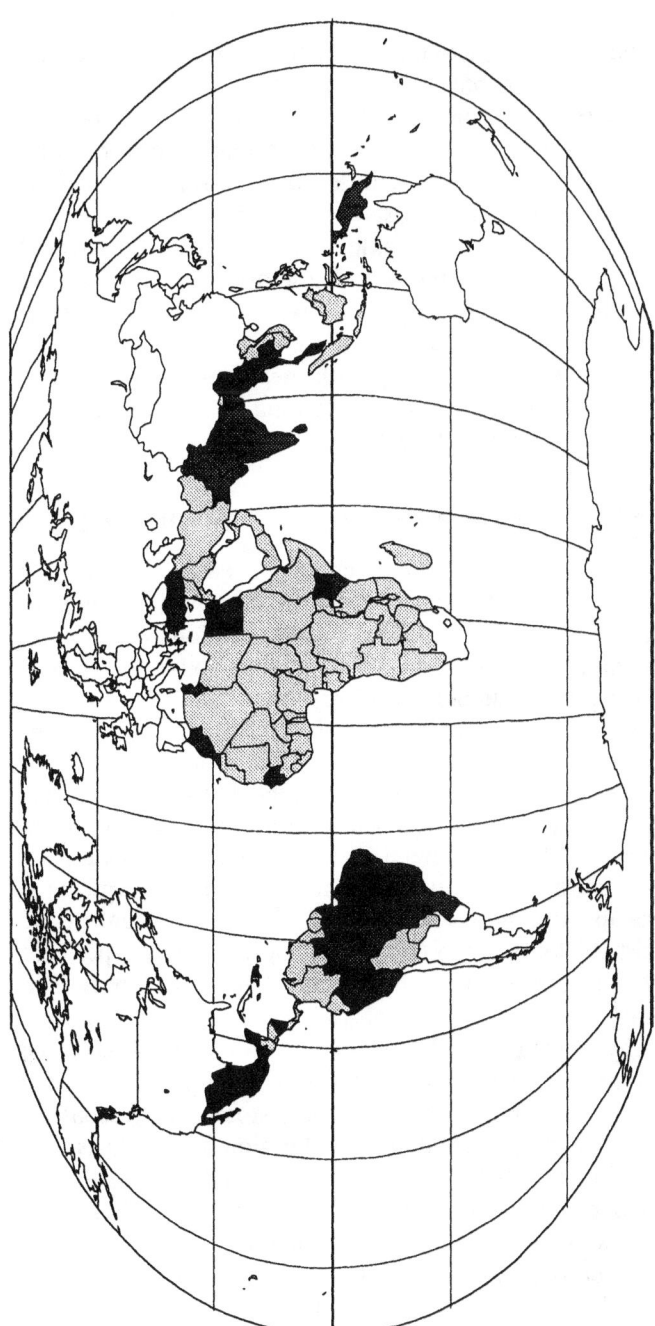

Figure 3.1 Areas associated with a high rate of travellers' diarrhoea

Note: The areas with dark shading have featured in epidemiological studies whereas information on the other shaded areas is based on anecdotal evidence or supposition

dysentery have been described in which the source of infection was a person who had recently returned from abroad with diarrhoea (NIH 1985; Cartwright 1992). Thus a clearer understanding of travellers' diarrhoea may provide an opportunity for health professions and promoters to address the need for better education and information for tourists to reduce a widespread but sometimes unnecessary and unpleasant aspect of the overall tourist experience of a destination. These are important reasons for studying and controlling travellers' diarrhoea both for the individual traveller, the communities of the sending and receiving country, and the tourism industry, with the widespread economic implications for both the tourist and destination area that is often required to provide medical treatment.

THE SYNDROME OF TRAVELLERS' DIARRHOEA

Travellers' diarrhoea is a syndrome characterised by a two-fold or greater increase in the frequency of unformed bowel movements. Commonly associated symptoms include abdominal cramps, nausea, bloating, urgency, fever and malaise (NIH 1985). The stools may be loose, liquid or watery but blood is present in only a minority of cases (Kollaritsch 1989b). The symptoms usually commence during the first few days of arrival in a high-risk area, with a peak rate of onset on the third or fourth day and with a small secondary peak during the second week (Pitzinger et al. 1991). Untreated, the diarrhoeal episodes last on an average for three to four days. The duration of symptoms is usually less in those above 40 years of age. Ten per cent of the cases persist for longer than one week, approximately 2 per cent for longer than one month, and less than 1 per cent longer than three months.

A minority of patients will have a more prolonged illness often with accompanying symptoms of fever, vomiting or abdominal cramps; or blood or mucus observed in the stools. The reasons for the variation in the presentation and duration of the illness are related to both the infecting organism and host factors. Although the illness is rarely severe in adults, occasionally hospitalisation may be necessary for parenteral rehydration. In children the illness may become chronic with small intestinal histological abnormalities and malabsorption (Msengi et al. 1988).

The causative agents: international perspectives

The principal aetiologic agents of travellers' diarrhoea have been identified as a result of specific but localised studies (Black 1990; Matilla et al. 1992). The range of aetiologic agents is similar throughout the world although differences in the mix vary according to the geographical location and the season. Assumptions are made as to the causative agents in areas where there have been no specific studies. In areas with a high incidence, the level of clinical and public health microbiology is usually limited and the investigation of cases of travellers' diarrhoea does not have a high priority in the national health programmes. It should be understood that even when faecal cultures are performed, that it is frequently not possible to identify causative organisms due to a failure to seek for all recognised pathogens, unrecognised pathogens and the relative insensitivity of the methods for detecting known pathogens or failure to collect specimens during the acute phase of the illness. There is usually only one enteropathogen isolated from a patient although mixed infections with two or more pathogens were reported.

Enterotoxigenic *E. coli* (also known as Enteropathogenic *E. coli*) (ETEC) are the predominant cause of travellers' diarrhoea throughout the world. ETEC adhere and multiply in the small intestine where they release enterotoxins. The toxins are either heat stable (ST) or heat labile (LT), implying that they can be destroyed by heat. One or both toxins may be released by individual isolates. Their detection in faecal samples is not straightforward and they are rarely sought in most routine microbiology laboratories due to a lack of both resources and expertise. Studies in travellers in Mexico have recorded it as a cause in 33 per cent to 72 per cent (median, 45 per cent) of cases. In Latin American countries other than Mexico, the median of five studies was 42 per cent (range, 26–72 per cent). In eight studies in Asia, ETEC have been found in 16 per cent (range, 0–37 per cent) and in three African studies in 36 per cent (range, 33–71 per cent) (Black 1990). Among Finnish tourists in Morocco, a seasonal difference was observed. In the autumn ETEC were isolated from 32 per cent of 111 cases of diarrhoea but from only 8 per cent of sixty cases in the winter (Mattila et al. 1992). These seasonal differences are important as they may indicate different sources and/or routes of infection. This in turn will influence the choice of preventive measures.

A case control study in England found ETEC in 5.8 per cent of 600 travellers returning from developed (mainly Mediterranean countries), 11.3 per cent in 36 from less developed countries and 0.9 per cent of 1,282 whose illness was not associated with recent travel abroad (Ahren *et al.* 1990). Enterotoxin-producing bacteria were identified in 20 per cent of 217 returning Swedish travellers with diarrhoea. The majority of the isolates were ETEC, although Enterotoxigenic Klebsiella, Morganella, Citrobacter, Pseudomonas and E-F group were also identified (Jertborn and Svennerholm 1991). Outbreaks of diarrhoea in cruise ship passengers have been attributed to ETEC infection (Snyder *et al.* 1984). Serologic responses to ETEC infection can be detected. A prospective study of ETEC serum antibody levels in Swedish travellers detected significant antibody response to *E. coli* heat labile enterotoxin (LT) and colonisation factors CFA I or II (Jertborn *et al.* 1988). Anti-LT responses did not correlate with a history of diarrhoea whereas anti-CFA responses were more frequent in those with symptomatic infections. A response in both the anti-LT and the homologous anti-CFA was seen following infection with ETEC among Bangladeshi women and children. The presence of antibody was not associated with a lower risk of LT-ETEC infection (Clemens *et al.* 1990). A less well-recognised and defined group the enteroadherent *E. coli*, which adhere to Hep 2 cells in culture but do not produce characteristic enterotoxins, has been associated with diarrhoea in travellers. It is not known how they cause diarrhoea (Mathewson *et al.* 1985).

Salmonella are a world-wide cause of gastro-enteritis attributed to food poisoning but are not a major cause of travellers' diarrhoea. They are nevertheless important as many travellers will still be excreting the organisms on their return home. The isolation rate in various studies ranges up to 33 per cent (Ahren *et al.* 1990; Black 1990). In a Moroccan study *Salmonella enteritica* was as common as ETEC in the autumn but rare in the winter (Mattila *et al.* 1992). It has been observed that salmonella are identified significantly more after travel to Southern Europe than to various tropical and subtropical areas (Speelman *et al.* 1983).

The *Shigella* species is associated with travellers' diarrhoea world-wide (Speelman *et al.* 1983; Black 1990). *Sh. boydii, Sh. flexneri* and *Sh. dysenteriae I* are particularly associated with travel to the tropics and subtropics. In 1984, there was a high rate of diarrhoeal illness in visitors to Albufeira, Portugal. *Shigella sonnei* was one of the causative organisms and five outbreaks of dysentery in the United Kingdom were traced to returning tourists from this resort (Cartwright 1992). The outbreaks occurred in different areas of the country but most affected young children. The causative bacteria carried markers which distinguished them from the strains which were already present in England and Wales. They were, however, the same as those in *Shigella sonnei* isolated from tourists returning from Albufeira with diarrhoea.

Campylobacter, the commonest cause of indigenous diarrhoea in the United Kingdom, has also been reported as a causative agent of travellers' diarrhoea (Speelman *et al.* 1983). Differences in reported rates range from 2 per cent to 28 per cent. In Morocco a seasonal variation was observed (Mattila *et al.* 1992), the significance of which has been discussed under the section of ETEC. *Vibrio cholerae* is a rare cause of travellers' diarrhoea even in visitors to endemic areas. *Vibrio parahaemolyticus* is, however, not uncommon in visitors to Thailand (Sriratanaban and Reinprayoon 1982) and South-East Asia (Taylor and Escheverria 1986). Associated with the ingestion of raw or improperly cooked seafood, *V. cholerae* non –01 and *V. fluvialis* have been isolated from travellers in Asia with travellers' diarrhoea (Gascon *et al.* 1993). These vibrios are part of the normal bacterial content of coastal waters in many parts of the world, contaminating seafood and in particular shellfish. These are killed by thorough cooking of the fish.

Aeromonas hydrophila (Kuijper *et al.* 1989), *Plesiomonas shigelloides* (Kain and Kelly 1989), *Providencia alcalifaciens* (Haynes and Hawkey 1989) are among other bacterial pathogens which have been reported in travellers' diarrhoea. Although these bacteria are not associated with large outbreaks of illness, they illustrate that in individuals there are many divergent species of bacteria capable of causing the common problem of travellers' diarrhoea.

The commonest intestinal parasite causing travellers' diarrhoea is *Giardia lamblia* and has long been associated with drinking tap water in St Petersberg (Leningrad) and in travellers to developing countries (Wright 1983). *Cryptosporidium* may cause travellers' diarrhoea although its incidence probably reflects the general distribution of the organism (Egger *et al.* 1990). *Entamoeba histolytica*, the cause of amoebiasis, is always a hazard to visitors to tropical and subtropical areas. The clinical features are, however, far more severe than those in normal travellers' diarrhoea.

It can be anticipated that enteroviruses will be widely spread in areas where there is a high incidence of travellers' diarrhoea. The precise role of viruses as a cause of travellers' diarrhoea is unknown as technical difficulties have precluded searching for them in most studies. Rota virus has been found in Mexican and Asian studies and seroconversions to Norwalk virus in some Peace Corps studies in Thailand and Honduras (Black 1990). In regions with a high incidence of travellers' diarrhoea, the faecal oral route of transmission is well established, with a consequent higher risk of exposure to wild strains of polio virus. All travellers should ensure that they have been fully immunised. *Coccidia* – cyanobacterium-like bodies and algal-like organisms – have been described as causing diarrhoea in visitors to Nepal (Egger *et al.* 1990) and the Caribbean (Long *et al.* 1990; Bendall *et al.* 1993; Lebbad and Linder 1993).

From this brief survey, it is apparent that travellers' diarrhoea is a widespread complaint with no single micro-organism causing the problem. For this reason, it is useful to turn to the epidemiology of travellers' diarrhoea to assess the scale and nature of the problem among international tourists in different destinations and resort areas.

Epidemiology

The study of any infection or communicable disease requires an understanding of its incidence, spatial and temporal distribution. The collection of data on travel-associated diseases poses particular problems. As has been noted already, travellers' diarrhoea is generally a mild disease of short duration not requiring medical attention and therefore unlikely to feature in any official health statistics. Data on those seeking medical attention or from whom specific pathogens have been isolated will not only be a very poor indicator of the numerator but will not provide any measure of the denominator. Although it is possible to count the numbers of returning travellers visiting their general practitioner, this does not include people who were ill but did not seek medical help. To determine the risk of acquiring illness in another country or resort requires information on both how many people went to the resort and how many were ill. The majority of the published information comes from short-term, intensive studies on small samples of travellers. These studies are expensive, involving either interviewers at the airport or the use of detailed questionnaires. They can be sustained for short studies but they are not viable for a long-term continuous study. The co-operation of tour operators and/or airlines is usually required and there is considerable sensitivity as to potential problems that may arise if a client's attention is drawn to illness acquired while on holiday.

A questionnaire study of 2,211 travellers returning from abroad to Scotland in summer 1977 revealed that 43 per cent had been ill predominantly with travellers' diarrhoea during their holiday or shortly after their return. Forty-five countries had been visited although the Mediterranean countries predominated. Visitors to Tunisia and Morocco had the highest rate of illness. A winter study showed a lower overall incidence of alimentary symptoms although the incidence for Tunisia remained high. A survey of 355 visitors to Scotland revealed an incidence of 5 per cent for alimentary illness (Reid et al. 1980) (see Chapter 2, this volume, for further details).

A large-scale study involving 16,568 travellers travelling home on charter flights to Switzerland and Germany used questionnaires completed during the flight (Pitzinger et al. 1991). The countries visited included some in the tropics, some in the subtropics and with North America as a control. Travellers' diarrhoea was defined as the occurrence of three or more watery or unformed stools or any number of such stools when accompanied by fever, abdominal cramps or vomiting. A total of 5.1 per cent of travellers to North America had travellers' diarrhoea whereas in most tropical countries the incidence exceeded 30 per cent. A lower level of 22.3 per cent was recorded for Thailand. In the subtropics Mexico had an incidence of 31 per cent and Tunisia 8.4 per cent. No correlation could be recognised between the star rating of a hotel and the incidence of travellers' diarrhoea. Overall the incidence was higher in those under 30 years of age. This probably reflects the different lifestyles of the younger adults who tend to be more adventurous in their eating and drinking habits.

An Austrian study involving 3,696 tourists (Kollaritsch 1989a) supports the high rates in subtropical countries and also seasonal variations. A study among those attending medical conferences in Mexico City showed attack rates for North Americans of 55 per cent, Australians 57 per cent, Europeans 39 per cent, and those from South America and the Far East 15 per cent (Lowenstein *et al.* 1973). Further breakdown of the European data showed higher rates in delegates from countries in Northern Europe as compared to those from Southern Europe. None of the prophylactic precautions either by medication or dietary restrictions decreased the risk of illness. The incidence of travellers' diarrhoea among 485 persons attending a European Congress in the United Kingdom was 2.8 per cent for the 143 British residents and 0.6 for 342 visitors (Freedman 1977).

Visitors to Mexico have been the subject of many studies into the causative organisms of travellers' diarrhoea and the effectiveness of various control measures (Black 1990). The median attack rate in fifteen of nineteen studies between 1974 and 1987 was 49 per cent (range 21–66 per cent). The study populations were mainly adult students, the number in each study varying from 19 to 188. Similar studies in Latin American countries had a median attack rate of 53 per cent (range 21–100 per cent), Asia 54 per cent (range, 21–57 per cent) and Africa 54 per cent (range, 37–62 per cent). The study populations in these areas were Peace Corps volunteers, adult tourists, students and military personnel. The rates in control groups of prophylactic studies in Egypt (Scott *et al.* 1990), Tunisia (Rademaker *et al.* 1989) and Turkey (Oksanen *et al.* 1990) were 26 per cent, 64 per cent and 46.5 per cent respectively.

Information from British package tourists

A different approach has been used in order to obtain a continuing profile of holiday resorts and regions (Cartwright 1992). Many tour operators use a client satisfaction questionnaire (CSQ) to assess the response of their clients to various aspects of their holiday. In the early 1980s, Thomson Holidays (now Thomson Tour Operations Ltd – TTO) agreed to include the questions 'Were you ill at any time during your holiday? If yes, please specify.'

Answers to the general questionnaires provided information as to the location and the timing of the holiday, the type of catering, and the age and sex of the client. The questionnaires are completed by clients over 16 years of age during the return flight to the UK. The data from the questionnaires are coded and entered into a computer by a commercial market analysis company. The specified illness is coded into 'stomach upsets', 'respiratory symptoms', 'combination of stomach upsets and respiratory symptoms', and 'other'. All diarrhoea and gastrointestinal symptoms are defined as subjective travellers' diarrhoea. A subset of the total data is analysed monthly using SPSS v 4.0 on an Apple Macintosh Quadra 700. In areas with a high incidence a more detailed analysis to hotel level and by client parameters such as age, sex, occupation and type of catering is undertaken.

In the summer seasons from 1984 to 1993 data from 2,756,321 questionnaires were analysed. In 1992 and 1993 over 600,000 questionnaires were analysed for each season. Data for the winter seasons from 1988 to 1993 have also been collected and analysed. This continuous study since 1984 has obtained information from nearly 6 million British package holiday tourists (Figure 3.2). The pattern for each year is similar, with the peak months being August and September. It would be tempting to believe that the reduction in peak rates from 1984 to 1991 represented an improvement in public health hygiene. While undoubtedly there was improvement in some resorts, the overall pattern is more likely due to changes in the destination regions and resorts included in the tour operator's programme. The highest rates recorded were in tropical Africa, southern and eastern Mediterranean countries and the Dominican Republic (Figure 3.3). A seasonal variation which was less pronounced in countries nearer the equator was observed (Figure 3.4). The reasons for seasonal variations are not fully understood but are multifactorial and include water availability, ambient temperatures and fly populations.

Doubts have been cast as to the value and accuracy of such a subjective-based study relying on such imprecise data. It is not possible to compare the incidence figures with those obtained from studies that have a clearly defined definition of travellers' diarrhoea. Nevertheless, the incidence levels in different countries in this study does not differ significantly from those obtained from short intensive studies. There has also been a good correlation with major public health changes in resorts, as shown by a dramatic fall in subjective travellers' diarrhoea in the resort of Salou (Figure 3.5) following the commission of a new drinking water supply in the Tarragona region of Spain.

This study is unique in providing a time dimension over ten years for many different resorts. It is limited by a number of factors such as the geographical coverage, the exclusion of children, and

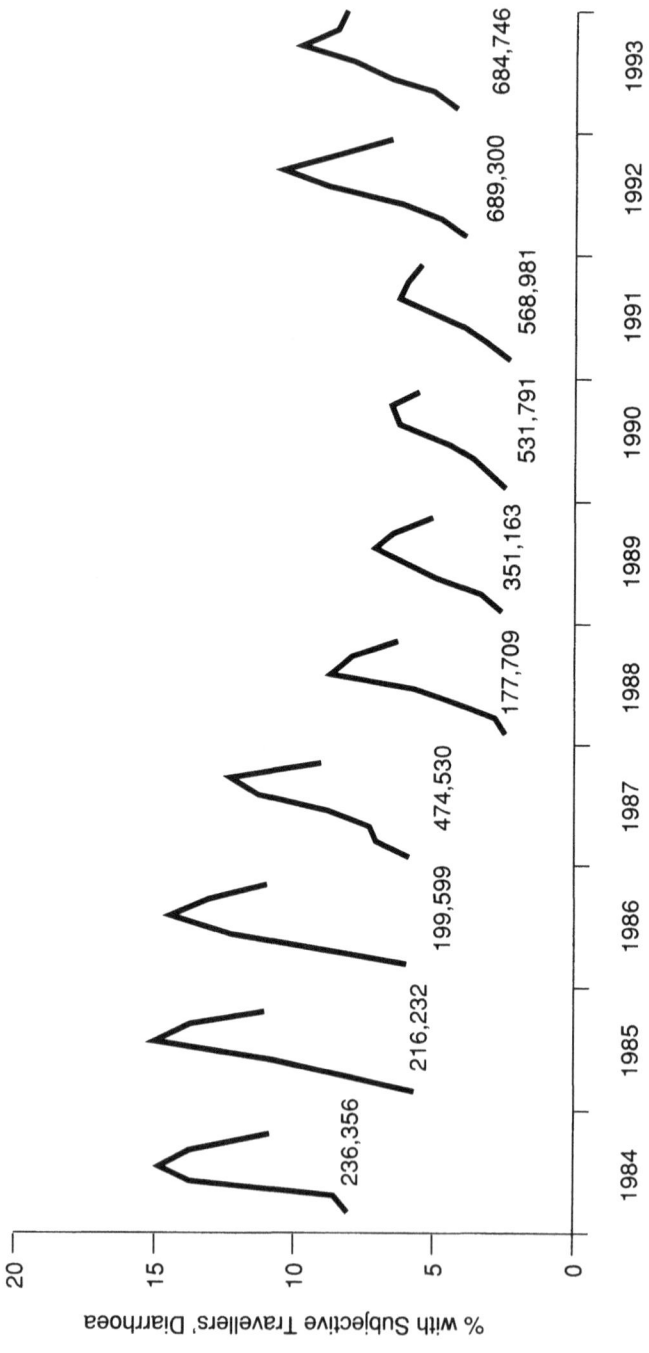

Figure 3.2 Subjective travellers' diarrhoea in British package holidaymakers, 1984–93

Source: Data obtained from Thomson Tour Operations Ltd client satisfaction questionnaires. The number of questionnaires examined each year is indicated.

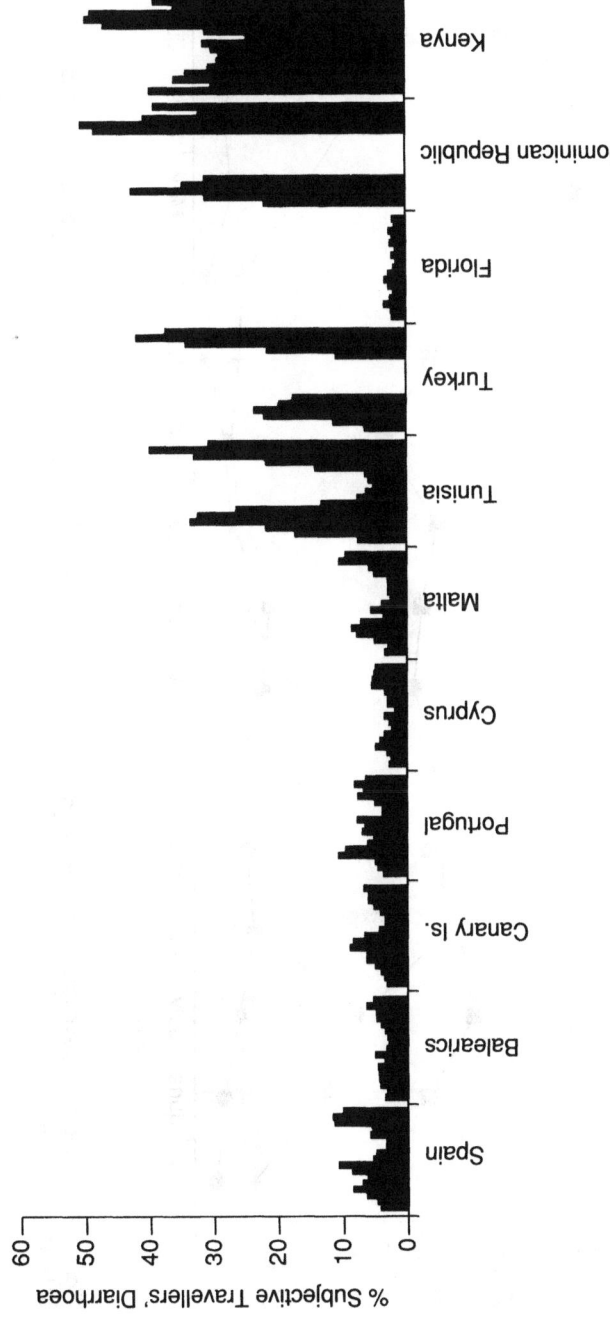

Figure 3.3 Subjective travellers' diarrhoea in British package holidaymakers, May 1991–September 1992

Note: There was no winter programme in Turkey or the Dominican Republic.

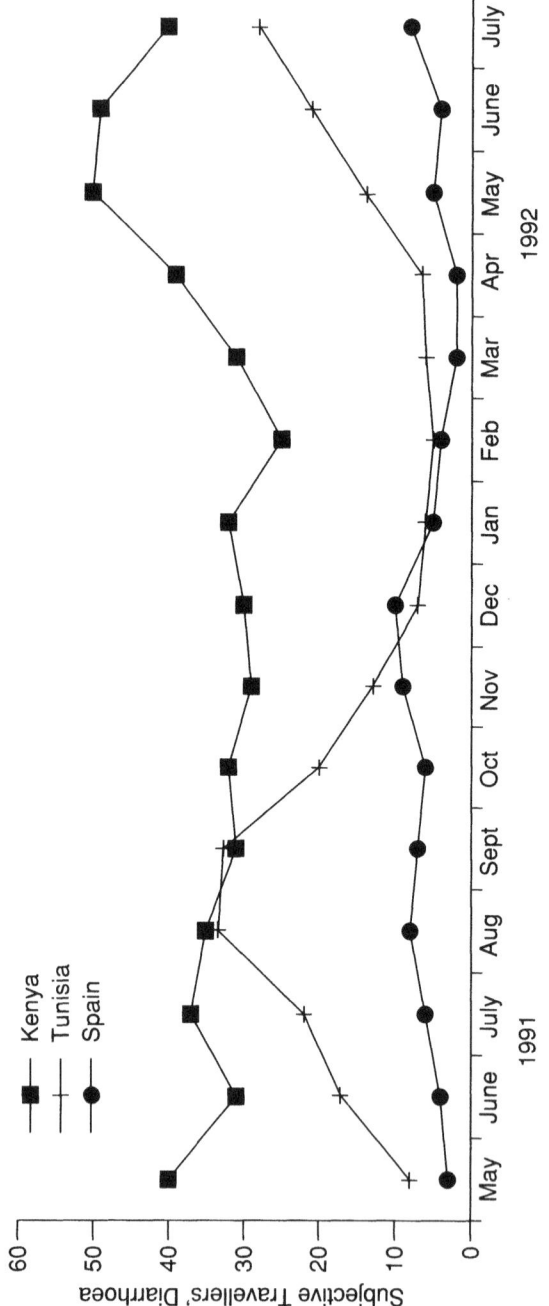

Figure 3.4 Subjective travellers' diarrhoea in British package holidaymakers showing differing seasonal variations between countries

the imprecise definition of travellers' diarrhoea. There is also the possibility of a bias in that the clients are all from one tour operator.

The Swiss as well as the TTO British studies rely on the close co-operation of tour operators and airlines. Such co-operation enables data to be collected from large numbers of travellers but is limited by the operator's desire not to remind their clients of the less enjoyable aspects of a holiday. The co-operation of the tourism industry requires an understanding by the investigators of the fears and requirements of the industry. It also requires a different approach by medical epidemiologists who are usually able to define exactly the criteria for inclusion into a disease category. The ongoing study of travel-associated disease has required a compromise but as the above study has demonstrated, it is possible to obtain useful epidemiological data sufficient for the purpose for which it is required. It is of paramount importance that the limitations of this and any similar studies are clearly understood and that the results are not given unsustainable meanings.

How then are the findings of the ongoing British study used? Areas with a high incidence of travellers' diarrhoea are highlighted. These may be areas where there is an unexpected increase or those which have a continuous high background level. The unexpected increase is invariably due to a local, short-term problem which has already been recognised and often dealt with by the local public health officials. The study results may be made available to those concerned to provide a monitoring mechanism on the effects of remedial actions. In areas with a high background the tour operator, either alone or in conjunction with other operators, will often approach the health and tourism departments in the area concerned.

The initial response is usually that there is not a problem and that other areas are equally as bad. The study results have been invaluable in explaining that this is not necessarily so and that they can be a useful monitoring tool to assess the effects of any remedial works. The confidential nature of the data is an essential factor in obtaining the co-operation of officials. The aim is co-operation for improvement not the public exposure of inadequate facilities. This study is being strengthened by the inclusion of data from other British and Scandinavian tour operators.

A further source of information in England and Wales is from epidemiological data collected by the Communicable Diseases Surveillance Centre of the Public Health Laboratory Service. This provides information on a limited number of enteric pathogens infecting British holidaymakers. These data are only available, however, if the holidaymaker consulted a doctor in the UK, if a faecal specimen was sent to a laboratory, if a pathogen was isolated, and if the isolate was reported together with the relevant travel history. The numbers are not representative of those infected and there is no information on the population at risk. However, for diseases such as typhoid fever and cholera, these data are extremely valuable, enabling international warnings to be given through the World Health Organisation.

PREVENTION OF TRAVELLERS' DIARRHOEA

Travellers' diarrhoea is essentially a preventable condition depending on the attainment and maintenance of high standards of public health and in particular those aspects concerned with safe water supplies, safe sewage disposal systems and effective food safety programmes. The challenge posed by many tourists is the desire to visit the less developed world and developing countries, yet enjoying the safety and hygiene which can be expected in the industrialised countries of Europe and North America. It is not only the standards within hotels which are important but also those of the resort, region and country. Improvements which reduce the incidence of travellers' diarrhoea will also have beneficial effects for the health of the indigenous population. The attainment of the appropriate standards requires the will of the politicians in the countries concerned with the provision of the appropriate resources and the establishment and implementation of necessary legislation. The recognition of the value to the indigenous population both in direct health terms and in the economic advantage of a thriving tourism industry is an important first step. All too often the problem is regarded as belonging to the health ministry as it involves health, only to then be referred to the tourism ministry as it involves tourists, whereas in reality it must involve at least both these ministries working together. It is essential that collaboration occurs between not only ministries of health and tourism but also those responsible for the environment, food production and power supplies. Inadequate electricity supplies can have a profound negative effect on the health of a community.

The international tourism industry plays a very important role in providing an important stimulus to ensure that necessary control programmes are formulated and implemented. The tour operators do not, however, have unlimited powers; they rely on persuasion and, as a last resort, the threat of sanctions by withdrawing their clients. Tour operators vary in their approach to matters affecting the health of their clients. Some have active client welfare departments which take a proactive approach while others have minimal sections who appear only to react to problems as a damage limitation exercise. The EC Package Travel Directive may become an important factor in encouraging tour operators to adopt the proactive approach as they become liable for all aspects of the package which they sell (Council Directive 1990).

Effective control requires the efforts and expertise of the receiving countries, the sending countries, international bodies such as the World Health Organisation and the World Tourist Organisation, the tourism industry and last, but by no means least, the individual tourist.

The most important preventive measures are those concerned with water, food and sewage. Water supplies vary both in quality and quantity. An adequate quantity of properly treated and distributed water is a fundamental public health requirement. The situation in Salou, Spain, in the late 1980s provides a telling example of the importance of water. The ongoing surveillance study had identified a problem in Salou with over 30 per cent of the tourists questioned reporting a diarrhoeal illness during the month of August in 1987 and 1988. In 1989 the incidence in June and July was exceeding that of previous years. The problem was not initially accepted locally but the occurrence of an outbreak of typhoid fever in July resulted in an in-depth investigation. Fourteen cases of typhoid fever were recognised involving British, Irish, Swiss and Spanish nationals. Three different strains of *Salmonella typhi* were isolated, indicating a sewage-contaminated source rather than a point source involving one person. At the time of the outbreak the water in the taps had a heavy salt content as the source wells were at a level that enabled salt water ingress. Hoteliers were coping by buying water from lorries which were filled from various sources, frequently rivers. There was no obvious public health control of the water quality. It was fortuitous that a new water supply to the region became operational within a few weeks of the outbreak. The surveillance system recorded a drop in the incidence of travellers' diarrhoea which has been maintained during successive years (Figure 3.5).

A similar reduction in the incidence of travellers' diarrhoea was observed among travellers to Albufeira in Portugal following an improvement in the water supply in 1984. If the quality of the water in an area is suspect, tourists should either boil the tap water or use bottled water, preferably uncarbonated. Care must also be taken regarding ice as it is a common misunderstanding that freezing destroys harmful pathogens. The majority are effectively preserved!

The other end of the water cycle within communities relates to sewage and its disposal, which may vary from the unregulated addition to rivers and the sea to highly sophisticated treatment works with safe solid and fluid effluents. Unregulated disposal may result in recreational waters becoming contaminated and becoming the source of infection. The EC Directive concerning the quality of bathing waters provides standards aimed at reducing the risk of acquiring infections by the recreational use of sewage-contaminated waters (Council Directive 1976). In hot climates the reuse of waste water may be a very important fact recognised by the WHO in their guidelines for the use of wastewater for agriculture and aquaculture (Mara and Cairncross 1989).

Food hygiene and safe food-handling are essential not only for the control of travellers' diarrhoea but also for the prevention of the classical forms of food poisoning. The maintenance of high food hygiene standards in accommodation, which forms part of a holiday package, is the responsibility not only of the local owner and manager, but also of the tour operator. The importance of good food standards and hygiene is recognised by most countries and the principles are incorporated in legislation. The European Community has taken steps to harmonise the legislation in member states. There are now Directives covering Food Hygiene; Meat and Meat Products; Poultry; Game; Fish and Shellfish; Milk and Milk Products; Eggs and Egg Products; Labelling of Foods; Composition (permitted colouring matter, emulsifiers, stabilisers, thickeners, pesticide residues, sweeteners, materials in contact with food and many more).

The Directive 93/43/EEC on the Hygiene of Foodstuffs requires member states to incorporate the Directive in their domestic laws

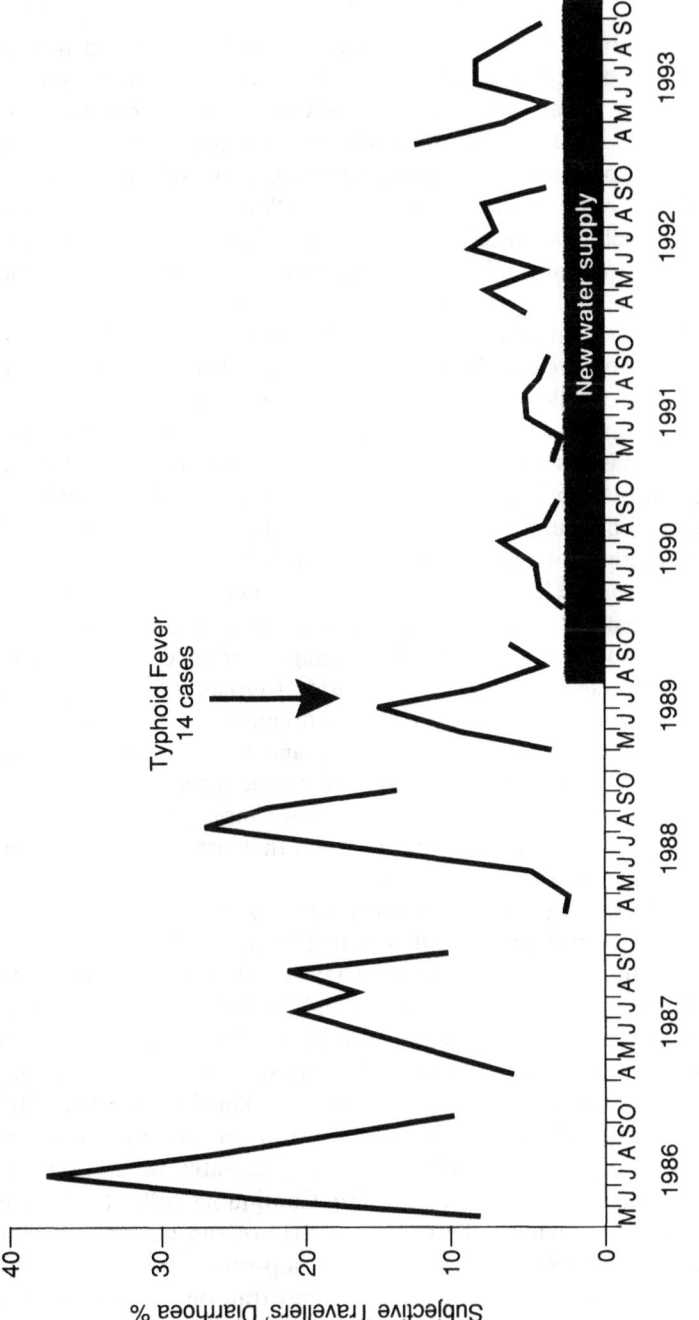

Figure 3.5 Incidence of subjective travellers' diarrhoea in British package holidaymakers visiting Salou, Spain, 1986–93

by December 1995 (Council Directive 1993). It stresses the importance of hazard analysis and critical control point systems (HACCP) as an approach in assessing food processes. Food businesses are required to identify, monitor and control all steps in their operation which are critical for food safety. There are particular requirements for all food-handlers to have a high degree of personal cleanliness and to wear suitable clothing. Employers must ensure that food-handlers are supervised and instructed and trained in food hygiene matters commensurate with their work activity. The legislation provides a framework for the enforcement of good food hygiene throughout the food cycle from the producer, processor, retailer and catering to the consumer.

If the tourist self-caters, it is important that the food available for purchase is of an acceptable quality including the absence of microbial pathogens if possible. However, for the majority of tourists who purchase prepared foods, the hygiene of the hotel or restaurant kitchen should be of a high standard.

The World Health Organisation has published guidance on the evaluation of national programmes to ensure food safety in addition to a training guide for managers of food service establishments (Jacob 1989). The World Tourism Organisation in co-operation within the WHO has organised a series of international workshops on food hygiene and tourism. The responsibility of the individual tourist should not be forgotten as it would appear that many travellers believe that simple personal hygienic practices are no longer necessary when they are away from home and especially when on holiday.

Hand-washing, after using the toilet and before eating food, is the most important facet of personal hygiene. Hands should be washed after any activity that may have resulted in them becoming contaminated and always before handling food. If at all possible, soap and running tap water should be used. Hot water is preferable, as even if the cold water is bacteriologically unsafe to drink, many or all of the bacteria will have been killed by the heat. The water should be as hot as is possible, although care must be taken not to scald the hands. Hands should preferably be air-dried or dried using a disposable hand towel. Continuous roller towels are satisfactory providing the container has not run out and all that is left is a well-used end of the towel. Loop-roller towels and multi-use towels should be avoided as they may transmit organisms from one person's hands to the next.

Toilet seats should not be handled if possible. Diarrhoeal-causing organisms may be present even in the absence of any faecal soiling. Hands must always be washed after using the toilet. Regular hand-washing is essential for all persons handling food, whether preparing food for themselves or catering for a large number of persons. The traveller who develops diarrhoea and/or vomiting should avoid preparing food for others and if possible should use a separate toilet.

The tourist should never assume that all food is equally safe and should follow some basic rules. Even in establishments with good levels of hygiene there are certain foods which are associated with a much increased risk of stomach illness. These foods should if possible be avoided or at least only eaten with the knowledge of the risk:

- shellfish and in particular uncooked oysters. Shellfish filter out and concentrate waterborne viruses and bacteria. Safety can only be guaranteed by thorough cooking;
- ice cream and ices, especially if not prepared by a recognised commercial manufacturer. Open ice-cream containers and scoops can easily become contaminated;
- dairy products made from unpasteurised milk;
- rare meat, steak tartar, raw fish;
- sauces and relishes left at ambient temperature. Hot spices do not kill microbes;
- food on which flies have settled;
- unwashed, unpeelable fruit or vegetables.

These foods are not a comprehensive list and any food where there is doubt about hygiene during preparations should be avoided.

CONCLUSION

Travellers' diarrhoea has spoiled many holidays and business trips yet is all too often regarded as part of travel. Indeed, as the commonest travel-associated illness, this attitude is easy to understand. It is however a condition which can largely be prevented, although the political will and investment required is huge. The important relationship with the standard of public health and therefore personal health of the indigenous population may not be fully recognised, but this may be a key in persuading governments to develop and apply control measures. The tourism industry can assist by taking part in surveillance programmes and conveying the results to the appropriate authorities. The individual tourist does not escape from a personal responsibility to maintain a high level of personal hygiene wherever they are.

REFERENCES

Ahren, C. M., Jertborn, M., Herclik, L., Kaijser, B. and Svennerholm, A. M. (1990) 'Infection with bacterial enteropathogens in Swedish travellers to South-East Asia – a prospective study', *Epidemiology and Infection* 105, 2: 325–33.

Bendall, R. P., Lucas, S., Moody, A., Tovey, G. and Chiodini, P. L. (1993) 'Diarrhoea associated with cyanobacterium-like bodies: a new coccidian enteritis of man', review, *Lancet* 341, 8845: 590–2.

Black, R. E. (1990) 'Epidemiology of travellers' diarrhoea and relative importance of various pathogens', review, *Reviews of Infectious Diseases* 12, Suppl. 1: 573–9.

Cartwright, R. E. (1992) 'Epidemiology of travellers' diarrhoea in British package holiday tourists', *PHLS Microbiology Digest* 9: 365–70.

Clemens, J. D., Svennerholm, A. M., Harris, J. R., Huda, S., Rao, M., Neogy, P. K., Khan, M. R., Ansaruzzaman, M., Rahaman, S. and Ahmed, F. (1990) 'Seroepidemiologic evaluation of anti-toxic and anti-colonisation factor immunity against infections by LT-producing *Escherichia coli* in rural Bangladesh', *Journal of Infectious Diseases* 162: 448–53.

Council Directive (1976) 'The quality of bathing water (76/160/EEC)', *Official Journal of the European Communities* L31: 1–7.

—— (1990) 'Package travel, package holidays and package tours (90/314/EEC)', *Official Journal of the European Communities* L158: 59–64.

—— (1993) 'The hygiene of foodstuffs (93/43/EEC)', *Official Journal of the European Communities* L175: 1–11.

Egger, M., Mausezahl, D., Odermatt, P., Marti, H. P. and Tanner, M. (1990) 'Symptoms and transmission of intestinal cryptosporidiosis', *Archives of Disease in Childhood* 65, 4: 445–7.

Freedman, B. J. (1977) 'Travellers' diarrhoea: does it occur in the United Kingdom?', *Journal of Hygiene (Cambridge)* 79: 73–5.

Gascon, J., Corachan, M., Valls, M. E., Gene, A. and Bombi, J. A. (1993) 'Cyanobacteria-like body (CLB) in travellers with diarrhoea', *Scandinavian Journal of Infectious Diseases* 25, 2: 253–7.

Haynes, J. and Hawkey, P. M. (1989) 'Providencia alcalifaciens and travellers' diarrhoea', *British Medical Journal* 299, 6691: 94–5.

Jacob, M. (1989) *Safe Food Handling: a Training Guide for Managers of Food Service Establishments*, Geneva: WHO.

Jertborn, M. and Svennerholm, A. M. (1991) 'Enterotoxin-producing bacteria isolated from Swedish travellers with diarrhoea', *Scandinavian Journal of Infectious Diseases* 23, 4: 473–9.

Jertborn, M., Svennerholm, A. M. and Iwarson, S. (1988) 'A prospective study of serum antibody responses to enterotoxigenic *Escherichia coli* in Swedish travellers', *Scandinavian Journal of Infectious Diseases* 20: 69–75.

Kain, K. C. and Kelly, M. T. (1989) 'Clinical features, epidemiology, and treatment of *Plesiomonas shigelloides* diarrhoea', *Journal of Infectious Diseases* 27, 5: 998–1001.

Kollaritsch, H. (1989a) 'Travellers' diarrhoea among Austrian tourists in warm climate countries: I. Epidemiology', *European Journal of Epidemiology* 5, 1: 74–81.

—— (1989b) 'Travellers' diarrhoea among Austrian tourists in warm climate countries: II. Clinical features', *European Journal of Epidemiology* 5, 3: 355–62.

Kuijper, E. J., Bol, P., Peters, M. F., Steigerwalt, A. G., Zanen, H. C. and Brenner, D. J. (1989) 'Clinical and epidemiologic aspects of members of Aeromonas DNA hybridization groups isolated from human faeces', *Journal of Clinical Microbiology* 27: 1531–7.

Lebbad, M. and Linder, E. (1993) 'Newly discovered organism behind diarrhoea. All patients had recently been abroad', *Swedish Lakartidningen* 90, 10: 951–2.

Long, E. G., Ebrahimzadeh, A., White, E. H., Swisher, B. and Callaway, C. S. (1990) 'Alga associated with diarrhoea in patients with acquired immunodeficiency syndrome and in travellers', *Journal of Clinical Microbiology* 28, 6: 1101–4.

Lowenstein, M. S., Balows, A. and Gangarosa, E. J. (1973) 'Turista at an international congress in Mexico', *Lancet* i: 529–31.

Mara, D. and Cairncross, S. (1989) *Guidelines for the Safe Use of Waste Water and Excreta in Agriculture and Aquaculture*, Geneva: WHO.

Mathewson, J. J., Johnson, P. C., Dupont, H. L., Morgan, D. R., Thornton, S. A., Wood, L. V. and Ericsson, C. D. (1985) 'A newly recognised cause of travellers' diarrhoea: enteroadherent *Escherichia coli*', *Journal of Infectious Diseases* 151: 471–5.

Mattila, L., Siitonen, A., Kyronseppa, H., Simula, I., Oksanen, P., Stenvik, M., Salo, P. and Peltola, H. (1992) 'Seasonal variation in etiology of travellers' diarrhoea. Finnish-Moroccan Study Group', *Journal of Infectious Diseases* 165, 2: 385–8.

Msengi, A. E., Philips, A. D., Ridson, R. A. and Walker-Smith, J. A. (1988) 'Travellers' diarrhoea among children returning to the United Kingdom from visits abroad', *Annals of Tropical Paediatrics* 8: 173–80.

NIH (1985) 'National Institute of Health Consensus Conference: Travellers' Diarrhoea', *Journal American Medical Association* 253: 2700–4.

Oksanen, P. J., Salminen, S., Saxelin, M., Hamalainen, P., Ihantola, V. A., Muurasniemi, I. L., Nikkari, S., Oksanen, T., Porsti, I. and Salminen, E. (1990) 'Prevention of travellers' diarrhoea by Lactobacillus GG', *Annals of Medicine* 22, 1: 53–6.

Pitzinger, B., Steffen, R. and Tschopp, A. (1991) 'Incidence and clinical features of travellers' diarrhoea in infants and children', *Pediatric Infectious Disease Journal* 10, 10: 719–23.

Rademaker, C. M., Hoepelman, I. M., Wolfhagen, M. J., Beumer, H., Rozenberg, A. M. and Verhoef, J. (1989) 'Results of a double-blind placebo-controlled study used ciprofloxacin for prevention of travellers' diarrhoea', *European Journal of Clinical Microbiology and Infectious Diseases* 8, 8: 690–4.

Reid, D., Dewar, R., Fallon, R. J., Cossar, J. H. and Grist, N. R. (1980) 'Infection and travel: the experience of package tourists and other travellers', *Journal of Infection* 2: 365–70.

Scott, D. A., Haberberger, R. L., Thornton, S. A. and Hyams, K. C. (1990) 'Norfloxacin for the prophylaxis of travellers' diarrhoea in US military personnel', *American Journal of Tropical Medicine and Hygiene* 42, 2: 160–4.

Snyder, J. D., Wells, J. G., Yashuk, J., Puhr, N. and Blake, P. A. (1984) 'Outbreak of invasive *Escherichia coli* gastroenteritis on a cruise ship', *American Journal of Tropical Medicine and Hygiene* 33, 281–4.

Speelman, P., Struelens, M. J., Sangal, S. C. and Glass, R. I. (1983) 'Detection of *Campylobacter jejuni* and other potential pathogens in travellers' diarrhoea in Bangladesh', *Scandinavian Journal of Gastroenterology* 84 (supplement): 19–23.

Sriratanaban, A. and Reinprayoon, S. (1982) '*Vibrio parahaemolyticus*: a major cause of travellers' diarrhoea in Bangkok', *American Journal of Tropical Medicine and Hygiene* 31: 128–30.

Taylor, D. N. and Escheverria, P. (1986) 'Etiology and epidemiology of travellers' diarrhoea in Asia', *Reviews of Infectious Diseases* 8 (Supplement): 136–41.

Wright, S. G. (1983) 'Parasites and travellers; diarrhoea', *Scandinavian Journal of Gastroenterology* 84 (Supplement): 25–9.

Chapter 4

HIV/AIDS and international travel: a global perspective

John D.H. Porter, Gil Lea and Bernadette Carroll

INTRODUCTION

At the end of June 1994, the World Health Organisation (WHO) estimated that over 16 million people world-wide had been infected with HIV. By the year 2000, WHO estimates that between 30 and 40 million people will be infected with the virus (Communicable Disease Report 1994). The most severely affected area at present is sub-Saharan Africa, where it is estimated that over 10 million people have been infected (WHO/GPA 1994) (Figure 4.1). Of this total, about half to two-thirds are in East and Central Africa. The most alarming current trends however, are in South and South-East Asia, where the epidemic is spreading in some areas as fast as it was a decade ago in sub-Saharan Africa. Over 2.5 million HIV infections have occurred in adults in this region, with the majority of reported infections appearing from two countries – India and Thailand (WHO/GPA 1994).

During the 1970s and 1980s there was a rapid expansion in international travel both for work and leisure. In 1985, close to 100 million travellers legally crossed international borders (World Tourist Organisation) while many millions crossed borders as refugees or displaced persons. This number is increasing every year and in 1990 in the United Kingdom, residents made 29 million visits abroad for business or leisure (Department of Employment 1990). Over 90 per cent of these visits were to countries in Europe and North America, while visits to Africa, Asia and Latin America accounted for 7 per cent of the total.

With the increase in the number of travellers has come the increased chance of sexual encounters between travellers and local residents. The relaxation of behavioural norms which can occur

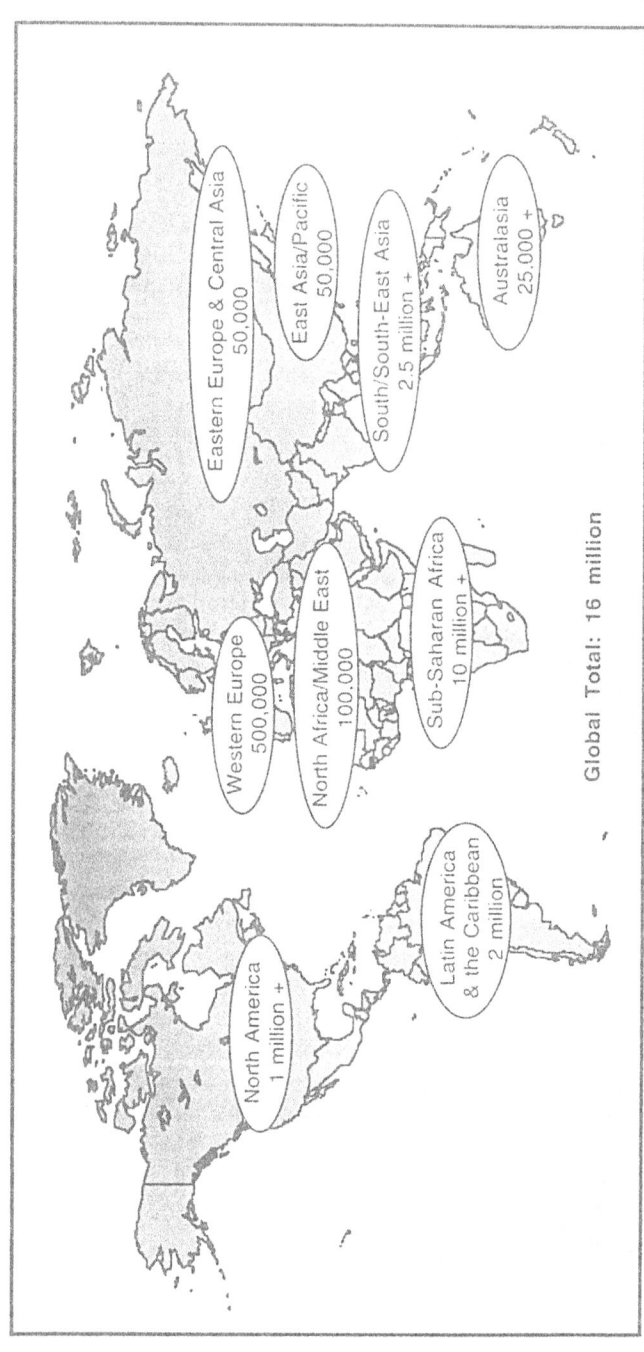

Figure 4.1 Estimated global distribution of cumulative HIV infections in adults, mid-1994

Source: Global Aids News (1994), no. 3

when away from home may increase the opportunities for sexually transmitted diseases (STDs), including HIV, to spread across international borders (Noone 1992). The evidence available suggests that rates of casual, unprotected sex are high among both short-term and long-term international travellers (DeSchryver and Meheus 1989). Behavioural data on UK travellers indicate that unprotected sexual intercourse occurs (Gillies *et al.* 1992). Information from the International Passenger Survey is that the average length of holiday visits for UK residents was between twelve and fourteen days, while business trips lasted on average seven days (Department of Employment 1990). These periods of time allow ample opportunity for sexual encounters!

This chapter will discuss the HIV/AIDS pandemic and the modes of transmission in different regions of the world, which have important implications for international tourists visiting such areas. It will examine which travellers are at risk and review the research that has been conducted into the knowledge levels, sexual behaviour and transmission of sexually transmitted diseases among travellers/tourists. Finally, it will address the area of prevention and what needs to be done to reduce the transmission of HIV infection.

THE INTERNATIONAL EPIDEMIOLOGY OF HIV/AIDS: A REGIONAL PERSPECTIVE

The Acquired Immunodeficiency Syndrome (AIDS) is the name given to the syndrome of disease which results from advanced suppression of the body's immune system following infection by the human immunodeficiency virus (HIV). AIDS is essentially a sexually transmitted disease (STD), with HIV being transmitted through unprotected sexual intercourse – vaginal, anal or oral – between men and women (heterosexual intercourse) or between men (homosexual intercourse). World-wide, STDs are the most commonly occurring group of infectious diseases after respiratory diseases (Noone 1992; Mulhall 1993). The role of international travel in the spread of STDs is illustrated by the rapid dispersion globally of penicillinase-producing strains of *Neisseria* gonorrhoea (Barlow and Sherrard 1992). In the UK in 1986, 20 per cent of the cases of primary or secondary syphilis, and 4 per cent of the cases of post-pubertal gonorrhoea reported, for which the location of exposure was known, were acquired abroad (Department of Health 1986). In 1990/91, nearly one-third of 314 reports of acute hepatitis B virus infection reported to the Communicable Disease Surveillance Centre in London were acquired abroad (Heptonstall and Mortimer 1991).

The transmission of other sexually transmitted diseases, including gonorrhoea, syphilis and chancroid, is associated with the same behaviours that expose individuals to potential HIV infection. Data suggest that STDs – especially chancroid and syphilis, which cause ulcerative lesions – greatly facilitate the sexual acquisition and transmission of HIV (WHO/GPA 1993a; Noone 1992). Like other STDs, HIV infection can also be transmitted through blood, blood products, or donated organs or semen (parenteral transmission) and from a woman to her foetus or infant (perinatal transmission). The routes of transmission are the same in every country although relative risks between the various modes of transmission may vary. For example, HIV transmission through blood transfusion of HIV-infected blood or blood products has now been virtually eliminated in industrialised countries, whilst this problem is still being actively addressed in most developing countries (WHO/GPA 1992). Beyond these differences in predominant patterns of transmission, it is behaviour not geographic location which poses the greatest risk factor for international tourists and travellers.

The HIV pandemic consists of many separate epidemics (in some cases even within a single country). Each epidemic has its own starting point and involves different types and frequencies of risk behaviours and practices. Studies to date indicate that about 60 per cent of adults infected with HIV-1 will develop AIDS within twelve to thirteen years of infection (WHO/GPA 1993a). Less is known about the natural history of HIV-2. Virtually all persons diagnosed as having AIDS die within a few years. Survival after diagnosis has been increasing in industrialised countries from an average of less than one year to about one to two years at present. However, survival time with AIDS in developing countries remains short – an estimated six months or less.

By the end of June 1994, a total of 985,119 AIDS cases had been reported to WHO (WHO/GPA 1994). WHO estimates that, when under-diagnosis, under-reporting, and delays in reporting are taken into account, nearly 4 million AIDS cases may actually have occurred world-wide (WHO/GPA 1994). Of these it is estimated that more than 750,000 are paediatric AIDS cases resulting from mother-to-child transmission, almost all of these having occurred in sub-Saharan Africa (WHO/GPA 1994). On a global scale, in 1994, over 75 per cent of cumulative HIV infections in adults are estimated to have been transmitted through heterosexual intercourse. The predominant modes of transmission vary, however, in different regions of the world.

Australasia, North America and Western Europe

In Australasia, North America and Western Europe, HIV spread extensively in the late 1970s and early 1980s. The people predominantly affected thus far have been homosexual or bisexual men and injecting drug-users. By mid-1994, over 1.5 million cumulative HIV infections in adults are estimated to have occurred in this region.

The distribution in cases between the different groups is individual to each country. For example, the predominant group affected in the United States is homosexual/bisexual men, whereas in Italy, two-thirds of cases are among injecting drug-users (WHO/GPA 1993b). Transmission of HIV infection among homosexual men appears to have decreased markedly during the 1980s, whereas infection among injecting drug-users has been increasing. The transmission of HIV through heterosexual intercourse increased during the latter half of the 1980s and the early 1990s. Up to one-third of new HIV infections in some urban centres in Scotland are now due to heterosexual transmission (WHO/GPA 1993b).

Latin America and the Caribbean

In the 1970s and 1980s infection was principally among homosexual and bisexual men, but during the late 1980s and early 1990s there has been increasing heterosexual transmission, principally among bisexual men and their female sex partners, and among female sex workers and their clients. In Brazil, the percentage of reported AIDS cases due to heterosexual transmission increased from 7.5 per cent in 1987 to 23 per cent in 1992. As of mid-1994, WHO estimated that over 1.5 million cumulative adult HIV infections had occurred in Latin America and the Caribbean. So, while in the early years of the epidemic the principal group at risk would have been homosexual travellers who were sexually active, now the concern will have extended to those heterosexual men who might make use of the services of female sex workers.

Sub-Saharan Africa

As of mid-1994, WHO estimated that over 10 million adult HIV infections had occurred in sub-Saharan Africa. Of this total, about half to two-thirds were in East and Central Africa, an area which accounted for only about one-sixth of the total population of the sub-Saharan region. At the end of June 1994, over 300,000 cumulative adult and paediatric AIDS cases had been reported in sub-Saharan Africa; however, because of the known extensive under-reporting, WHO estimates that more than 2 million AIDS cases had occurred in this region as of mid-1994; constituting over two-thirds of the current global total. Since heterosexual transmission is predominant, the number of HIV infections in men and women is nearly equal, with females outnumbering males by a ratio of 6 to 5. Consequently, the travellers at most risk in sub-Saharan Africa may be those heterosexual men who have sex with local prostitutes.

South and South-East Asia

Although the extensive spread of HIV in South and South-East Asia began only in the mid-1980s, the progression of the pandemic in this region has been rapid. As of mid-1994, WHO estimates that over 2.5 million HIV infections have occurred in adults. While India and Thailand account for the majority of infections, rapid HIV spread into specific populations has been seen elsewhere in the region. As of the end of June 1994, almost 9,000 AIDS cases have been reported from this region, although the true figure is likely to be considerably higher. Heterosexual transmission of HIV appears to be increasing rapidly in other vulnerable groups. In Thailand as of late 1991, a prevalence of 21 per cent was seen in female prostitutes, and of 5.6 per cent in people attending STD clinics. Studies of HIV prevalence in female sex workers demonstrate a rising trend in at least two cities in India. A study among STD patients in Pune, West India, found an HIV prevalence of almost 9 per cent in 1991 and 17 per cent in 1992 (WHO/GPA 1993). Again, the major concern would be for male travellers who have sex with prostitutes.

Areas which currently have a low HIV incidence

East Asia and the Pacific, Eastern Europe and the former USSR, and North Africa and the Middle East are currently thought to have a low incidence of HIV infection. By mid-1994 WHO estimated that over 50,000 cumulative adult HIV infections had occurred in East Asia and the Pacific. There were estimated to be over 50,000 cumulative HIV infections in adults in Eastern Europe and Central Asia, with sexual transmission the predominant route of transmission. In North Africa and the Middle East as of mid-1994 it was estimated that there were approximately 100,000 cumulative adult HIV infections.

TRAVEL, TOURISM AND HIV/AIDS RISKS

The international traveller or tourist may be exposed to the risk of HIV infection through three principal routes: sexual intercourse with an HIV positive partner, inoculation with HIV-infected blood/blood products or sharing HIV contaminated needles used by injecting drug-users. Seventy five per cent of people with HIV have acquired their infection through heterosexual intercourse and the major source of HIV risk for the traveller is unprotected intercourse.

Every sexually active traveller who engages in 'unsafe' sexual behaviour is potentially at risk from HIV infection. The risk of acquiring HIV from sexual activity depends on the possibility that a sexual partner is infected, and the type and number of sexual contacts with the infected partner. Although the probability that a partner is infected may be higher in some countries than others, it is clear from the epidemiological situation that there is a risk of exposure to HIV infection from sexual contact throughout the world (Von Reyn *et al.* 1990).

Although transfusion remains associated with a substantial risk of HIV infection in some areas of the world, the likelihood that a blood transfusion would be required during international travel is low. Estimates are that 1.3 in 10,000 international tourists from the USA require blood transfusion within a two-week period as do 5 in 10,000 Swedes (Noone 1992). WHO recommends the screening of all blood received for donation to protect the blood supply; such systems are increasingly being implemented in developing countries especially in large urban areas (Von Reyn et al. 1990). Parenteral transmission also occurs through infected needles and other skin-piercing equipment. If the tourist is an injecting drug-user, then they must ensure that they use 'clean' equipment. Reusable skin-piercing equipment for tattoos or acupuncture, razors and other cutting instruments should be avoided. Medical treatment in developing countries should be by tablet rather than by injection where this is an alternative.

It has been estimated that British travellers are 300 times more likely to develop AIDS than residents who do not travel (Feachem and Phillips-Howard 1988). Reasons for an increased risk of HIV transmission in travellers has been linked to changes in their behaviour whilst abroad. Alcohol use has been demonstrated to alter sexual practices and tourists are thought more likely to engage in sexual activity with different partners or local prostitutes. At the same time they may be visiting countries where the prevalence of HIV infection is higher than in their own country (Ellis 1987; Conway et al. 1990a; Higson et al. 1990; Robertson and Plant 1988).

Research on travel, tourism and HIV/AIDS

As with all epidemics caused by transmissible pathogens, AIDS has been seen in many countries as an imported problem. What this perspective fails to recognise is that with the explosion of international tourist travel in the past thirty years, it is virtually impossible to prevent the spread of infectious disease across international borders (Hawkes and Hart 1993). The early studies on HIV and tourist travel were related to ethical implications of restricting the freedom of movements of individuals (Hawkes and Hart 1993). In the next research phase came reports of Europeans or Americans infected during visits abroad and travel was found to be an independent risk factor for infection in specific countries such as France (Vittecoq 1987) and regions such as East Africa (Carswell et al. 1989). However, there has been little work on the reasons why travel should be a risk factor for HIV and few studies on the relationship between travel and people's behaviour (Hawkes et al. 1994).

Knowledge and attitudes

A limited number of studies have investigated knowledge and attitudes to HIV infection among travellers/tourists. Porter *et al.* (1991) report two studies conducted at the Travel Clinic, Hospital for Tropical Diseases in London, to determine the knowledge and attitudes to HIV among persons attending the clinic for pre-travel advice. The studies aimed to determine whether prospective British tourists considered themselves to be at risk of acquiring HIV/AIDS and how they protected themselves; whether certain demographic groups were at greater risk because of less knowledge and poor protection; and whether they wanted more information about HIV transmission. Two separate studies were conducted, the initial one to determine the general knowledge of travellers about AIDS used self-completed questionnaires to interview 100 subjects. The results were then used to define the questionnaire for the second study.

The two studies demonstrated a difference in knowledge and attitudes between different ethnic groups and showed that despite the lack of knowledge of AIDS among many travellers there were few requests for more information about the disease. Men were more likely to have bought condoms than women, and white respondents were three times more likely to have bought condoms than persons from other ethnic groups (Table 4.1).

Despite sixty-three participants (25 per cent) not knowing if AIDS was present in the country to which they were travelling, only seventy-two (29 per cent) requested more information about AIDS, presumably indicating that they did not feel they were at risk.

Allard and Lambert (1992) report a similar survey which studied the perceived risk of AIDS among Canadian travellers where knowledge of transmission was good, although the risk of acquisition of HIV infection from a contaminated blood transfusion was underrated. Fourteen per cent of 331 travellers did not think that avoiding sexual intercourse was protective against HIV, and many thought that condoms were more effective if used with fellow tourists than with locals. This was especially true of travellers who considered AIDS as being particularly severe but difficult to prevent.

A study conducted in Korea in 1991 to determine the knowledge of AIDS among travellers and the use of condoms (Choi

Table 4.1 AIDS awareness among travellers attending the Travel Clinic at the London Hospital for Tropical Diseases

Factor	Total	Yes	Odds ratio	95%CI
A Are travellers at greater risk of AIDS because they travel?				
Male	125	37	1.2	0.6–2.2
Female	118	31		
White	211	68	5.7	1.6–24.2
Other	39	3		
Single	132	39	1.1	0.6–2.1
Other	118	32		
Holiday travellers	132	36	0.9	0.5–1.6
Other travellers	118	35		
B Is AIDS present in the country to which you are travelling?				
Male	126	96	1.2	0.6–2.1
Female	124	91		
White	211	170	7.8	3.8–16.3
Other	49	17		
Single	132	97	0.9	0.5–1.6
Other	118	90		
Holiday travellers	132	88	0.4	0.2–0.7
Other travellers	118	99		
C Have you ever bought a packet of condoms?				
Male	113	100	6.8	3.3–14.3
Female	111	59		
White	202	150	3.3	1.4–8.1
Other	28	13		
Single	108	88	1.4	0.8–2.6
Other	111	75		
Holiday travellers	108	85	1.2	0.6–2.1
Other travellers	113	78		

Source: Porter et al. 1991

et al. 1992) surveyed 571 people who completed a self-administered questionnaire. Most respondents were knowledgeable about the cause of AIDS and the main routes of HIV transmission. Among men who had been sexually active in the previous five years (81% of all respondents), 46% had practised multiple sex partnerships, 24% had paid money for sex, 8% had had same-gender sex, and 46% of married men had had extramarital sex. A total of 54% of sexually active men never used condoms and only 14% always used them.

Sexual behaviour and behaviour change

Travel and the pursuit of international tourism may induce a feeling of freedom from inhibitions and home ties and result in less responsible behaviour among both domestic and international tourists. This may contribute to an increased number of sexual encounters, whether with other tourists or with people in the host community. A survey of 978 people aged between 16 and 40 years of age was conducted among UK tourists in 1990 (Conway *et al.* 1990b). The main aim of the study was 'to assess the extent of risk behaviours for HIV transmission amongst a sample of adults from Nottingham who travelled abroad'. Eight per cent of the sample interviewed stated that they had formed a 'new romantic or sexual relationship on their last trip abroad' and seventeen (5 per cent) travellers reported a relationship which included sexual intercourse. Twelve of the seventeen people reporting sexual intercourse were carrying condoms, but only five of these reported using them on all occasions. Single people and tourists unaccompanied by a partner were more likely to report sexual intercourse with a new partner than married or accompanied tourists (see Chapter 7, this volume, for full details of this study).

The significance and difficulty of obtaining corroborating evidence from social survey-based research on tourists' sexual behaviour is apparent from the study by Daniels *et al.* (1992). They undertook a study in a London genito-urinary clinic (GUM) in which 250 attendees were asked about their sexual behaviour whilst abroad. They found that eighteen (20 per cent) women, twenty-six (51 per cent) heterosexual men and nineteen (36 per cent) homosexual men had had sex with a local foreign contact on holiday. Although both heterosexual and homosexual men were statistically more likely to have sex abroad with a local inhabitant, women were more likely to have unprotected sex with a local partner (Daniels *et al.* 1992).

Likewise, Barlow and Sherrard's (1992) study using GUM clinic attendees reported data from a survey of 18,237 UK-born patients at St Thomas's Hospital, London, in which subjects were asked about their experience of sexual intercourse outside the United Kingdom. While London may not be typical of the situation among all UK residents, due to the cosmopolitan nature of London's population, it found that white respondents were more likely to have had sex abroad than black respondents and among both white and black groups, men were more likely to report sex than women. The highest incidence of sex abroad was among white men, with black men having the highest incidence of multiple partnerships abroad.

Lister and Robinson (1993) studied STDs and travel among sixty-eight patients visiting the GUM clinic at University College Hospital, London who reported having had sexual intercourse abroad with a new or casual partner in the preceding six months. Thirty-five (51 per cent) were diagnosed as having a current STD and in fifteen cases a disease pathogen was isolated. The data reported an association between unprotected intercourse and infection.

A more detailed profile of a specific group of international tourists emerged from a study by Hawkes *et al.* (1994) at the Hospital for Tropical Diseases, which derived information from patients attending an outpatient clinic for a 'post-tropical check-up'. The clinic sees a particular client-group – the longer-term holidaymaker and business traveller rather than the shorter-term tourist who visits a destination for one to two weeks. A total of 782 people were approached and 96 per cent agreed to complete a self-administered questionnaire. The study revealed that:

- 141 (18.5 per cent) of the sample reported having sex with new partners during their most recent trip;
- 61 per cent of those reporting sexual activity were men;
- 52 per cent had sex with one partner; the remainder had sex with two or more partners;
- 64 per cent did not use condoms or used them infrequently and nineteen men paid for sex;
- 6 per cent of the 141 patients who had been sexually active abroad had received treatment for an STD on their return.

Those people reporting sex abroad were different from those who did not in several ways: they were more likely to be travelling on an overland tour; more likely to have been abroad longer; six times more likely to have paid for sex in the last five years; and twice as likely to have been treated for an STD in the last five years. Sixteen of these people were HIV infected with the prevalence higher in those born in East, Central and Southern Africa than elsewhere (18 versus 0.7 per cent). Four British men were HIV infected and one of these reported having sex with men. Consequently, targeted health promotion to business travellers visiting high-risk countries may prove valuable in the light of this study.

Prostitution

High levels of HIV infection have been reported among male and female prostitutes in Europe, Africa, the Americas and Asia (Johnson and Laga 1988; Ungchusak et al. 1991; Bhave et al. 1990). In Thailand, for example, as of late 1991, overall median rates of 21 per cent were seen in female prostitutes (WHO/GPA 1993). Although it can be assumed that there are some people who travel abroad with the primary intention of having sexual encounters (see Hall, Chapter 9, this volume) it is probable that the distinction between a person who has sex whilst travelling, and a 'sex tourist', is not only difficult and arbitrary, but may also be potentially misleading (Mulhall 1993). Nevertheless men and women certainly do travel specifically for the purpose of having sex and this group needs to be targeted with information to prevent transmission of STDs and HIV. Several countries in the world, particularly in South-East Asia, have large-scale, well-organised sex industries catering both for the indigenous and for the international tourist market. Thailand has received particular attention.

HIV is a growing problem in Thailand. Despite prostitution being made illegal in 1960 (Cohen 1988), the commercial sex industry is large and diverse. It is estimated that approximately half a million young women, mainly in the 16–24 age group, work in the sex industry. Most sex workers are female but there is also a thriving male sector for homosexuals (Ford and Koestsawang 1991). The risks of HIV transmission within the sex industry vary according to the social status of the clientele. Higher-status customers are likely to be better educated and more aware of the risk of HIV and other sexually transmissible infections, and as such are more likely to comply with condom use. Other sexually transmitted diseases are common among the female prostitutes: 70 per cent have some form of STD (Ford and Koestsawang 1991) (for a fuller discussion of prostitution and sex tourism see Chapter 9, this volume).

Mulhall et al. (1993) report a survey of Australian tourists to Thailand and their intended sexual behaviour in which only 34 per cent of the sample reported a definite intention not to have sex in Thailand. Regarding choice of sexual partner, 24.5 per cent more men than women said they would have sex with a Thai national.

However, 82 per cent of the sample reported that they would use condoms 100 per cent of the time, which is an encouraging sign.

Wilke and Kleiber (1992) have conducted studies of German tourists contacts with sex workers in several less developed countries which have large sex industries. As part of their research programme, ninety-four German male tourists who had had sex with Thai men were interviewed in Pattaya in 1992. The men were aged between 20 and 60 years and reported having had sex with an average of eight Thai men/boys during their stay and 41 per cent reported having had sex with five or more men/boys. A wide variety of sexual practices were reported, with 17 per cent reporting 'never' using a condom, 15 per cent 'sometimes' and 68 per cent 'always'. Condom use was reported to be more consistent during receptive intercourse with 82 per cent of men always using them.

Alcohol use

The use of alcohol may contribute to more sexual risk-taking on holiday (DeSchryver and Meheus 1989). It may also contribute to road traffic accidents and this may take place in countries where there is a higher risk of HIV from unscreened blood products. In the Nottingham study on sexual behaviour, questions were included on alcohol consumption (Conway *et al.* 1990). Drinking was more frequent abroad for 75 per cent of the respondents, 21 per cent drank the same as at home and only 4 per cent drank less. Of the sample, 49 per cent reported drinking every day whilst abroad compared with only 6 per cent who drank every day at home. A total of 26 per cent reported getting 'very drunk' at least once during their time abroad. Thus, studies that report less inhibition among international tourists indicate that alcohol may be a significant risk factor to the sexual behaviour of specific groups of tourists who run the danger of HIV infection (see also Chapter 6, this volume, for information on alcohol consumption by British tourists in Malta).

WHAT CAN BE DONE TO IMPROVE HIV PREVENTION?

Preventive approaches which are effective in achieving safe behaviour at home may increase safe behaviour abroad. Sound health education at home should precede travel (Noone 1992). The problem is that there is ample evidence to show that even though tourists understand how HIV is transmitted, they continue to take risks (Mulhall et al. 1993). Interventions are required which will produce alterations in behaviour due to understanding. What form of education is effective in altering sexual behaviour? It is clear that this is one area which future research needs to address in view of the apparent risk behaviour of tourists who are aware of the potential effect of HIV transmission.

Advice to tourists

Advice about prevention of HIV infection should be offered to international tourists regardless of their destination. A Department of Health Travel Safe leaflet which gives information on the subject is also available free (Department of Health 1993). Tourists may reduce the risk of HIV infection if they are informed about how the virus is transmitted, and if they adhere to the simple precautions relating to sexual behaviour and receipt of injections or blood (von Reyn et al. 1990). However, it might not be possible to ensure these medical standards if a true emergency occurred in a rural area in a high-risk region.

Any interaction between a health care worker and an intended tourist is an opportunity for education. Both domestic and international tourists need to be told of the extent of HIV/AIDS and other STDs in the countries they are visiting and to understand the importance of using condoms if having casual sex. Tourists may wish to consult their national embassy, mission or consulate in the country of destination for advice in selecting health care facilities that provide adequate sterilisation methods and screened blood. Plasma expanders (rather than blood) should be considered if urgent resuscitation is necessary (von Reyn et al. 1990). A useful table has been constructed by the Society of Occupational Medicine for advising tourists on how to reduce the risk of HIV infection (Figure 4.2).

Advice to HIV-infected tourists

HIV-infected tourists should be advised to have a medical consultation prior to deciding on their holiday destination. Live virus vaccines may be contra-indicated and so a destination which

- Discover all you can about the extent and pattern of HIV and other STDs in the countries you are visiting.
- Find out whether HIV screening is a prerequisite for entry and, if so, arrange a test and counselling session before departure.
- Be sure you understand what is meant by 'safe sex'.
- Arrange adequate medical insurance.
- Consider taking 'travel packs' of injecting equipment with you. Be aware, however, of these possible problems:
  (a) You may have difficulties clearing customs.
  (b) Local doctors may feel offended if you suggest using your equipment, rather than theirs.
  (c) It may be difficult to ensure that your equipment is used.
- Accept no blood for transfusion unless it has been screened for HIV or there is a high degree of confidence about its safety.
- Travel prepared. If having casual sex, be certain to use a condom.
- Take with you the names and addresses of reliable sources of advice from people with local knowledge of the countries you are visiting.
- Read the WHO leaflet for travellers on HIV infection.

Source: A. Noone, Society of Occupational Medicine, 1992

Figure 4.2 Advice to travellers on reducing the risk of HIV infection

involves a risk of yellow fever should usually be avoided. There is a lowered resistance to other infections and this should be taken into consideration before the resort is chosen. There may also be entry restrictions and the policy of the chosen country should be checked with the embassy or consulate.

CONCLUSION

It is the tourists' behaviour, and more importantly their change of behaviour, which puts them at risk of HIV infection. These behaviours are the same for each country but the risk of acquiring the infection is greater in some countries compared with others (Noone 1992). HIV infection is now found in all regions of the world and, to a certain extent, international and domestic tourists are at risk in all destinations. The estimated and projected annual

AIDS incidence for regions of the world show increases through to 2000 (Figure 4.3) indicating that the risk of a traveller acquiring HIV infection will increase through to the next century.

At present the prevention message is safer sex with condoms, but it is evident from even the little research that has been conducted on behaviour of international tourists, that the processes of education currently being used have not sufficiently altered patterns of sexual behaviour. The relation between information and behaviour change is not a direct one and contextual factors may affect a tourist's behaviour despite his/her adequate knowledge and positive attitudes. Consequently, further research is needed to devise education strategies and approaches which are effective in leading to safer behaviour among domestic and international tourists (Noone 1992).

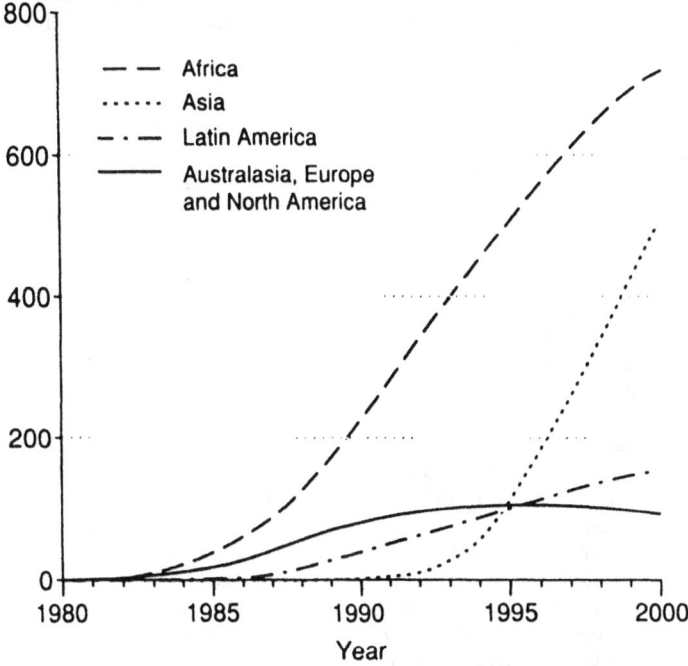

Figure 4.3 Estimated and projected annual AIDS incidences by 'macro' region, 1980–2000

Note: * number of new cases every year   Source: WHO

Finally, there is a paucity of studies on sexual behaviour among tourists, despite the studies included in this volume, particularly in relation to the factors that influence their behaviour. This needs to be remedied, especially *vis-à-vis* better approaches to educating people on how to keep themselves healthy and free of the HIV virus. Studies are clearly needed to investigate the factors influencing sexual behaviour patterns in tourist destination areas. Such research needs to look at the social, economic and associated factors influencing both the behaviour of the tourists and the interaction between them and the host populations (Hawkes and Hart 1993). These studies would help to identify public health interventions to assist with HIV prevention and to help the international and domestic tourist to reduce the risk of HIV infection.

REFERENCES

Allard, R. and Lambert, G. (1992) 'Knowledge and beliefs of international travellers about transmission and prevention of HIV infection', *Canadian Medical Association Journal* 145: 353–9.

Barlow, D. and Sherrard, J. (1992) 'Sexually transmitted diseases', *PHLS Microbiology Digest* 9, 3: 129–31.

Bhave, G. G., Wagle, U. D., Tripathis, S. P. and Seth, G. S. (1990) 'HIV serosurveillance in promiscuous females of Bombay, India', *Sixth International Conference on AIDS*; San Francisco, USA.

Carswell, J. W., Lloyd, G. and Howells, J. (1989) 'Prevalence of HIV-1 in East African lorry drivers', *AIDS* 3: 759–61.

Choi, K. H., Catania, J. A., Coates, J., Hyung, L. D. and Hearst, N. (1992) 'International travel and AIDS risk in South Korea', *AIDS* 6, 12: 1555–7.

Cohen, E. (1988) 'Tourism and AIDS in Thailand', *Annals of Tourism Research* 15: 467–86.

Communicable Disease Report (1994) 'AIDS and HIV-1 infection worldwide' 4, 46: 221–2.

Conway, S., Gillies, P. and Slack, R. (1990a) *The Health of Travellers*, Nottingham: Department of Public Health and Epidemiology, University of Nottingham and Nottingham Health Authority.

Conway, S., Gillies, P. and Slack, R. (1990b) 'Sexual behaviour in international travellers – a pilot study', Abstract number 3010, *Sixth International Conference on AIDS*, San Francisco, USA.

Daniels, D. G., Kell, P., Nelson, M. R. and Barton, S. E. (1992) 'Sexual behaviour amongst travellers: a study of genitourinary medicine clinic attenders', *International Journal STD and AIDS* 3, 6: 437–8.

Department of Employment (1990) *International Passenger Survey*, London: Department of Employment.

Department of Health (1986) *'New Cases Seen at NHS GUM Clinics in England. Summary Information from SBH60 Returns*, London: Department of Health.

—— (1993) *Health Advice for Travellers* (T3), London: HMSO.
DeSchryver, A. and Meheus, A. (1989) 'International travel and sexually transmitted diseases', *World Health Statistical Quarterly* 42: 90–9.
—— (1992) 'International travel and sexually transmitted diseases', *World Health Statistical Quarterly* 42: 90–9.
Ellis, M. (1987) 'AIDS and the foreign traveller', *Travel Medicine International* 5: 527–60.
Feachem, R. and Phillips-Howard, P. A. (1988) 'Risk to UK heterosexuals of contracting AIDS abroad', *Lancet* 2: 394–5.
Ford, N. and Koetsawang, S. (1991) 'The socio-cultural context of the transmission of HIV in Thailand', *Social Science and Medicine* 33, 4: 405–15.
Gillies, P., Slack, R., Stoddart, N. and Conway, S. (1992) 'HIV-related risk behaviour in UK', *AIDS* 6: 339–41.
Gilmore, N., Orkin, A. J., Duckett, M. and Grover, S. A. (1989) 'International travel and AIDS', *AIDS* 3: S225–30.
Hawkes, S. J. and Hart, G. J. (1993) 'Travel, migration and HIV', *AIDS Care* 5, 2: 207–14.
Hawkes, S. J., Hart, G. J., Johnson, A. M., Shergold, C., Ross, E., Herbert, K. M., Parry, J. V. and Mabey, D. (1994) 'Risk behaviour and HIV prevalence in international travellers', *AIDS* 8: 247–52.
Heptonstall, J. and Mortimer, J. (1991) 'HIV infection and foreign travel', *British Medical Journal* 302: 352.
Higson, R. W., Strunin, L., Berlin, B. M. and Hereen, T. (1990) 'Beliefs about AIDS, use of alcohol and drugs and unprotected sex among Massachusetts adolescents', *American Journal of Public Health* 80: 295–9.
Johnson, A. M. and Laga, M. (1988) 'Heterosexual transmission of HIV', *AIDS*, 2 (supplement 1): 549–56.
Lister, P. and Robinson, A. (1993) 'STD in travellers presenting to a GUM clinic', *International Journal of STD and AIDS* 4: 59–61.
Mulhall, B. P. (1993) 'Sexually transmissible diseases and travel', *British Medical Bulletin* 49, 2: 394–411.
Mulhall, B. P., Hu, M., Thompson, M., Lin, F., Lupton, D., Mills, D., Maund, M., Cass, R. and Millar, D. (1993) 'Planned sexual behaviour of young Australian visitors to Thailand', *Medical Journal of Australia* 158, 8: 530–5.
Noone, A. (1992) 'Travel and HIV infection', from *What employers should know about HIV and AIDS*, London: Society of Occupational Medicine, 13–19.
Porter, J. D. H., Philips-Howard, P. A. and Behrens, R. H. (1991) 'AIDS awareness among travellers', *Travel Medicine International* 1: 28–32.
Robertson, J. and Plant, M. (1988) 'Alcohol, sex and risks of HIV infection'. *Drugs and Alcohol Dependency* 22: 75–8.
Ungchusak, K., Thanprasertsuk, S., Vichai, C., Sriprapandh, S., Pinichapongsa, S. and Kunasol, P. (1991) 'Trends of HIV spreading in Thailand detected by national sentinel serosurveillance', Seventh International Conference on AIDS, Florence, Italy.
Vittecoq, D. (1987) 'AIDS after travelling in Africa: an epidemiological

study in seventeen caucasian patients', *Lancet* 1: 612–14.
Von Reyn, C. F., Mann, J. M. and Chin, J. (1990) 'International travel and HIV infection', *Bulletin of the World Health Organisation* 86, 2: 251–9.
Wilke, M. and Kleiber, D. (1992) 'Sexual behaviour of gay German (sex) tourists in Thailand', poster presentation, Eighth International AIDS Conference Third STD World Congress, Amsterdam, The Netherlands.
World Health Organisation (1985) 'International Health Regulations (1969)', *Weekly Epidemiological Record* 60, 40: 311.
WHO/GPA (World Health Organisation/Global Programme on AIDS) (1992) *Current and Future Dimensions of the HIV/AIDS Pandemic*, Geneva: World Health Organisation.
—— (1993a) *The HIV/AIDS Pandemic: 1993 Overview*, Geneva: World Health Organisation (WHO/GPA/CNP/EVA/93.1).
—— (1993b) 'WHO estimate of HIV infection tops 14 million', Geneva: 1–17.
—— (1994) *The HIV/AIDS Pandemic: 1994 Overview, Geneva: World Health Organisation (WHO/GPA/SEF/94.4)*.

Part II

Tourism, tourist behaviour and risks to health

Chapter 5

Off the beaten track
The health implications of the development of special-interest tourism activities in South-East Asia and the South Pacific

Brenda Rudkin and C. Michael Hall

INTRODUCTION

> Tropical travel carries risks. Before ... travel we need to organise vaccinations in a timely manner, advise on protection from insect biting and on water and food-borne disease, and be aware of chronic illness which may complicate travel arrangements. On return we need to know that we are dealing with a traveller.
>
> (Ellis-Pegler 1992: 111)

The romantic image of South-East Asia and the South Pacific has long held a fascination for the international traveller. As travellers increasingly seek to experience 'unspoilt' natural ecosystems and indigenous Pacific cultures, they invariably venture off the beaten tourist track. However, expectations by 'alternative' travellers that remoteness provides isolated indigenous peoples an idyllic 'laidback' lifestyle without the pressures of polluted urban living and an abundance of locally produced or gathered foods, is not the reality. Many of these Pacific communities live in areas with inadequate housing, unreliable fresh water and poor sanitation: conditions that can lead to severe illness for host and guest alike, and which affects the tourist's experience of the destination. Furthermore, medical personnel, health facilities and supplies may be absent or inadequate at the local level. Indeed, most Pacific Island economies face rising populations and deteriorating balance deficits, straining infrastructure and health budgets.

This chapter was prompted by the authors' research into sustainable tourism development in the South-West Pacific and by their own health experiences as a consequence of such research.

Undoubtedly, tourism is seen as a critical element of economic development in South-East Asia and the South Pacific. The microstates of the region have few, if any, other development alternatives. However, health requirements of both travellers and local people have not generally been considered in the tourism development process. Similarly, despite media publicity of deaths among Australian and New Zealand holidaymakers from tropical diseases (e.g. Australian Associated Press 1991; Howarth 1992) and reports of tropical diseases in return travellers (e.g. *New Zealand Herald* 1993a), many tourists have not been warned of the potential health dangers of visiting South-East Asia and the South Pacific, even though relevant health literature is available (e.g. Wilson and Baker 1992; Department of Health 1993). According to the World Health Organisation (cited in PATA Advisory Council 1992), for every 100,000 people who travel overseas to tropical areas:

- 50,000 have health problems;
- 30,000 get travellers' diarrhoea;
- 3,000–4,000 will contract malaria;
- 8 will die;
- 2 will contract typhoid; and
- 0.1 will contract cholera.

Therefore, the authors argue that it is essential that the health dimensions of travel in the region be considered, particularly in the development of special-interest travel opportunities. Within the European Community, a recent EC Directive on Package Holidays actually places a legal requirement to make such information available, due to potential risks.

Specific data on travel-related illness is generally unavailable in Australia and New Zealand and even less so in Pacific Island microstates (Ellis-Pegler 1992). Therefore, the authors have drawn data from a wide range of sources, including interviews with staff of infectious disease units in Australia and New Zealand, other health professionals, and special-interest travel operators, in order to ascertain the level of awareness of travel-related health issues in Pacific countries.

This chapter is divided into three main sections. First, a discussion of special-interest tourism and its characteristics. Second, a review of three of the main diseases affecting travellers in the region: malaria, cholera/diarrhoea, and dengue fever. Third, an examination of the potential health implications of special-interest tourism development in the region. This final section focuses on the health implications of the development of nature-based and cultural tourism, which promotes contact with regions away from the main tourist centres. It is argued that such travellers are exposing themselves to malaria and other infectious diseases, such as dengue fever and typhoid, which are prevalent among some South Pacific communities. Similarly, warm clear waters laden with colourful coral and marine life and numerous sunken war wrecks are a diver's paradise, but a lack of knowledge of the dangers that lurk in the waters could result in dire consequences for the unprepared, including pollution, coral cuts, food poisoning and decompression sickness (Nicholls 1992).

SPECIAL-INTEREST TOURISM

Special-interest tourism can be said to occur when the traveller's motivation and decision-making are primarily determined by a particular special interest (Hall and Weiler 1992). Special-interest tourism is often equated with 'active' or 'experiential' travel. According to Heywood (1990: 46), the increased active component of travel is illustrated by the trends in tourism 'towards conservation, scholarship, science and environmental awareness'. The active involvement of travellers in the cultural and/or physical environment they are visiting is regarded as a key element of special-interest travel, as is the tourist's search for novel, authentic and quality tourist experiences. As Tabata (1989: 70) observed: 'The special-interest traveller wants to experience something new, whether it is history, food, sports, customs or the outdoors. Many wish to appreciate the new sights, sounds, smells and tastes and to understand the place and its people.'

Special-interest travel, particularly nature-based and cultural-based tourism, is becoming an increasingly important element of travel marketing and promotion of the Pacific Island states and several areas in South-East Asia, for example, hill-tribe trekking in northern Thailand or diving in the South Pacific (Hay 1992; Hall 1994a, 1994b). The European Union-funded Tourism Council of the South Pacific (TCSP) has undertaken a series of visitor surveys in member countries which indicated that between 50 and

80 per cent of all tourists to the region stated that the natural environment was one of the principal attractions of the host country (Kudu 1992).

> For island states that have very few resources, virtually the only resources where there may be some comparative advantage in favour of [island microstates] are clean beaches, unpolluted seas and warm weather and water, and at least vestiges of distinctive cultures.
>
> (Connell 1988: 62)

Although traditional recreational tourism is important in destinations such as Bali, Fiji, Phuket and Tahiti, special-interest travel, such as diving holidays, cultural tours and ecotourism activities, are increasingly being promoted throughout the region. For example, marine tourism is being promoted by Fiji, Vanuatu, the Solomon Islands, Indonesia and Thailand; cultural tourism is becoming a significant market segment in Malaysia and Indonesia; while 'ecotourism', often tied into the creation of new national parks, is being promoted heavily throughout the region (Hall 1994a).

The geographical distribution of special-interest travel activities is substantially different from that of recreational tourism. Whereas recreational tourism tends to be resort centred and focused on 'sun, sand, sea, and surf', special-interest travel activities tend to be dispersed and occur in areas away from mass tourism. Indeed, as noted above, one of the motivational factors of special-interest tourists is regarded to be the desire for novelty and authenticity in the tourist experience. Therefore, contact with areas and peoples that are not exposed to mass tourism is probably fundamental to the success of any special-interest travel operation. However, the very factor that may make an area attractive to special-interest tourists, that of relative isolation, also has potential health implications for host and guest alike. First, tourists who fall ill may place significant demands on local health services (if they are available), and the availability of services should be taken into account in the promotion of destinations. Second, the local population may be at risk of diseases transmitted by tourists. Third, tourists may be at risk from exposure to local diseases with the returning tourist potentially introducing diseases into his or her country of origin (Alleyne 1990). For example, the opening up of the former

Soviet Union to tourists is reported to have led to increases in occurrences of diphtheria in visitors to Russia and the Ukraine (Thompson 1993). Similarly, in Singapore all reported cases of malaria, 60 per cent of typhoid and 40 per cent of hepatitis A cases occurred in Singaporeans who contracted the disease whilst overseas (Shaw 1993). Nevertheless, it should be acknowledged that diseases do not distinguish between special-interest travellers and recreational tourists: given the presence of diseases throughout the region, all travellers would appear to be at risk.

THE EXTENT OF TRAVEL-RELATED ILLNESS IN AUSTRALIA AND NEW ZEALAND

One of the great difficulties in evaluating the extent of travel-related diseases in Australia and New Zealand is the lack of a specific travel disease database. While both countries have comprehensive disease-reporting mechanisms and produce regular bulletins on communicable diseases, sources of exposure to diseases are rarely reported. Therefore, disease information is available only at an aggregate level. Furthermore, in the case of tropical diseases not all are notifiable and, as in the case of one of the authors, one individual may have multiple cases. In most cases it is up to the individual doctor to note the areas visited by a patient. In addition, problems in identifying disease sources arise when people have visited multiple destinations.

As far as can be ascertained, the only published systematic survey of travel-associated disease in either Australia or New

Table 5.1 Travel-associated illness reported at the Infectious Diseases Unit, Auckland Hospital, July–December 1989

	DIAGNOSES					
	Total	Malaria		Diarrhoea	Dengue	Other
		Prophylaxis	Treatment			
Phone calls	141	46	29	20	3	43
Outpatient clinics	18	–	6	1	4	7
Hospital admissions	29	–	9	4	5	11
Total	188	46	44	25	12	61

Source: Wallace *et al.* 1992: 315.

Zealand is a study of travel-related illness undertaken at the Infectious Diseases Unit at the Auckland Hospital from July-December 1989 (see Table 5.1). The survey reported on 140 telephone consultations, 18 outpatient assessments and 29 hospital admissions. Significantly in terms of the relative impact of travel-related illness, the twenty-nine admissions constituted 20 per cent of the total admissions (127) during the survey period (Wallace *et al.* 1992). Malaria was the most common problem for which consultation was sought, with the next major diagnostic groups being diarrhoeal disease and dengue fever. Although a clear profile of travel-related illness in Australia and New Zealand is not available, evidence suggests that the pattern of disease reported in the Wallace *et al.* (1992) study is broadly representative of cases in the two countries (Ellis-Pegler 1992).

Malaria

Malaria is increasing as a problem disease for Australian and New Zealand travellers in South-East Asia and the South Pacific (Cook 1992; Ellis-Pegler 1992; Wallace *et al.* 1992). Malarial cases in travellers are reported to have doubled in the past decade (Howarth 1992). Malaria is caused by *Plasmodium*, a single-cell parasite. There are four types which cause malaria in humans: *Plasmodium falciparum* (commonly known as cerebral malaria), *P. vivax*, *P. ovale* and *P. malariae*. The parasite produces attacks of fever varying in severity and frequency, with the most serious symptoms being caused by *P. falciparum*. Malarial parasites are injected into the human bloodstream by the bite of an infected *Anopheles* mosquito. The number of cases of malaria is rising world-wide. Malarial parasites now infect an estimated 489 million people every year, killing up to 2.8 million people, which is far more than AIDS, and causing up to 100 million cases of acute illness (Turley 1990; *The Economist* 1993).

The World Health Organisation (WHO) announced in 1955 that the disease would soon be eradicated (*Newsweek* 1993). However, such optimism was not to be met. The WHO approach to eradicating malaria was two-fold. First, attempting to halt the passing-on of malaria by attacking infected mosquitoes with residual pesticides such as DDT. Second, to destroy malaria parasites in the human blood through treatment with anti-malarial drugs. Unfortunately, the success of the strategy was short-lived. The relatively high cost of anti-malarial programmes for developing countries meant that such programmes were either stopped or severely curtailed when foreign aid was withdrawn. The widespread and often indiscriminate use of chemical pesticides has meant that many malaria carriers have now developed high genetic resistance. In addition, the use of insecticides often had numerous unintended side-effects on 'friendly' insects which reduced local support for spraying programmes. Malarial parasites, such as *P. falciparum*, have also developed resistance to anti-malarial drugs. The development of transport and development infrastructure in developing countries has also hastened the spread of malarial-carrying mosquitoes and parasites. Finally, many developing countries have not been able to place enough investment into health, sanitation and education (Turley 1990). All of these problems are represented to varying degrees in special-interest tourism destinations in the Asia-Pacific region (see World Health Organisation 1993b, 1993c).

In Thailand, where public health officials have managed to control malaria for several decades, the country's population of 55 million people is increasingly at risk from a resurgence of malaria for two reasons. First, the location of Thailand between two major reservoirs of malaria strains. Second, the increasing drug resistance of malarial strains.

In the densely forested highlands that separate Thailand from Burma on one side and Cambodia on the other, the *falciparum* parasite has become increasingly resistant to treatment (Nosten et al. 1991). In addition, social and political changes are forcing people into closer contact with disease-bearing areas. Burma's unstable political situation has pushed thousands of refugees across the Thai border in recent years, and their constant movement makes disease control extremely difficult.

According to *Newsweek* (1993), about 15,000 cases of malaria (70 per cent involving *falciparum*) occur annually among the 30,000 Karen tribespeople living along the frontier. In many hill-tribe villages, infant mortality rates approach 30 per cent. Many of the hill-tribe villages have already been ravaged by HIV and the increasing resistance of malaria to treatment poses another severe health risk. However, given the growing popularity of hill-tribe trekking by Western tourists and the growth of river rafting near the Thai–Burma border, malarial control is a major issue in the health of special-interest tourists, particularly as previous prophylaxic regimes appear to be becoming inadequate.

The situation on the Burma border is dwarfed by the problem that is developing on the Cambodian border. The Pailin region of Cambodia, which is a major gem field, is noted for its rabies and its virulent malaria. Approximately 250,000 miners per year enter Thailand's Trat province with many infected by the drug-resistant *falciparum*. So far, Thai health authorities have been able to keep the disease under relative control. However, the liberal use of anti-malarial medications in Thailand has led to increasing drug resistance in malarial strains. According to *Newsweek*,

> Chloroquine and Fansidar, still marginally effective in most parts of the world, are virtually useless against the *falciparum* parasite in Thailand. Backup drugs such as mefloquine and halofantine are fast losing their effectiveness, and so is the old standby quinine. Experts say that without new therapies, Asia could face wholly untreatable strains of malaria by the end of the decade.
>
> (*Newsweek* 1993: 14)

Resistance to malarial medication in the South Pacific is an increasing problem in Papua New Guinea, the Solomons, Vanuatu and several other South Pacific islands. The Solomon Islands has one of the highest rates of malaria in the world, with Honiara, the capital on the island of Guadalcanal, having one of the largest number of cases reaching almost 800 cases per thousand population in 1991, down from a high of over 900 cases in 1990 (Honimae 1992). Given the role that tourism is playing in the economic development of the Solomons, through such activities as scuba-diving and ecotourism projects, the high incidence of malaria should clearly be of concern to tourism operators and travellers themselves.

Precise figures about the proportion of *Plasmodium falciparum* infections that are resistant to chloroquine in the Pacific Islands are unavailable. It is known that a 'significant number of travellers to nations such as the Solomon Islands and Papua New Guinea develop malaria due to *Plasmodium falciparum* while taking chloroquine' (Auckland Hospital Infectious Diseases Unit, personal communication, 30 September 1992). Although exact details are unknown, it appears that chloroquine-resistant *Plasmodium falciparum* is quite prevalent and that its frequency approaches that of the worst affected parts of Africa and South-East Asia.

Dengue fever

Like malaria, dengue fever is a mosquito-borne viral disease transmitted by *Aedes aegypti*, which is endemic throughout the topics. Dengue belongs to the flavivirus group of viruses. In recent years epidemics of dengue fever have occurred in Fiji, French Polynesia, Vanuatu, New Caledonia and other Pacific Islands. As a result of an increase of dengue in South-East Asia and the Pacific Islands and increased travel to this region from Australia and New Zealand, it is expected that the disease will present itself more frequently in Australian and New Zealand tourists returning from tropical areas. For example, Mills (1991) in a study of the clinical spectrum of dengue fever in travellers, reported on cases of travellers to Fiji, Bali, India, Singapore and Malaysia.

The prevention of dengue fever in tourists at present depends on avoiding infection as there are no vaccines available to prevent the disease. The behaviour of the dengue vector is substantially different from that of the Anopheline mosquito responsible for malaria:

> *Aedes aegypti* prefers to feed on humans during the daytime and most frequently is found in or near human habitations. Personal mosquito avoidance measures are the most important means of reducing the risk of acquiring dengue infection.
>
> (Mills 1991)

However, there is clearly a need for medical advice on the different health measures required for dengue fever and malaria to be conveyed to the tourist. The focus often remains on malaria, with little preventive information on dengue fever being supplied to Australian and New Zealand travellers in the South Pacific and South-East Asia.

Dengue is also endemic to the tropics of northern Queensland. The vector of the dengue virus, *Aedes aegypti*, is known to occur only in Queensland. Outbreaks of dengue fever occurring in Townsville and Cairns in 1992, both major tourism centres, indicate the potential of the disease to spread in tropical Queensland (Sinclair 1992). Although the outbreak of dengue fever did receive some publicity in the national media, as far as can be ascertained, travellers to the region did not receive formal warning of the outbreak by tour operators. However, the threat of dengue fever is regarded as so serious by the city of Rockhampton on the central Queensland coast that they have placed four flocks of chickens, known as 'sentinel hens', on the outskirts of the city in order to check for the arrival of dengue-carrying mosquitoes (*New Zealand Herald* 1993b). And in March 1995 an outbreak of dengue fever was reported in a Cairns suburb (*New Zealand Herald* 1995).

Cholera and diarrhoea

Cholera is a disease endemic in many less developed countries. Cholera is essentially a disease of poverty, poor health and housing, and malnutrition, and often accompanies natural disasters such as floods and earthquakes. The seventh world pandemic that started in Indonesia in 1961 reached South America in 1991 after traversing Asia and Africa. The arrival of the pandemic heralded the first significant occurrence of cholera and subsequent mortality for a century in South America (Godlee 1991).

WHO (1993a) currently advises that cholera vaccination is not a legal requirement for international travel and that travel does not need to be restricted on account of cholera. According to the *New Zealand Medical Journal* (1991: 274) 'Cholera vaccination has no part to play in the control of epidemics and the current inactivated vaccines give protection for three months in half the inoculated. The main problem concerns the traveller who is at low risk.' Nevertheless, travellers to Asia from New Zealand are being warned of a new strain of cholera which is sweeping through Asia. Tens of thousands of cases of a new strain of *Vibrio cholarae* (serotype 0139), have been reported by the World Health Organisation in India, Bangladesh, Nepal, China, Malaysia, Thailand, Hong Kong and Singapore. The New Zealand Ministry of Health's Adviser on Public Medicine, Dr Arvind Patel, has stated that the cholera vaccine already of relatively limited use against the usual strains of cholera, was probably of no use against the new strain. The new strain of *Vibrio cholarae* was regarded as five times as lethal as the common strain, killing 5 per cent of those infected. Dr Patel explicitly noted the danger of the new strain for tourists and commented that although food prepared in top-quality hotels was unlikely to be a problem, food and drink from other sources were likely to be suspect (Townsend 1993). In October 1993 the New Zealand Ministry of Health started to issue official warnings to travellers regarding the dangers presented by the new strain. Similar to the effects of cholera but much more prevalent are diarrhoeal diseases (Barer 1989). By far the most common cause of travellers' diarrhoea is the enterotoxigenic *E. coli*, which may affect between 20–50 per cent of tropical travellers (*New Zealand Medical Journal* 1991). Therefore, advice about food and oral rehydration are probably more important than vaccination for many travellers. While knowledge of 'Delhi belly', or other such euphemisms, seems good amongst the backpacking fraternity and is often noted in guidebooks such as *Lonely Planet*, awareness of tropical diarrhoea does not seem to be as prevalent amongst more up-market special-interest travel groups in the South Pacific. This may partly be because of improved food hygiene by operators. However, it may also be a result of an unwillingness of some operators to disclose such perils of travelling or perhaps even a lack of field experience.

HEALTH IMPLICATIONS FOR SPECIAL-INTEREST TRAVELLERS

By their very nature, special-interest travellers are seeking to get off the conventional tourism routes and away from mass tourist resorts. In doing so they are also potentially exposing themselves to a range of diseases that for hygiene, sanitation, health education and environmental reasons are not found in many of the resort areas of the region. As the above discussion indicates, tropical diseases that were previously thought to be under control are becoming increasingly virulent and threatening to travellers. Nevertheless, many travel operators and national and regional tourism bodies are often failing to acknowledge such health threats perhaps because of a fear of scaring potential visitors away or because of the damage it could do to a country's or region's image.

An example of the manner in which decision-making processes ignore the health dimensions of special-interest tourism can be provided from an ecotourism development in the Solomon Islands. In October 1988 a proposal for a rainforest wilderness trail traversing Guadalcanal 'under the control of an indigenous company of customary landowners' (Sofield 1992: 96), was proposed from within the Prime Minister's Office by Trevor Sofield, the then Australian High Commissioner, as an alternative to logging rainforest. The proposed walk was to start at Aola on the north coast of Guadalcanal and end at Lauvi Lagoon on the southern Weather Coast. However, the coastal area of the Weather Coast has only poor quality agricultural land and is beset by health problems, such as malaria, and by natural disasters including cyclones, flooding and earthquakes. Health facilities and the general level of sanitation, hygiene and water quality are grossly inadequate for local people, let alone tourists. Malaria is a major problem on the Weather Coast and has been described by the Director of Health Services of Guadalcanal Province as 'crippling attempts at developing a tourism industry and it would appear to be getting worse not better. In short, it is a major social, economic and health disaster in this small developing country' (Guadalcanal Province 1991: 2).

Despite such health warnings, and widespread local concerns surrounding the Lauvi Lagoon tourism resort project, the Tourism Council of the South Pacific (TCSP) (1991) produced a report highlighting the potential of the area for ecotourism development. Indeed, the Solomon Islands Tourism Development Plan, 1991–2000, (TCSP 1990) stated that the Lauvi Lagoon:

> has potential for development of a small scale nature-oriented attraction with associated visitor accommodation and other services. There appears to be scope for developing and managing the crocodile populations for tourist viewing, this being the major attraction. Other attractions which should be developed are trails in the surrounding forest, and trips to the outlying reef. It may also be possible to integrate custom and traditional villages with tourism depending on the wishes of the people.
> (Tourism Council of the South Pacific 1990: 359)

The proposal that diving and snorkelling trips to the reef could be provided was especially surprising, given that local people will neither swim in the sea nor around Sahulu Island, just south of Lauvi Lagoon, because of the number of sharks in the water (Hall and Rudkin 1993). However, the lagoon area, and the Weather Coast in general, provide the breeding ground for mosquitoes and a number of intestinal diseases, at least in part because of poor water quality and sanitation, as well as a number of other diseases including leprosy and tuberculosis (Guadacanal Province 1991). Following substantial local opposition, the ecotourism development proposal was dropped (temporarily) with Ezekiel Âlebua, a government minister and developer, concluding that given the opposition to the resort project, it may be appropriate to divert TCSP funding into the Lees Lake area in the highlands of Guadalcanal which had substantially fewer health problems than the lagoon (Rudkin 1995), although it should be noted that malaria does still exist in the region (Bennett 1987).

In January 1993 cyclone Nina devastated many of the villages along the Weather Coast. In the village nearest the lagoon not a single house was left standing. The airstrip was covered with logs and other debris. It took several days of clearing by the local people before flights could resume. Nevertheless, despite health, social, environmental and broader development concerns the proposals for ecotourism development in the region are still being pursued (Hall and Rudkin 1993), with no provision for the access of water supply, sanitation for the locals or any economic benefits generated through the development to improve the inadequate health or educational facilities of the area (Rudkin 1995).

The proposed ecotourism development on the Weather Coast of Guadalcanal is not an isolated example of inadequate consideration of health matters in special-interest tourism promotion in the South Pacific. Studies of ecotourism developments in the region provide evidence that the health dimension is being all but ignored within the tourism development process (Hay 1992; Sofield 1992; Hall 1994a; Rudkin 1995), both in terms of the local people and in the potential impacts of travellers on the already scarce health resources of many countries in the region. Furthermore, the ignorance of health issues is not restricted to tourism developers, as many operators and travel agents are also either ignorant or naïve about the health dangers that exist for those travellers who intend to venture outside of the main tourist resorts. For example, a patient with severe *P. falciparum* malaria admitted to Auckland Hospital in 1992 that he 'had taken antimalarial prophylaxis regularly through eighteen months of tropical travel, only to stop in the last few weeks in Indonesia when he was told, incorrectly, that there was no malaria risk' (Ellis-Pegler 1992: 110).

Another area of special-interest tourism in the Asia-Pacific region in which the health risks have not received the attention they deserve is that of diving. Countries such as the Solomon Islands, Fiji and Vanuatu have invested heavily in the promotion of their underwater attractions at remote locations. As with other forms of special-interest tourism, it is the isolation of many dive sites which represents a potential health threat. Decompression sickness is probably the most well-known hazard for diving, particularly if it is exacerbated by flying home from a diving holiday (Edmonds *et al.* 1992). For example, the carrying of portable personal decompression chambers is now compulsory for Australian commercial diving operators, although such measures are not enforced in the Pacific Islands. However, in reality the greatest marine health threat arises from contact with stinging fish and shells and ciguatera fish poisoning.

The South-East Asia–South Pacific region abounds with hazardous fish and shells. While media attention is often focused on the danger of shark attack, in reality there is far more danger from contact with poisonous animals, including stonefish (*Synanceia trachynis, S. verrucosa*), stingrays, jellyfish, fire coral, butterfly cod (*Pterois volitans*), cone shells (*Conus sp.*), sea snakes and the blue-ringed octopus (*Hapalochlaena maculosa*) (Wilson and Gillett 1971; Edmonds 1978; Colfelt 1985). Cone shells, for example, have been responsible for many serious stings and a number of fatalities as divers collect shells as souvenirs. Several of the cones are highly dangerous as their venom is a powerful neurotoxin and can only be safely collected with tongs and should be placed in a thick collecting bag or pail, particularly as their harpoon can penetrate heavy clothing.

Ciguatera fish poisoning is the result of consuming marine fish that have become contaminated via the food chain with toxins produced by a benthic species of dinoflagellate (*Gambierdiscus toxicus*). According to Lange *et al.* (1992: 2049), 'this organism flourishes as a consequence of environmental insult to tropical and subtropical reef ecosystems'. Ciguatera fish poisoning is endemic in South-East Asia and the South Pacific (Edmonds 1978; Bagnis *et al.* 1979; Ruff 1989), although 'the condition is not reportable to public health authorities either nationally or internationally, so its incidence is not clearly known, and its epidemiology is incompletely understood' (Lange *et al.* 1992: 2049). Many species of tropical and subtropical fish are affected by ciguatera poisoning with neither freshness nor cooking having any bearing on fish toxicity. Edmonds (1978) recommends that large, carnivorous fish be avoided, particularly as ciguatera poisoning occurs sporadically and unpredictably, and may gradually spread from one area to another. There is no sure way of avoiding ciguatera poisoning apart from not eating fish, somewhat humorously Edmonds (1978: 169) suggests to 'try out a sample on the neighbour's cat, and observe for a few hours', while another approach 'is to feed the older members of the family first, and if they remain unaffected after several hours, the fish may be fed to the children with safety. Some cultures may reverse this process'. Despite such a comic approach, Edwards does have a significant point to stress in terms of the health of the international traveller. Many divers and visitors to more remote communities and islands will be staying in an environment in which fish is part of the staple diet. Furthermore, for many divers part of the experience in visiting these places will be the possibility of eating the fish they have caught. Ciguatera is therefore potentially a major problem for special-interest travel health and as Lange *et al.* (1992: 2052) concluded: 'international travel is an important risk factor for [ciguatera fish poisoning], and that the health risk might even be comparable to that of acquiring hepatitis A, a threat against which specific precautions are routinely recommended and administered'.

CONCLUSION

At present few potential health problems exist if travellers contain their sightseeing and experiences to the more popular Asian and Pacific destinations, although there is some evidence to suggest that increased resistance of some diseases to either treatment or spraying of vectors may lead to their becoming a health risk even in the larger resort areas. Nevertheless, for the growing number of special-interest tourists who are intent on being off the beaten track, numerous health problems abound. Armed with comprehensive medical insurance, prophylactics, and a well-stocked medical kit, many feel that they are safe. However, the sheer isolation of many of the regions that they are visiting is itself a health risk, particularly as many tropical diseases such as malaria and dengue fever are re-emerging as health threats, a feature reflected in the recent outbreak of dengue fever in the Cook Islands in 1995. Williams (1995) reported that 350 people had been treated for dengue fever between March and April 1995. One outcome of the outbreak was that visitor arrivals to the capital – Rarotonga, the site of the outbreak, dropped. As a result a significant number of stopovers to the Cook Islands' capital severely dented the local tourism economy.

Special-interest travel is a rapidly emerging form of tourism marked by a desire of its participants to avoid many of the traditional tourist locations. However, the search for novel, 'tourist-free' destinations and activities does in itself represent a health threat to participants. By being off the beaten track, special-interest travellers from Australia and New Zealand, as elsewhere around the world, are also exposing themselves to diseases and health risks that are not to be found in recreational tourism resorts. While risk is an essential element of the excitement of travel for many special-interest tourists, tourist operators, travel agents and government tourist agencies have often not been providing an honest appraisal of some of the health risks involved. Given a better understanding of the health risks involved in visiting some of the destinations where special-interest tourism is being promoted, it may well be the case that some tourists will re-evaluate the health risks involved and select an adventurous, yet not so potentially dangerous, form of leisure-taking.

REFERENCES

Alleyne, G. (1990) 'The health/tourism interaction', *The Courier* 122, 67–8.
Auckland Hospital Infectious Diseases Unit (1993) personal communication, 30 September.
Australian Associated Press (1991) 'Tourists warned of malaria', *The Dominion* 9: December.
Bagnis, R., Kuberski, T. and Laugier, S. (1979) 'Clinical observations of 3009 cases of ciguatera (fish poisoning) in the South Pacific', *American Journal of Tropical Medicine and Hygiene*, 28: 1067–73.
Barer, M. (1989) 'Diarrhoea and intestinal infections', in R. Dawood (ed.) *Travellers' Health: How to Stay Healthy Abroad*, 2nd edn, Oxford: Oxford University Press, 21–42.
Bennett, J. A. (1987) *Wealth of the Solomons: A History of a Pacific Archipelago, 1800–1978*, Honolulu: University of Hawaii Press.

Colfelt, D. (1985) *100 Magic Miles of the Great Barrier Reef: The Whitsunday Islands*, Rose Bay: Windward Publications.
Connell, J. (1988) *Sovereignty and Survival: Island Microstates in the Third World*, Sydney: Research Monograph No. 3, Department of Geography, University of Sydney.
Cook, G. C. (1992) 'Malaria: an underdiagnosed and often neglected medical emergency', *Australia and New Zealand Journal of Medicine* 22: 69–82.
Department of Health (1993) *Fare Well: Health Aspects of International Air Travel*, Wellington: Department of Health, Te Tari Ora, New Zealand.
Edmonds, C. (1978) *Dangerous Marine Animals of the Indo-Pacific Region*, Newport: Diving Medical Centre Monograph on Identification, First Aid and Medical Treatment, Wedneil Publications.
Edmonds, C., Lowry, C. and Pennefather, J. (1992) *Diving and Subaquatic Medicine*, 3rd edn, Oxford and Sydney: Butterworths.
Ellis-Pegler, R. B. (1992) 'Travel to the tropics: going away and coming home', *Communicable Disease New Zealand* 92, 12: 109–11.
Evening Post (1993) 'Warning on new cholera strain issued', 19 October.
Godlee, F. (1991) 'Cholera pandemic', *British Medical Journal* 302: 1039–40.
Guadalcanal Province (1991) *The State of Health of the People of Guadalcanal Province*, Honiara: Guadalcanal Province.
Hall, C. M. (1994a) *Tourism in the Pacific: Development, Impacts and Markets*, South Melbourne: Longman Cheshire.
—— (1994b) 'Ecotourism in Australia, New Zealand and the South Pacific: Appropriate tourism or a new form of ecological imperialism?', in E. A. Cater and G. A. Bowman (eds) *Ecotourism*, Chichester: Wiley/Royal Geographical Society: 137–58.
Hall, C. M. and Rudkin, B. (1993) 'Ecotourism as Appropriate Tourism? A Case Study from the Solomon Islands', Paper presented at the Thirteenth International Congress of Anthropological and Ethnological Sciences, Symposium on Tourism as a Determinant of Culture Change, 30 July.
Hall, C. M. and Weiler, B. (1992) 'Introduction. What's special about special interest tourism?', in B. Weiler and C. M. Hall (eds), *Special Interest Tourism*, London: Wiley, 1–14.
Hay, J. E. (ed.) (1992) *Ecotourism Business in the Pacific: Promoting a Sustainable Experience, Conference Proceedings*, Auckland: Environmental Science, University of Auckland.
Heywood, P. (1990) 'Truth and beauty in landscape – trends in landscape and leisure', *Landscape Australia* 12, 1: 43–7.
Honimae, J. (1992) 'Malaria research tracks down a killer', *The Solomons Voice*, 29 April: 9.
Howarth, A. (1992) 'Take your malaria medicine', *The Dominion*, 22 September: 13.
Isaacs, R. and Ellis-Pegler, R. B. (1987) '*Plasmodium falciparum* resistance to quinine and sulfadoxime-prymethamine in the Solomon Islands', *Medical Journal of Australia* 146: 449–50.

Kudu, D. (1992) 'The role and activities of the Tourism Council of the South Pacific, particularly in relation to ecotourism development', in J. E. Hay (ed.) *Ecotourism Business in the Pacific: Promoting a Sustainable Experience, Conference Proceedings*, Auckland: Environmental Science, University of Auckland, 154–60.

Lange, W. R., Snyder, F. R. and Fudala, P. J. (1992) 'Travel and ciguatera fish poisoning', *Archives of International Medicine* 152: 2049–53.

Mills, G. D. (1991) 'Clinical spectrum of dengue fever in travellers', *New Zealand Medical Journal* 104: 228–30.

Newsweek (1993) 'Mosquitoes on the comeback killer trail', 15 September, Section 2: 14.

New Zealand Herald (1993a), 'Travellers catch typhoid', 4 August, Section 1: 24.

—— (1993b) 'Guard chickens', 3 November, Section 2: 2.

—— (1995) 'Dengue alert', 20 March, section 1: 15.

New Zealand Medical Journal (1991) 'Cholera rampages on', 26 June: 274.

Nicholls, D. (1992) 'Sea anemone sting while SCUBA diving', *New Zealand Medical Journal*, 24 June: 245.

Nosten, F., Ter Kuile, F. and Chongsupajaisiddhi, T. (1991) 'Mefloquine-resistant *falciparum* malaria on the Thai–Burmese border', *Lancet* 337: 1140–3.

PATA Advisory Council – Development Committee (1992) *Position Paper – Tourism and Health*, Woollahara: Dain Simpson Associates.

Rudkin, B. (1995) 'Ecotourism: passage to sustainable development?' Masters thesis, Massey University, Albany, Auckland, in progress.

Ruff, T. A. (1989) 'Ciguatera in the Pacific: a link with military activities', *Lancet* 1: 201–5.

Shaw, M. (1993) 'Catching the travel bug', *GP Weekly*, 10 March: 28–9.

Sinclair, D. P. (1992) 'The distribution of *Aedes aegypti* in Queensland, 1990 to 30 June 1992', *Communicable Diseases Intelligence* 16, 19: 404–6.

Sofield, T. (1992) 'The Guadalcanal Track ecotourism project in the Solomon Islands', in J. E. Hay (ed.) *Ecotourism Business in the Pacific: Promoting a Sustainable Experience, Conference Proceedings*, Auckland: Environmental Science, University of Auckland, 89–100.

Tabata, R. (1989) 'Implications of special interest tourism for interpretation and resource conservation', in D. Uzzell (ed.) *Heritage Interpretation, Volume 2, The Visitor Experience*, London: Belhaven, 68–77.

The Economist (1993) 'One bite is one too many', 21 August: 31–2.

Thompson, L. (1993) 'Diphtheria cases rise in Russia', *New Zealand Herald*, 5 October, Section 3: 3.

Tourism Council of the South Pacific (1990) *Solomon Islands Tourism Development Plan, 1991–2000*, Suva: Tourism Council of the South Pacific.

—— (1991) *Solomon Islands Nature Sites Development Project: Lauvi Lagoon*, Suva: Tourism Council of the South Pacific.

Townsend, K. (1993) 'New killer cholera', *New Zealand Herald*, 19 October, Section 1: 1.

Turley, R. (1990) 'Worldwide search for solutions', *Geographical Magazine*, February: 22–7.
Wallace, E., Thomas, M. G. and Ellis-Pegler, R. B. (1992) 'Travel-associated illness', *New Zealand Medical Journal* 105: 315–16.
Williams, L. (1995) 'And then there was dengue', *Pacific Islands Monthly*, June: 27.
Wilson, N. and Baker, M. (1992) 'Choosing vaccinations for the traveller', *New Ethicals*, October: 47–55.
Wilson, B. R. and Gillett, K. (1971) *Australian Shells*, Sydney: A. H. & A. W. Reed.
World Health Organisation (1993a) *International Travel and Health: Vaccination Requirements and Health Advice Situation as on 1 January 1993*, Geneva: World Health Organisation.
—— (1993b) 'World malaria situation in 1991, Part I', *Weekly Epidemiological Record* 68, 34: 245–52.
—— (1993c) 'World malaria situation in 1991, Part II', *Weekly Epidemiological Record* 68, 35: 253–9.

Chapter 6

Dimensions of holiday experiences and their health implications
A study of British tourists in Malta

Nicola Clark and Stephen Clift

INTRODUCTION

This chapter describes some of the findings from two surveys of British tourists in Malta conducted in March 1993 and March 1994 which explored aspects of holiday experiences relevant to individual well-being, health risks and problems with health. These studies are part of a broader interdisciplinary programme of research – the Travel, Lifestyles and Health project (Clift and Page 1994) – concerned with investigating links between travel and health and with contributing to the development of practical initiatives in travel health promotion (see Chapter 11, this volume). A particular concern of the project has been to explore the cultural assumption that holidays provide a setting conducive to romantic and sexual relationships with new partners (see Clift 1994a, 1994b) and to undertake empirical investigations of the sexual behaviour of tourists/travellers while abroad (see Clark and Clift 1994; Black, Clift and Wijisurendra 1994; Clift and Wilkins 1994).

During the course of the project, the opportunity arose to conduct health-oriented surveys of British tourists on holiday in Malta during March 1993 and again in 1994, utilising the services of Tourism Studies students engaged in a field course on the island. These surveys tested the feasibility of conducting face-to-face interviews with tourists while on holiday and allowed the health dimensions of tourism in both a positive and negative sense to be explored. Findings from the earlier study have been fully described elsewhere (Clark, Clift and Page 1993, 1994; Page, Clift and Clark 1994) and only a brief summary will be provided here as a basis for a more detailed discussion of the 1994 survey.

BRITISH TOURISTS IN MALTA – 1993 STUDY

In the first study, 785 British tourists on Malta in March 1993 were interviewed using a structured questionnaire. Interviews were conducted at fourteen sites across the island over one and a half days by forty-two Tourism Studies students participating in a tourism field course. Questions were asked regarding: pre-travel health advice; health precautions taken; behaviour while on holiday which posed health risks; health problems experienced and actions taken in response to them.

Few holidaymakers sought health advice prior to travel but 14 per cent referred to travel agents and 13 per cent consulted GPs regarding health issues. Twenty-three per cent had read something on health issues prior to travel and 15 per cent reported reading *Health Advice for Travellers* (Department of Health 1992). Many tourists took preparations and medicines with them: 76 per cent suncream; 61 per cent painkillers; 24 per cent travel sickness tablets; 29 per cent insect repellant; and 30 per cent anti-diarrhoea tablets. A total of 28.5 per cent of tourists also had prescribed medicines with them, the incidence of which increased markedly with increased age.

In terms of health problems, 37 per cent of respondents reported experiencing some health problem while on holiday. However, these were mostly minor – headache 20 per cent, sunburn 16 per cent, sore throat 9 per cent and diarrhoea 7 per cent (this figure being close to the level of diarrhoea among tourists in Malta in March 1992 found by Cartwright – personal communication) (see Cartwright, Chapter 3 of this volume for a detailed discussion of travellers' diarrhoea). Self-medication was the most commonly reported response to health problems (10 per cent), but 6 per cent of tourists changed their plans and 4.5 per cent had to stay in bed. Those who consulted a doctor amounted to 1.4 per cent, and 0.4 per cent had to visit the hospital in Malta. For half of those reporting a health problem, the difficulty affected them for only one day, but 17 per cent were affected for three or more days.

A number of interesting associations were found between tourist characteristics, their activities on holiday, and health. Thus the following groups – younger tourists, those who smoked, those who had sought pre-travel advice and tourists with medicines with them – were all significantly more likely to be ill than older tourists, non-smokers and those who did not seek health advice and take medicines with them. These patterns served to replicate findings previously reported in the works of Cossar and his associates in Glasgow (see Chapter 2, this volume).

Associations were also found between the experience of diarrhoea and eating food from street vendors ($X^2 = 10.34$ $p < 0.01$), and between swimming in swimming pools and a constellation of symptoms including sore throat, headache, sunburn and diarrhoea.

Data on alcohol consumption and exposure to the sun also revealed interesting patterns. A marked age trend in alcohol consumption was apparent, with 64 per cent of visitors under 30 drinking more in Malta than at home, decreasing with age, to only 39 per cent of the over-sixties drinking more on holiday. In addition, while 76 per cent of all visitors reported having protective suncream, 16 per cent reported sunburn. Burning, despite suncream, was more common in the younger age groups. Thus, of the under-30s, 81 per cent took suncream to Malta, but 23 per cent got sunburned, whereas only 65 per cent of those in their sixties took suncream, and 10 per cent reported being burned.

The first survey served to establish the feasibility of undertaking face-to-face interviews on health issues among tourists while on holiday. It also provided data on the incidence of health problems and factors associated with symptoms which were reassuringly consistent with the findings of previously reported studies. Nevertheless, it has to be conceded that the health problems and symptoms reported were on the whole minor and short-lived, and that only a small proportion of tourists had any kind of problem which interfered with their holiday.

The study also had a number of shortcomings. The lack of a matched control group who were not on holiday, for example, made it impossible to conclude that the pattern of symptoms observed were in all cases a consequence of travelling to, and holidaying in, Malta – the people surveyed may well have experienced a similar range of minor health problems had they stayed at home. Nevertheless, certain aspects of the survey findings, particularly levels of sunburn, and the associations between swimming in pools and symptoms, indicate specific holiday-related health issues which would not have been observed in a comparable survey back home in England in March!

A second shortcoming of the study was the lack of any attention given to sexual activity while on holiday and the possible risks associated with unprotected sex with new partners. It was, however, considered inappropriate and potentially insulting to approach strangers in the street while on holiday and ask them highly personal and potentially worrying questions about their sexual activity. While Ford and his associates succeeded in doing this in Torbay using young interviewers to approach tourists in the same age group (see Chapter 8, this volume), it was considered problematic to attempt questioning on sexual activity in Malta given the context of the interview, the very wide age range of the interviewees, and the relative youth of the fieldworkers.

A further limited feature of the 1993 survey was its strong focus on precautions to avoid health problems and tourists' experiences of unpleasant symptoms and illness, with no consideration given to potentially positive aspects of holidays. Ideally, holidays provide opportunities for enjoyment, relaxation and new activities and these features of holidays could serve to enhance a sense of well-being and promote health in a positive and holistic sense, embracing emotional, mental, social and spiritual dimensions.

In planning a second survey of British tourists in Malta, therefore, it was decided to give a much stronger emphasis to the positive health dimensions of tourism and to attempt to address, at least indirectly, the issue of romantic and sexual relationships on holiday and the potential risks which may be involved.

A number of studies have explored tourist motivations, activities and experiences which have both positive and negative implications for health, and these influenced the conception and design of the second investigation. In a 'psychographic' study of American tourists in North Carolina, for example, Gitelson and Kerstetter (1990) found four distinct factors motivating their trip: relaxation ('to get away from it all', 'release tension' and 'relax'); exploration ('to see interesting sights', 'explore new places' and 'view scenery'); excitement ('do exciting things', 'be entertained' and 'experience luxury') and social factors (including 'share a familiar place with others', 'return to a favourite vacation site' and 'do something with the family'). The explorer dimension was the most highly rated in the over sixties, and by middle-class households. Relaxation was more important to summer visitors than those visiting in other seasons, and excitement was a greater motivator in winter than in the autumn and spring.

Gladwell (1990) reports three distinct types of travellers who use Inns in Indiana State Park: knowledgeable travellers (self-confident, family and education orientated), budget-conscious travellers (often with children under 6 and low income and educational levels) and travel planners (who sought relaxation, educational and historical opportunities on vacation). These three groups responded differently to a questionnaire designed to explore their travel motivations and experiences on holiday. Knowledgeable travellers, for example, agreed that 'my idea of a good vacation is to travel to a quiet and peaceful location for maximum relaxation' whereas the other groups did not. Knowledgeable travellers were more likely to 'seek thrills and adventure' and agree that 'the most important part of my vacation is meeting new people'. Travel planners were more likely to endorse cultural and historical influences for the choice of their holiday destination than were budget-conscious travellers, who tended to show no interest in educational, sporting or camping holidays.

Clark and Clift (1994) investigated the health and risk behaviour of single British students aged 18–25 during their last holiday abroad, in which holiday experience was assessed using a specially devised holiday experience questionnaire. Factor analysis of thirty-two items revealed five distinct factors: 'Social Life and Relationships' (e.g. 'I was on the lookout for excitement and a good social life'), 'Enjoyment' (e.g. 'I thoroughly enjoyed myself and had a good time'), 'Personal Development' (e.g. 'I felt I broadened my outlook on life'), 'Health Concerns' (e.g. 'I made sure I was well supplied with medicines, creams, plasters, etc.') and 'Rest-Activity' (e.g. 'I returned home feeling rested and refreshed').

Significant sex differences emerged with men scoring more highly on the Social Life and Relationships factor and women more highly on the Health Concerns factor. In terms of sexual health, those tourists scoring highly on the first factor appeared to be at potentially higher risk since it served to identify young people who were seeking an exciting nightlife; were willing to engage in casual sexual relationships; felt less inhibited than at home; were prepared to use drugs if offered to them; and who consumed more alcohol than at home. The picture emerging from this factor confirms the association between sexual activity, alcohol consumption and recreational drug-taking reported by Ford (1991) (see Ford and Eiser, Chapter 8, this volume) and Conway, Gillies and Slack (1990) (see Gillies and Slack, Chapter 7, this volume). High scores on the remaining factors, in contrast, all have positive health implications whether in terms of enjoyment, personal well-being and freedom from stress, personal growth and development, active avoidance of health problems or the pursuit of exercise and relaxation.

BRITISH TOURISTS IN MALTA – 1994 STUDY

Aims of the study

The 1994 survey in British tourists to Malta had the following aims:

- to collect basic information on health problems experienced on holiday as a point of comparison with the earlier study;
- to explore the extent to which the dimensions of holiday emerging from the study of students (Clark and Clift 1994) described above could be identified in a more diverse and representative cross-section of British tourists surveyed during the course of their holiday;
- to assess the relevance of age, sex and holiday companions on the quality of tourists' holiday experiences;
- to explore the positive and negative health implications associated with different holiday experience profiles identified.

METHODOLOGY

Design

Data were collected from British tourists by structured face-to-face interviews in fifteen different sites on Malta. A team of thirty-six undergraduate Tourism Studies students undertook interviews under the close supervision of senior staff. A total of three hours was devoted to training to ensure that interviewers were very familiar with the questionnaire and the data that were required. The need to be thorough and accurate in recording information was stressed and ways of approaching tourists in a tactful and polite manner were practised. Interviewers were also given specially prepared identification cards, with a photograph, indicating that they were collecting data as part of a UK health authority-funded research project. Interviewers worked in small teams for mutual support and safety.

Sampling

Given the context of the interviews and the fact that individuals approached were at liberty to refuse to participate in the survey, it is not possible to guarantee a random sample of the British tourist population on the island. In addition, it was considered important to obtain, as far as possible, equal numbers of men and women and an even distribution of individuals across the age range from the upper teenage years to the sixties and above.

Interviewers were asked to attempt to interview at least one male and one female in each of six age groups, giving a total of twelve interviews per interviewer. The only other criterion employed was that tourists should have been on the island for at least three days.

The questionnaire

The questionnaire had four sections: demographic and holiday details; details of any health problems experienced on holiday: a shortened version of the Holiday Experience Questionnaire (developed by Clark and Clift 1994); and probes on tourists' attitudes to a return visit.

RESULTS

Sample interviewed

A total of 413 tourists were interviewed, 48.3 per cent men and 51.7 per cent women, with a fairly even spread from visitors in their teens through to their seventies.

Information collected on respondents' holiday companions showed that the most common pattern was for visitors to be on holiday with their spouse.

Coding of age and holiday companions

For the purposes of further analysis, respondents were divided into three age groups (teens, twenties and thirties; forties and fifties; sixties and seventies) and two categories according to companions (those with a presumed sexual partner and those

Table 6.1 Sex, age group and holiday companionship in the sample of British tourists in Malta

Sex	Age group		
Men	Teens-30s	40s–50s	60s–70s+
Without a partner	36(50%)	9 (15.8%)	10 (14.5%)
With a partner	36 (50%)	46 (84.2%)	59 (85.5%)
			$X^2=12.7$, df=2, p<0.005
Women	Teens-30s	40s–50s	60s–70s+
Without a partner	40 (54.1%)	24 (35.3%)	18 (25.7%)
With a partner	34 (45.9%)	44 (64.7%)	52 (74.3%)
			$X^2=12.7$, df=2, p<0.005

without a partner). Table 6.1 reports the composition of the total sample according to these variables and sex.

For men and women, a significant age difference emerges in the proportions of visitors with a sexual partner. The percentages are clearly higher among the middle-aged and oldest group than among the teens to thirties group. The difference between men and women in the middle-aged group is also significant, with women more likely to be without a 'partner' than men ($X^2 = 5.1$, df = 1, p < 0.05).

Problems with health

Visitors were asked the simple question: 'Have you had any problems with your health during your stay?' A total of fifty-four tourists (13.1 per cent of the sample) had had such problems and Table 6.2 reports details. Percentages sum to more that 100 per cent since a few tourists reported more than one problem. A total of 5.1 per cent of the sample reported vomiting, diarrhoea and upset stomachs and these were generally attributed to food/water or excessive alcohol consumption. Sunburn/sunstroke was reported by only 3 per cent of the sample and in several cases respondents reported having fallen asleep on the beach as the reason for burning. Alcohol consumption was implicated in at least three cases. Most people with a minor health problem took action themselves to treat it with preparations brought with them from the UK, e.g. aftersun, strepsils (throat lozengers), anti-diarrhoeals. Four

Table 6.2 Health problems experienced by British tourists while on holiday in Malta

Problem reported	n	% of those with problems (n = 54)	% of total sample (n = 413)
Diarrhoea, vomiting, upset stomach	21	38.9	5.1
Sunburn/sunstroke	13	24.1	3.1
Upper respiratory tract problems	7	13.0	1.7
Ear infection	4	7.4	1.0
Minor accidents/aches	4	7.4	1.0
Hangover	3	5.6	0.7
Insect bites	2	3.7	0.5
Other	5	9.3	1.2
All	54	–	13.1

people consulted a local doctor (7.4 per cent of those with problems; 1.0 per cent of the total sample). Two of the consultations were for alimentary symptoms (one vomiting and one diarrhoea), one was for dehydration and the fourth was for an ear infection.

RESPONSES TO THE HOLIDAY EXPERIENCE QUESTIONNAIRE

Table 6.3 reports the pattern of responses to the holiday experience items for the entire sample (the numbers represent the order of items in the questionnaire and n varies slightly from item to item due to missing cases which were higher for the more sensitive items on drugs and 'romantic' relationships). If the items are rank-ordered in terms of endorsement (strongly agree and agree) and split into four groups (75 per cent +, 50–74 per cent, 25–49 per cent and up to 24 per cent), the following patterns emerge.

Very highly endorsed items

Over 95 per cent of visitors to Malta said they were 'more cheerful with the change of climate' and were having 'a really good time'. The dominant theme emerging is that tourists were able to 'relax more than I do at home', 'leave the stresses of life behind' and 'spend time just watching the world go by'. As a result, most agreed that 'they recharged their batteries'. Linked with this is the finding that most people took advantage of the tourist resources of the island and 'travelled around looking at the scenery' and 'visited a lot of cultural sites'.

Highly endorsed items

It is clear that the sun is a major attraction for a majority, but not all, tourists: 73.7 per cent 'spent time just sitting in the sun', 65.5 per cent had 'tried to build up a good suntan', while 72.8 per cent had been 'careful to avoid getting sunburned'. The picture emerging is that tanning is a majority pursuit, but a sizeable minority (44.5 per cent) disagreed that getting a tan was important. The 27.2 per cent who disagreed that they had 'been careful to avoid getting sunburned', may not have actually suffered sunburn but may have had skin types that rapidly tan rather than burn, or may have routinely kept out of the sun for reasons other than sunburn avoidance.

A second theme is that people feel more energetic and are more active and outgoing when on holiday. Sixty-two per cent 'felt more energetic than I do at home'; 62.7 per cent had 'taken more exercise that I do at home'; and 57.4 per cent had felt 'more outgoing and sociable than at home'; 52.1 per cent had felt 'less inhibited than I am at home'. On the other hand, large proportions of tourists also disagreed with these statements and had not felt *more* outgoing and energetic or less inhibited. In fact, 62.3 per cent agreed that they had 'enjoyed getting away from people'. This may mean the people left behind at home, or people on holiday, but whichever group is referred to, the sense is one of valuing solitariness or the company of a partner or immediate group.

A third issue endorsed by 56.8 per cent of tourists was that their holiday had 'broadened my outlook on life'. This may well reflect the fact that most tourists had travelled about and visited 'a lot of cultural sites on the island'.

Finally, in this group, 65.7 per cent of tourists said they had been careful to avoid infections. This endorses the results from an earlier survey of health issues among tourists in Malta (see Clark *et al.* 1993; Page *et al.* 1994) which revealed that high proportions of visitors took preparations and medications with them and avoided patterns of eating and drinking that could have carried a risk of infection.

Table 6.3 Responses by British tourists in Malta to items in the Holiday Experience Questionnaire

Items 'During my holiday in Malta I've ...'		N	% Strongly agree	% Agree	% Disagree	% Strongly disagree
27	felt more cheerful with the change of climate	411	66.9	29.7	2.7	0.7
14	enjoyed myself and had a really good time	409	58.2	38.4	2.4	1.0
1	travelled around looking at the scenery	413	48.7	42.6	4.6	4.1
8	been able to leave stresses of life behind	411	50.6	36.0	8.5	4.9
26	recharged my batteries	410	42.0	44.1	9.0	4.9
16	relaxed more than I do at home	409	46.2	39.6	8.1	6.1
11	spent time just watching the world go by	412	42.7	37.9	14.1	5.3
25	visited a lot of cultural sites on the island	411	43.8	36.5	12.7	7.1
5	spent time just sitting in the sun	411	34.8	38.9	17.5	8.8
22	been careful to avoid getting sunburned	408	34.8	38.0	14.2	13.0
12	been careful to avoid infections	411	32.1	33.6	19.0	15.3
18	tried to build up a good suntan	409	32.0	33.5	21.8	12.7
7	taken more exercise than I do at home	412	24.8	37.9	20.4	17.0
20	enjoyed getting away from people	408	29.9	32.4	25.0	12.7

Table 6.3 continued

Items 'During my holiday in Malta I've ...'	N	% Strongly agree	% Agree	% Disagree	% Strongly disagree
2 felt more energetic than I do at home	413	24.7	37.3	28.1	9.9
3 broadened my outlook on life	412	14.8	42.0	28.6	14.6
28 been more outgoing and sociable than at home	411	23.1	34.3	30.2	12.4
9 been less inhibited than I am at home	412	20.1	32.0	34.5	13.3
4 drunk more alcohol than I would do at home	412	25.5	19.9	25.2	29.4
24 reflected on the meaning of life	409	11.5	21.0	33.3	34.2
15 developed more as a person	409	8.3	21.3	43.3	27.1
21 felt disappointed about some aspects of my stay	410	7.8	22.7	34.4	35.1
6 had an exciting nightlife	412	10.0	20.4	32.0	37.6
19 enjoyed flirting with people I've met here	402	13.7	15.4	22.6	48.3
13 sometimes felt anxious and under stress	411	3.4	9.2	30.2	57.2
23 had a romantic relationship with someone new	402	3.5	4.2	10.4	81.9
10 found it difficult to unwind	412	3.4	4.9	33.5	58.3
17 been offered drugs by someone I've met	404	2.7	1.5	6.7	89.1

Moderately endorsed items

Three themes emerge when items endorsed by less than 50 per cent but more than 25 per cent of tourists are considered. The first reflects an outgoing, extroverted lifestyle: 30.4 per cent, almost a third, said they 'had an exciting nightlife', 29.1 per cent 'enjoyed flirting with people' and 45.4 per cent had 'drunk more alcohol than I would at home'. The second theme relates to 'personal development' with 32.5 per cent agreeing they had 'reflected on the meaning of life' and 29.6 per cent had 'developed more as a person'. Finally, 30.5 per cent had been 'disappointed by some aspects of my stay'. Unfortunately, no further information was collected on this issue. The percentage is surprising since 96.6 per cent agreed that they had 'a really good time' during their stay. Clearly, even though the holiday was generally enjoyed, there may have been some minor irritations or problems which made the experience a little less enjoyable than it could have been.

Weakly endorsed items

Four items were agreed with by less than 25 per cent of respondents. Two were negatively worded statements relating to the broad theme of relaxation and rest: only 8.3 per cent said they had found it 'difficult to unwind' on holiday and 12.6 per cent said that they had 'sometimes felt anxious and under stress'. These figures may reflect the fact that 13.1 per cent of people questioned reported problems with their health on holiday. Just 7.7 per cent of tourists (n = 31) reported having 'a romantic relationship on holiday' (3.5 per cent 'strongly agreed' which may reflect the strength of the romance!). Finally, 4.2 per cent of tourists (n = 17) reported being offered drugs.

SEX, AGE, PARTNERSHIPS AND HOLIDAY EXPERIENCES

In order to assess the effect of sex, age and partnerships on holiday experiences, a series of three-way analyses of variance were undertaken. For the purpose of these analyses, responses to items were coded numerically from 0 to 3 with 3 representing 'strongly agree' for positively worded items, and 'strongly disagree' for negatively worded items.

Table 6.4 Age differences in holiday experiences among British tourists in Malta

Items 'During my holiday in Malta I've...'	% agreement		
	Teens–30s	40s–50s	60s–70s
Statements with the highest levels of agreement in the youngest age group			
drunk more alcohol than I would do at home	63.7	41.2	29.7
spent time just sitting in the sun	80.2	68.2	71.5
had an exciting nightlife	45.9	20.7	22.5
been offered drugs by someone I've met	9.0	0.8	2.2
tried to build up a good suntan	81.4	64.3	50.7
enjoyed flirting with people I've met	42.5	20.5	22.1
enjoyed getting away from people	73.6	59.7	52.9
had a romantic relationship with someone new	14.4	1.6	5.3
Statements with the highest levels of agreement in mid-life			
visited a lot of cultural sites on the island	71.2	85.7	84.7
taken more exercise than I do at home	47.3	74.6	68.1
relaxed more than I do at home	86.2	90.5	81.0
recharged my batteries	76.8	94.4	88.3
Statements with the highest levels of agreement in the oldest age group			
been careful to avoid sunburn	61.4	78.4	80.1
spent time just watching the world go by	74.0	80.2	87.7
been careful to avoid infections	56.6	68.2	73.9
reflected on the meaning of life	22.8	35.2	40.9

Sex differences

Two significant main effects due to sex were found: men were more likely to have drunk more alcohol than women (52.3 vs. 38.7 per cent) and more likely to have flirted with people they had met (43.6 vs. 25.0 per cent).

Age differences

No fewer than sixteen items showed main effects due to age. Table 6.4 reports the percentage of each age group agreeing with the statements involved. These are divided into three patterns: those statements showing a decline in agreement with age; those showing an increase in agreement with age, and those showing higher levels of agreement in mid-life.

Effect of partnerships

Five items showed main effects due to the partnership variable. All of them reflect the restraint associated with having a current partner, on patterns of social and sexual behaviour. People without a partner were more likely to have had an exciting nightlife (41.3 per cent) than those with a partner (24.8 per cent); those alone were also less inhibited (59.4 per cent) than respondents with a partner (48.6 per cent); those alone were more likely to have been offered drugs (9.5 per cent) than those with a partner (1.4 per cent); people without a partner were much more likely to have enjoyed flirting (48.6 per cent) than those with one (19.1 per cent), and those alone were more likely to have actually entered into a romantic relationship (17.7 per cent) than those with a partner (2.6 per cent).

Interactions

The items with the strongest main effects due to 'partnership' also showed significant interaction effects between age and partnership. An exciting nightlife, flirting and romantic relationships were more common among younger tourists but this was particularly so for those without partners. Table 6.5 reports the results for these three items in greater detail. The groups reporting the highest frequency of 'romantic' relationships are young, unattached people (25 per cent). It is clear, however, that among the unattached a clear age function emerges, with levels of reported romance falling in mid-life (3 per cent) and then rising again among the oldest group (12.5 per cent). This pattern is echoed weakly among the 'attached' group.

One interaction emerged between age group and sex for the item: 'I've enjoyed myself and had a really good time'. The pattern

Table 6.5 Percentage levels of agreement among British tourists in Malta to three social life/relationship items by age and partnership

	Without a partner			With a partner		
Item	Teens–30s	40s–50s	60s–70s	Teens–30s	40s–50s	60s–70s
Exciting nightlife	56.6% (43/76)	18.2% (6/33)	25.9% (7/27)	34.2% (24/70)	21.5% (20/93)	21.6% (24/111)
Enjoyed flirting	60.5% (46/76)	30.3% (10/33)	36.0% (9/25)	22.9% (16/70)	16.9% (15/89)	18.7% (20/107)
Romantic relationship	25.0% (19/76)	3.0% (1/33)	12.5% (3/24)	2.9% (2/70)	1.1% (1/89)	3.7% (4/108)

observed was that among the youngest age group, men and women were similar in levels of enjoyment, for the middle-aged group women enjoyed themselves more than men, while for the oldest group, men appeared to enjoy themselves more than women.

FACTOR ANALYSIS OF THE HOLIDAY EXPERIENCE QUESTIONNAIRE

Complete data for the holiday experience questionnaire were available for 383 tourists. For the purposes of this analysis, item responses were coded from 0 to 3 with 3 representing 'strongly agree' for positively worded statements and 'strongly disagree' for negatively worded statements. This effectively ensured that all loadings would be consistently positive or negative. Principal Components Analysis identified eight factors with eigen values greater than 1.00. A plot of eigen values, however, indicated the start of a 'scree' from the fourth factor, suggesting that no more than three factors should be retained for rotation. Table 6.6 reports the item loadings on the three varimax factors which emerged. All loadings less than ±0.3 are omitted. Simple structure is closely approximated with only six out of twenty-eight items having loadings in excess of ±0.3 on two factors. Two items (20, 12) failed to load on the three rotated factors above ±0.3, but they were associated with factor 2 and 3 respectively.

Table 6.6 Three factors extracted from the Holiday Experience Questionnaire completed by British tourists in Malta

Item 'During my holiday in Malta I've . . .'	Factors 1	2	3
'Sun, sex and sangria'			
6 had an exciting nightlife	0.62		
23 had a romantic relationship with someone new	0.60		
19 enjoyed flirting with people I've met here	0.58		
17 been offered drugs by someone I've met	0.58		
4 drunk more alcohol than I would do at home	0.57		
28 been more outgoing and sociable than at home	0.52		0.42
9 been less inhibited than I am at home	0.49		0.41
18 tried to build up a good suntan	0.49		
5 spent time just sitting in the sun	0.48		
22 been careful to avoid getting sunburned	0.32		
Relaxation and enjoyment vs. stress			
10 found it difficult to unwind		0.67	
14 enjoyed myself and had a really good time		0.66	
13 sometimes felt anxious and under stress		0.61	
26 recharged my batteries		0.57	0.34
8 been able to leave the stresses of life behind		0.56	0.32
16 relaxed more than I do at home		0.56	
11 spent time just watching the world go by		0.48	
27 felt more cheerful with the change of climate		0.47	
21 felt disappointed about some aspects of my stay		0.40	
20 enjoyed getting away from people			
Personal development and activity			
15 developed more as a person			0.67
3 broadened my outlook on life			0.66
24 reflected on the meaning of life			0.60
7 taken more exercise than I do at home			0.53
2 felt more energetic than I do at home			0.51
1 travelled around the island looking at the scenery	−0.35		0.48
25 visited a lot of cultural sites on the island	−0.40		0.44
12 been careful to avoid infections			

Note: * loadings < 0.30 are omitted

Interpretation of the factors

The first factor can be labelled using the popular phrase 'sun, sex and sangria'. The loadings clearly reflect not only stereotypical notions of a beach/nightclub holiday involving sunseeking, alcohol consumption and 'romance' – but also the link between alcohol, drugs and sexual activity on holiday which emerged in the earlier survey (Clark and Clift 1994) and in the work of Ford (1991) and Conway, Gillies and Slack (1990). The second factor has nine positive loadings and the central theme is the contrast between enjoyment and relaxation vs. stress, anxiety and disappointment. This factor clearly suggests that for some tourists their holiday was enjoyable and helped them unwind, relax and leave the stresses of life behind, while for others, their experiences on holiday had not been so positive. The third factor reflects a more outgoing, active holiday pattern with a strong emphasis on personal reflection and development. Tourists high on the third factor feel they have developed more as a person and broadened their outlook on life. This involved being more outgoing socially, leaving the stresses of life behind, being more energetic than usual, and travelling around the island to see both the scenery and historical/cultural sites.

The items which have loadings on two factors are interesting as they highlight the different tourist patterns. Being 'more outgoing and sociable' and 'less inhibited' can take two forms: one is in the context of pursuing an active nightlife, perhaps aided by consumption of alcohol, and the second relates to being more outgoing during the day in travelling and visiting places of interest. 'Leaving the stresses of life behind' and 'recharging my batteries' also appear to take two forms – either through the enjoyment and relaxation which comes from being on holiday, especially in a sunny climate, or through greater activity and energy associated with going outwards, to visit places of interest, and looking in, to reflect on 'the meaning of life'. Finally, 'visited a lot of cultural sites on the island' and 'travelled around the island looking at the scenery' positively defines factor 3 but is negatively loaded on the first factor. This indicates that tourists interested in the 'sun, sex and sangria' were not so interested in culture and scenery!

DISCUSSION

Health problems experienced on holiday

Different rates of reported illness and sunburn were found between the 1993 survey and the second study. Clark et al. (1993) discovered that 37 per cent of tourists reported some form of health problem during their visit, whereas in the 1994 study, incidence levels were much lower. For example, 8.8 per cent of the 1993 sample reported sore throats compared with 1.7 per cent of the current study. The percentages reporting diarrhoea, however, are more comparable, with 7 per cent in 1993 and 5.1 per cent in 1994.

It is likely that the differences between 1993 and 1994 are due to the nature and format of the questionnaires employed. The survey instrument used by Clark et al. (1993) listed specific ailments, and these were read out to respondents by the fieldworker. This may have led to more comprehensive answering on symptoms than the questionnaire used in the 1994 study, which simply asked if visitors had had any health problems and then asked for a description. In the second survey tourists may have forgotten minor ailments, or considered them too trivial to mention without a specific prompt.

The third possibility for the apparent drop in reported illness rates between 1993 and 1994 involves people's perceptions of illness. Whilst it is inappropriate to discuss perceptions of health and illness at great length here (see Blaxter 1990 for a concise review) there are several commonly identified; absence of disease, ability to function normally, health as a reserve (which can be strengthened or used up), health as physical fitness, and health as mental well-being and balance (Herzlich 1973; Pill and Stott 1982; Blaxter and Patterson 1982). It seems likely, for example, that headaches (the symptom that so inflated the 1993 illness rates) are not considered 'health problems', since they are not caused by pathogens, are not generally incapacitating, and are not contagious. It is also rare for their sufferers to change their routine because of them (so social functioning continues as normal) or to consult medical personnel about them. Thus when asked if they had suffered health problems, the 1994 visitors did not spontaneously generate 'headaches' as a symptom.

DIMENSIONS OF THE HOLIDAY EXPERIENCE

The second survey provides interesting insights into the quality of tourists' holiday experiences and associated implications for health risks and positive well-being. The pattern of responses to individual items provides a graphic picture of the varied aspects of tourist experience and an added dimension is provided by the significant differences association with age, sex and the nature of holiday companions. The main themes are clarified still further by the application of factor analysis, which reveals three distinct factors. These correspond closely to factors previously identified in a smaller-scale study investigating a more restricted sample of undergraduate students (Clark and Clift 1994).

Sun, sex and sangria

The first factor brings together a diverse range of items and corresponds to one of the popular stereotypes of the summer holiday. Interestingly too, younger respondents and those on holiday without a sexual partner score more highly on this factor.

With respect to the first component – 'sun' – the results from the survey provide valuable information on British attitudes to sunbathing and their behaviour in the sun. These have clear implications for health, given the linkage of sunburn and malignant melanoma, and for health promotion, given the adoption of the *Health of the Nation* targets which aim to reduce incidence of skin cancer in the population. Public information campaigns mounted by the Health Education Authority, District Health Promotion Units, chemists and manufacturers of sun-protective products, have attempted to persuade the British public that sunbathing can have harmful effects. The data from the 1994 survey suggest that the 'Safe-Sun' message has had some impact on sunbathing practices of those holidaying abroad. Thus, it is encouraging that 72.8 per cent of respondents reported being careful not to burn. This could be taken as evidence that these visitors understand the risks associated with sunburn and translate this understanding and concern for their future well-being into practical action to avoid sunburn. However, more than a quarter of respondents disagreed with this statement and thus may be increasing their risks of skin damage and more serious consequences in the longer term.

Whilst the messages on suntanning and whether it can be done safely are more complex than a simple condemnation of sunburning, this sample are still clearly courting tanned skin. A huge two-thirds were actively trying to suntan in Malta. The innovative young, rather than taking on the encouraged pale look, were the most likely to be sunbathing to go brown. This hardly heralds the new decade of sunwise travellers, who are happy to return to the pre-Coco Chanel chic of untanned skin. It may be a reduction in fashion consciousness, or desire to bare flesh, which contributes to the reduction in suntanning with age in this sample. Alternatively, the over-sixties may be pioneering the adaption of holiday behaviour, so that a suntan is not a desired outcome of a week's winter break.

The fact that the whole sample attributed feeling more cheerful, at least in part, to the change in climate between grey Britain and sunny Malta, may indicate that safer sun messages are more likely to succeed than sun-avoidance messages. The authors feel that health educators should face the challenge that people enjoy sitting and being in the sun, and that they must integrate this into their health promoting strategies (see Chapter 12, this volume, for a further elaboration of this point of view by Weston). We must find ways to promote an outdoor lifestyle without the associated risks of skin exposure to sun; and place more emphasis on protective clothing rather than low-protective factor creams, which are rendered less effective by perspiration and towel drying.

Reference to 'sex' in labelling the first dimension may be presumptuous since specific questions were not asked about sexual activity. Given the circumstances of the study, however, it would have been inappropriate to have done so, and an indirect series of questions were formulated which assess the extent to which tourists engaged in activities which could lead to sexual activity. Thus, 29.1 per cent enjoyed flirting and 7.7 per cent admitted to having had a 'romantic relationship'. Both items showed clear sex, age and relationship status variations. In addition, factor analysis identified a meaningful pattern of circumstances, dispositions and behaviours likely to facilitate flirting and the forming of new relationships. A total of 30.4 per cent of tourists reported having an 'exciting nightlife' and it seems highly likely that increased opportunities for socialising in clubs and bars contributed to the finding that 45.4 per cent of tourists consumed more alcohol than usual – and probably too, for the 4.2 per cent incidence of being offered drugs. The holiday atmosphere, the climate, night-time socialising and consumption of alcohol also appear to be factors in encouraging 57.4 per cent of tourists to be 'more outgoing and sociable' than at home and 52.1 per cent to feel 'less inhibited' than at home. The pattern observed and its association with a younger, unaccompanied group of tourists, is entirely consistent with the broad pattern emerging from earlier studies (see Gillies and Slack, Chapter 7, and Ford and Eiser, Chapter 8, this volume) and clearly indicates a range of social, contextual and psychological factors which enhance the likelihood of sexual activity and the possible risks associated with it. It is important, therefore, that health promotion activities are planned in the light of these patterns. Ways need to be found to encourage safer behaviour despite the operation of forces that may render it less likely and work is required in the settings where people are meeting and entering into new and often short-lived relationships. The relevance and value of the Torbay model of outreach work with young people is clearly supported by our findings (see Ford, Inman and Mathie, Chapter 14, this volume).

Relaxation and enjoyment versus stress

The second dimension of holiday experiences clearly highlights that the promise of rest and relaxation which holidays offer is realised for a large majority of tourists of all ages. Krippendorf's (1987: 38) observation is strongly supported by the findings from this survey: 'People go away in order to recharge their batteries, consume peace, climate, landscape and foreign cultures, and then they return to defy everyday life for a while longer. Tourism is the big regeneration machine.'

No fewer than 96.6 per cent of respondents agreed that they had enjoyed themselves and 'had a really good time', with 58.2 per cent agreeing strongly. And in line with Krippendorf's view, 86.1 per cent felt they had indeed 'recharged' their batteries, 86.6 per cent had left the 'stresses of life' behind and 85.7 per cent felt they had been able to 'relax more' than at home. Holidays do indeed allow people to escape the pressures of life and offer opportunities for regeneration so that everyday life can be defied 'a while longer'. It is also of particular interest that while this aspect of holiday experience was common across all age groups, the highest levels of endorsement were found among tourists in mid-life – the forties to fifties age group. This clearly makes sense, given the fact that work pressures and family responsibilities may well be greatest in this age group – certainly compared with the more elderly group, most of whom have retired.

The extent to which the theme of rest and relaxation is endorsed by tourists serves to emphasise the importance attached to this issue and throws into greater relief the degree of frustration and disappointment felt when holidays do not live up to tourists' expectations. The large majority of respondents had had 'a really good time', but 3.4 per cent did not; and even larger percentages had not 'been able to leave the stresses of life behind' (13.4 per cent), had 'found it difficult to unwind' (8.3 per cent), had 'sometimes felt anxious or under stress' (12.6 per cent), had not 'relaxed more' than at home (14.2 per cent), and had not 'recharged' their batteries (13.9 per cent). A fairly large 30.5 per cent of tourists had, in fact, 'felt disappointed' by some aspect of their stay. There is no evidence available from this survey to suggest that stress and lack of relaxation on holiday had detrimental effects on physical health, but it is easy to imagine that a sense of personal well-being and the quality of interpersonal relationships would not be enhanced by a poor, disappointing holiday and that such negative holiday experiences could result in a lingering sense of missed opportunity and resentment on returning home. Sources of stress on holidays, their impact on the holiday and longer-term consequences should be explored further in future research.

Personal development and activity

The final factor identified in this research clearly relates to a more humanistic/spiritual dimension of health with a strong emphasis on personal growth and a broadening of perspective on life. No fewer than 56.8 per cent of tourists, for example, felt that their holiday had helped to 'broaden my outlook on life'; 29.6 per cent went further in agreeing that they had 'developed more as a person', and for 35.2 per cent their holiday had offered them an opportunity to reflect on 'the meaning of life'. It is particularly interesting that agreement with the last statement showed a significant age trend with endorsement among tourists aged 60–70+ at almost twice the level found among the youngest age group (40.9 compared with 22.8 per cent). Reflection on the meaning of life is clearly a preoccupation more commonly found in the elderly.

Unfortunately the survey generated no data on whether these patterns and trends would emerge in a study of experiences and preoccupations 'at home', nor on what aspects of the physical and cultural environment on Malta (if any) prompted some tourists to reflect on the deeper meaning of life. It is significant, however, that two items relating to travel around the islands to view the landscape and absorb the culture, also define the third dimension. Since the Maltese islands are famous for their churches and neolithic temples – it may be that tourists' self-exposure to such monuments is motivated by, and in turn stimulates, a concern for self-development and a widening of perspective on life. Further research exploring these issues in greater depth would certainly be of value, perhaps including a comparative exploration of the extent to which a range of tourist destinations differentially stimulates such reflections and the conclusions visitors draw from their experiences.

Apart from the spiritual dimensions of personal development and 'meaningfulness' in life, the third dimension is also defined – more mundanely perhaps, by a sense of greater energy and increased exercise. Interestingly, 62.0 per cent of tourists reported feeling 'more energetic' and 62.7 per cent reported taking 'more exercise' than at home. Both items also show significant age trends, with the highest levels of agreement found among tourists in mid-life (fourties to fifties). Responses to the issue of exercise, in particular, show marked differences across age – with 47.3 per cent of tourists in their teens to thirties taking more exercise, compared with 74.6 per cent of those in their forties and fifties. Again, the lack of comparative data on respondents' activity and exercise patterns 'at home' makes it difficult to interpret these findings.

CONCLUSION

Malta emerges as a very safe destination for tourists with respect to physical health problems. While a minority of tourists were found to experience serious difficulties and needed to consult local doctors or visit a hospital – the vast majority reported no such difficulties or very minor symptoms.

This picture emerging from the first study prompted a change of focus in the second survey towards an investigation of tourists' experiences of their holiday and longer-term implications these might have not only for health problems but equally importantly for the positive promotion of health in a more holistic sense. The findings from the second study revealed three dimensions of holiday experience and demonstrated substantial variation in experience according to sex, age and holiday companions. Each dimension has clear relevance to potential health risks or the promotion of health, and further research is needed to test the implications identified.

ACKNOWLEDGEMENTS

The authors would like to thank Dr R. Goodenough, Ms J. Wilkinson, Ms R. Hardiman and the students on the 1994 Malta fieldtrip for their help in collecting these data.

REFERENCES

Black, P., Clift, S. and Wijisurendra, S. (1994) 'Sexual health risk behaviour abroad among GUM clinic attendees', unpublished paper, Canterbury Christ Church College.

Blaxter, M. (1990) *Health and Lifestyles*, London: Routledge.

Blaxter, M. and Patterson, E. (1982) *Mothers and Daughters: a Three Generational Study of Health Attitudes and Behaviour*, London: Heinemann Educational Books.

Clark, N. and Clift, S. (1994) *A Survey of Student Health and Risk Behaviour on Holidays Abroad*, Travel, Lifestyles and Health Working Paper No. 3, Canterbury Christ Church College.

Clark, N., Clift, S. and Page, S. (1993) *A Safe Place in the Sun? Health Precautions, Behaviours and Health Problems of British Tourists in Malta*, Travel, Lifestyles and Health Working Paper No. 1, Canterbury Christ Church College.

—— (1994) 'A safe place in the sun: health precautions, advice and problems of British tourists in Malta', *Travel Medicine International* 12: 47–50.

Clift, S. (1994a) *Romance and Sex on Holidays Abroad: a Study of Magazine Representations*, Travel, Lifestyles and Health Working Paper No. 4, Canterbury Christ Church College.

—— (1994b) 'Travel, holidays abroad and sex: a study of magazine representation', poster presentation, Second International Biopsychosocial Impact of AIDS Conference, Brighton.

Clift, S. and Page, S. (1994) 'Travel, lifestyles and health', *Tourism Management* 15: 69–70.

Clift, S. and Wilkins, J. (1994) 'Gay men, tourism and sexual health', unpublished paper, Canterbury Christ Church College.

Conway, S., Gillies, P. and Slack, R. (1990) *The Health of Travellers*, Department of Public Health Medicine and Epidemiology, University of Nottingham and Nottingham Health Authority.

Department of Health (1992) *Health Advice for Travellers* (T4), London: HMSO.
Ford, N. (1991) *Sex on Holiday: the HIV Related Sexual Interaction of Young Tourists Visiting Torbay*, Occasional Working Paper No. 14, Exeter: Institute of Population Studies, University of Exeter.
Gitelson, R. and Kerstetter, D. (1990) 'The relationship between sociodemographic variables, benefits sought and subsequent vacation behaviour: a case study', *Journal of Travel Research*, Winter 1990: 24–9.
Gladwell, N. (1990) 'A psychographic and sociodemographic analysis of State Park Inn Users', *Journal of Travel Research*, Spring 1990: 15–20.
Herzlich, C. (1973) *Health and Illness; a Social Psychological Analysis*, London: Academic Press.
Krippendorf, J. (1987) *The Holiday Makers: Understanding the Impact of Leisure and Travel*, Oxford: Heinemann.
Page, S., Clift, S. and Clark, N. (1994) 'Tourist health: the precautions, behaviour and health problems of British tourists in Malta', in A. V. Seaton (ed.) *Tourism: the State of the Art*, Chichester: Wiley.
Pill, R. and Stott, N. E. H. (1982) 'Concepts of illness causation and responsibility: some preliminary data from a sample of working class mothers', *Social Sciences Medicine* 16: 43–52.

Chapter 7

Context and culture in HIV prevention
The importance of holidays?

Pamela Gillies and Richard Slack

INTRODUCTION

'British girls on sex spree in the sun don't give AIDS a thought' screamed a headline in a UK tabloid newspaper (Kinnersley 1991). In spite of the confidence with which the journalist maintained the occurrence of 'one long merry-go-round of sex, sex and more sex' at the holiday resort he visited, there is in fact very little good scientific evidence on the extent of sexual activity of young adults abroad. Information on the meaning of sexuality in young adults, and those factors that influence sexual activity is also scant. Yet such qualitative data are crucial to understanding sexual behaviour in the context in which it occurs and thereby to planning interventions in relation to the prevention of HIV and other sexually transmitted diseases (or STDs).

It could reasonably be claimed that recent new-found interest in sexual behaviour among holidaymakers is driven by concerns related to the HIV/AIDS pandemic. This has caused academic researchers and clinicians, as well as the aforementioned journalist, to speculate about the seriousness of the potential threat to health posed by the risk of acquiring HIV and STD infection through unprotected sexual intercourse abroad (Feachem and Phillips-Howard 1988; Behrens and Porter 1990; Ellis 1990; Hawkes and Hart 1993). It is well recognised that the spread of STDs, particularly gonorrhoea, is associated with population movement and tourism (De Schryver and Meheus 1989): thus the sexual habits of the more than 31 million UK residents who travel abroad each year (Baty and Templeton 1991) assume particular interest.

This chapter describes the findings from an exploratory study of young adults' sexual behaviour at home and whilst on holiday.

It seeks to locate the results within a conceptual framework which privileges the social construction of sexuality. By so doing, it argues that sexual behaviour research could unravel the social and cultural factors that shape sexuality and thereby make a significant contribution to our understanding in this field. Such research may also proffer insights into the design of innovative approaches for public health and health promotion interventions which endeavour to change sexual behaviours in a variety of contexts.

The chapter begins by outlining the study methods employed. The findings are then discussed in relation to previous work. Survey data on sexual behaviour are reviewed, followed by consideration of the evidence for 'personal' and 'social' factors associated with sexual activities. Ways in which sexual practices, particularly lack of condom use, may increase the chance of individuals becoming infected with sexually transmitted disease including HIV, are then appraised. Topics covered include gender, sexual identity, sexual culture, alcohol and other drug use, social systems and structures. Finally, the limitations of data notwithstanding, the implications of the argument for the international traveller and for agencies concerned with the public health will be explored.

SURVEYING THE SCENE: STUDY METHODS

Design of the study

The study comprised a cross-sectional, anonymous, self-completed questionnaire survey of the general population from one location within the health district of Nottingham, England. It was felt important to attempt to survey a general population sample rather than a specific target group, such as travellers abroad on so-called 'sex tourist' holidays. By undertaking preliminary work with the 'ordinary' traveller, it was hoped a wider perspective of sexual behaviour of UK residents abroad might be gained.

The sample

A random sample of 1,030 adults aged 16–40 years old and stratified by age and sex, was selected from the age-sex register of an urban general practice in Nottingham. One in every three patients aged between 16 and 40 years registered with the practice was initially selected. Of these, thirty were excluded for a variety of reasons: (a) recent demise; or (b) recent move to different location; or (c) having reading or learning difficulties. This left 1,000 individuals who were sent questionnaires.

The questionnaire

The questionnaire was designed to be self-completed and was anonymous. It comprised a series of closed and open questions covering basic demographic details and recent travel abroad within the last two years; health experience whilst abroad in relation to sunburn, sickness, diarrhoea and accidental injury. In addition, questions were asked about alcohol use, non-prescribed drug use and sexual behaviour at home and abroad. Finally attitudes and beliefs about HIV/AIDS were surveyed and these questions derived from a Department of Health and Social Security national survey (DHSS and the Welsh Office 1987).

The decision to use a postal questionnaire rather than in-depth household interviews was taken to contain costs in what was an exploratory survey. However, in a separate study of sexual behaviour, albeit in a selected population of genito-urinary medicine clinic attenders in Nottingham, no difference was recorded in responses to simple sexual activity questions in self-completed as opposed to interview responses (James et al. 1991). This suggests that the quality of the data for straightforward questions about behaviour may not have been adversely affected by the decision to select a questionnaire as opposed to the face-to-face interview method for data collection. The questionnaire was piloted with a random sample of thirty staff within Queens Medical Centre, Nottingham, resulting in only minor changes to the questionnaire (Conway et al. 1990).

Questionnaires were sent to eligible participants with a covering letter signed by their general practitioner, a reply-paid (freepost) envelope for return of the completed script, and a postcard (also reply-paid) for those who wished to receive a broadsheet summary of the findings of the survey. The covering letter from the GP reiterated the anonymous nature of the survey and stressed that GPs would not have access to the answers of individual patients. Using local GPs as the 'source' of such questionnaire surveys is known to be more effective in encouraging response

Context and culture in HIV prevention 137

than sources unknown to the respondent such as university research departments (Jacoby 1991). Four weeks after the first 1,000 questionnaires were sent out to patients, one postcard reminder was sent. Whilst two reminders are recommended for maximising response to postal questionnaires, this was precluded by resource constraints. However, postcard reminders have been shown to be as effective in increasing response as sending out questionnaires again, whether one or two reminders are sent (Roberts *et al.* 1993). The postcard technique is also considerably less expensive.

Can questionnaires provide accurate information about sensitive subjects like sexual behaviour?

Many have levelled criticism at sexual survey approaches which use questionnaires or structured interview schedules. Such criticisms concern two key areas. The first is whether these methods can produce reliable and valid information, that is 'truthful' responses (Herold and Way 1988; Muhondwa 1988; Maddox 1989). The second and more difficult area to study is whether such techniques are sensitive enough to cultural and sub-cultural diversity, in relation to norms, values and language, to provide rich and meaningful insights and to locate findings properly within those social contexts in which behaviours occur (Parker 1992; Van Landingham *et al.* 1994).

Reliability and validity of sexual survey data

In the preliminary study reported here, limited resources allowed the assessment of reliability only through internal consistency techniques within the questionnaire itself. A high degree of consistency was found in relation to sensitive questions such as condom use and other rather more innocuous behaviours such as suntan oil use (Conway *et al.* 1990). Consistency of response does not of course guarantee the validity of the data. As reviewed by Dare and Cleland (1993), there is on balance some good evidence, most notably from the British National Sexual Attitudes and Lifestyle Survey (Johnson *et al.* 1994), that sexual surveys can provide both valid and reliable aggregate data.

Understanding sexual activity in context

Parker (1991, 1992), has applied social construction theory to studies of sexual culture in Brazil (Raffaelli *et al.* 1994) and to consideration of AIDS education. He has argued that current gaps in our understanding of human sexuality and sexual diversity severely hinder efforts to prevent HIV transmission through educational interventions. Thus whilst sexual behaviour surveys can provide limited information on aspects of sexual practice such as condom use or anal sex, the findings may be less helpful in attempts to understand the meaning and significance such practices may have for individuals. These 'meanings' may be crucial in interpreting 'risky' sexual practices such as, for example, receptive anal intercourse in both men and women. The notion of transgression is a powerful erotic force in the sexual culture of Brazil (Parker 1992). Therefore whilst anal intercourse may be socially proscribed, it holds a pivotal role in the erotic imagination and sexual life of Brazilians. Intervention which entreated individuals to desist from anal sex would clash with a cultural way of being sexual which brings the greatest sexual satisfaction. It is clear that such reading of sexual life cannot be gleaned from simple questionnaire studies. In fact, Parker (1991) undertook an ethnography of sexual culture in Brazil and has built upon this work with a series of questionnaire and interview studies in the Brazilian and other cultures (Raffaelli *et al.* 1994; Gillies and Parker 1993). Such detailed work, although vital to a better understanding of the social processes, systems and influences which shape sexuality, was none the less beyond the scope of the present survey.

The study described here aimed simply to establish the extent of sexual activity in a representative sample of people from one region of an English city and to begin to identify those factors associated with casual sex whilst on holiday. This preliminary investigation sought to identify whether there existed sufficient risk-related activity to support the input of scarce local public health resources into fashioning a preventive sexual health intervention for local holidaymakers abroad.

SURVEY FINDINGS AND DISCUSSION

Response rate to the survey

A good response to such surveys is important to the interpretation of findings since it allows researchers to adduce the level of representativeness of respondents and thereby the extent to which the findings may be generalised to the urban population from which the sample was drawn. In this survey, of the 1,000 questionnaires sent, twenty were returned because the addressee had left or died, and two were mistakenly sent to people over the age of 40 years owing to inaccuracies in the age-sex register. Of the 978 questionnaires that reached the appropriate destination, 548 were returned, giving an overall participation rate of 56 per cent. The age and gender of respondents is given in Table 7.1.

Although comparisons with other surveys are problematic due to differing methodologies, it is interesting that surveys in the health-related field, whether they used postal or doorstep interview techniques, tend to achieve response rates of remarkably similar magnitude. For example, the National Survey of Sexual Attitudes and Lifestyles reported a 63 per cent response rate to household interviews (Johnson *et al.* 1994); the Trent Health Lifestyle postal survey, 61 per cent (Roberts and Magowan 1992); and a postal survey in Doncaster of 19 year olds' knowledge, attitudes and behaviours in relation to HIV/AIDS recorded 58 per cent response (Galt *et al.* 1989). These levels of response do give cause for concern about the representativeness of those replying.

Table 7.1 Response to the Nottingham survey on travel and health by age and sex

Age	Male		Female		Total	
	N	%	N	%	N	%
16–20	43	44	66	68	109	57
21–25	33	35	52	64	85	40
26–30	37	40	64	66	101	52
31–35	55	55	63	63	118	65
36–40	51	47	77	71	128	65
Total* and average %	219	45	323	67	541	56

*Note:** Missing values = 7

This means the findings cannot be generalised. Johnson *et al.* (1994) did however demonstrate convincingly that their respondents were in fact mostly similar, in terms of demographic characteristics, to the population from which they were drawn. In this study, data were not readily available from the general practice records to allow such comparisons to be made. Data that were available on age and sex of the population suggested, however, that there may have been important differences between those who did and did not respond. As has been found in many surveys (Roberts and Magowan 1992; Galt *et al.* 1989; Catania *et al.* 1992; Leigh *et al.* 1993; Spira *et al.* 1993; Johnson *et al.* 1994), significantly more women (67 per cent) than men (47 per cent) responded in this study (women = 323; men = 221; X^2 = 47; df = 1; p<0.001). The proportion of men responding was extremely similar to that of 44 per cent found by Johnson *et al.* (1994) in the recent national survey. Johnson *et al.* noted that the lower rate amongst men was due to greater difficulty in contacting men in the household rather than due to direct refusals to participate. This cannot, however, account for the lowered male response rate to postal questionnaires in this and other studies (e.g. Galt *et al.* 1989; Roberts and Magowan 1992). Data from household interview studies suggest that non-responders, as well as being male, tend to be less well educated, fat, young, smokers and drinkers (Sonne-Holme *et al.* 1989; Smith and Nutbeam 1990). Whilst such associated factors paint a rather unflattering picture of the male non-responder who is never at home when interviewers come calling because he is always out eating and drinking, they still do not explain non-response to postal questionnaires. A riddle yet to be unravelled.

In this study, only one-third of men in the 21–25 age group (35 per cent) responded to the questionnaire. Since the 16–24 year age group is the age at which people reported the greatest numbers of sexual partners in the national survey of 16–59 year olds (Johnson *et al.* 1994), it is unsettling to have the lowest level of response within this group of men. Possibly the young men are all out eating, drinking and wooing young women and though this may sound light-hearted, it is a serious point since it suggests how the findings of this study may be biased – they may under-report sexual activity on holiday in young men. Interpretation of the findings reported in this preliminary study must therefore be approached with some caution.

Travelling types

Travel abroad in the last two years was reported by 66 per cent of the sample (354/548), with most of these trips being completed by holidaymakers (318/354; 90 per cent) for periods of up to two weeks (in 41 per cent of trips; 146/354). Twenty-nine per cent of all trips were to Spain.

There were no differences within the sample between those who had travelled abroad and those who had not, in terms of gender or age group. Travellers were, however, significantly more likely to be of higher occupational grouping, single rather than married, and in paid employment or students rather than unemployed (Table 7.2). It is not surprising that travel experience appears to be related to disposable income.

Table 7.2 Characteristics of travellers abroad in the Nottingham survey

Characteristics	Travelled abroad in last 2 years		Not travelled abroad in last 2 years	
	N	%	N	%
Socio-economic grouping				
I–II	100	78	28	22
III (non manual)	113	66	58	34
III (manual)	58	56	45	44
IV–V	39	52	36	48
	$X^2 = 18.8$; df = 3: $p < 0.001$			
Marital status				
Married	210	62	131	38
Single	143	70	60	30
	$X^2 = 4.0$ df = 1; $p < 0.05$			
Employment status				
In paid work	281	68	132	32
Unemployed	36	43	48	57
Student	37	79	10	21
	$X^2 = 23.7$; df = 2; $p < 0.001$			

Health effects of the holiday?

Although the vast majority of travellers had taken suntan oils or lotions with them when they left to go abroad (82 per cent; 289/354), over two-thirds had suffered from some degree of sunburn (68 per cent; 207/304). Men were particularly prone to sun-related problems and were less likely than women to take suntan oils on holiday, less likely to use them, and more likely to suffer from severe sunburn (Conway *et al.* 1990). One in four reported diarrhoea (26 per cent; 91/354) and one in ten had a bout of vomiting (12 per cent; 41/354). Sickness was attributed to alcohol excess by over half of those who reported vomiting (22/41; 54 per cent).

Whilst one in five travellers reported having suffered accidental injuries such as insect bites (12 per cent), cuts (5 per cent), bruising (5 per cent) (possibly due to falling in a dizzy state from too much sun or alcohol consumption!) and blisters (2 per cent). Only four (1 per cent) were so badly injured that they needed medical care. None the less, the catalogue of bilious adventures and diarrhoea attacks, to say nothing of roasted and blistered skin, leads one to speculate about just how happy and 'healthy' the holidays taken turned out to be, and to ponder the opportunities for romance which form the focus of the remainder of this chapter.

Sexual activity 'in' the sun

The findings from this preliminary survey may help us place newspaper reporting about the extent of sexual activity on holiday within a wider context. Thirty of the travellers abroad in this sample (8 per cent) said they had formed a new romantic attachment on their last trip. Of these, only half (17; 5 per cent of the total sample of travellers) indicated that their romantic attachment had included sexual intercourse. All of the reported sexual relationships abroad had been heterosexual and none had included payment for sex.

The numbers of travellers abroad reporting sexual intercourse with new partners were therefore relatively small, twelve men (8 per cent) and five women (2 per cent). Comparisons with other studies are difficult due to differing methods, differing samples and the paucity of general population surveys. However, one study of 1,229 men and women aged 15–46 years who were guests in a

Table 7.3 Factors emerging from the Nottingham survey associated with sexual intercourse abroad with a new partner

Factor	Number having sex abroad		χ^{2*}	P
	Yes	No		
Sex				
Male	12	133	5.2	<0.02
Female	5	203		
Marital status				
Single	15	128	14.7	<0.001
Married	2	207		
Age (years)				
≤20	8	64	10.08	<0.01
>20	9	269		
Travelling				
Without a partner	17	122	24.77	<0.001
With a partner	0	213		
Sexual partners in UK in last 2 years†				
≥20	12	29	12.7	<0.001
≤20	5	89		
Drug use				
Ever	7	12	10.02	<0.01
Never	8	95		
Alcohol use abroad				
Getting very drunk	11	30	16.46	<0.001
Not getting very drunk	3	68		

Notes:
All degrees of freedom = 1
* With Yates correction † For those travelling without a partner (n = 139)

youth hostel in Copenhagen during the summer of 1987 provides a useful source for comparison. Of the respondents to a self-completed questionnaire, 95 per cent were foreign visitors. In all, 13 per cent of men and 9 per cent of women reported having had sexual intercourse during their stay in Copenhagen (Worm and Lillelund 1989). Unfortunately, the researchers did not manage to separate new partner activity from intercourse with travelling companions and steady partners. They do report, however, that forty-nine foreign male tourists had had sex with local Danish men and women during their visit. One can therefore calculate that casual sexual intercourse with a new partner abroad was recorded in approximately 6.7 per cent of the male tourists in the Copenhagen youth hostel sample, a proportion remarkably close to the 8 per cent for men recorded in the Nottingham study. Comparable data for women were not available.

In the Nottingham study, significantly more of those reporting new sexual activity were single (n = 15) rather than married (n = 2), although the two married respondents were travelling without their partners, and were under 20 years of age (see Table 7.3). This is perhaps not surprising given that nearly two-thirds of the Nottingham holidaymakers travelled with their partners (214; 61 per cent).

Although young men were under-represented in this study, these findings tend to challenge the notion that 'rampant', young, sexually marauding female and male adults on holiday are the norm. They are, in fact, in line with the results from the national sexual survey which show that mean numbers of sexual partners reported in the last year for the age range 16–44 years were 1.2 for men and 1.0 for women (Johnson *et al.* 1994). The average by age showed a higher level in the younger age range for men, with a mean of 1.4 partners during the last year in the 16–24 age range compared with 1.0 for women of the same age. Average partner turnover then stayed the same for women with increasing age but decreased slightly for men to 1.2 in the 25–34 age range and 1.1 in the 35–44 age band.

To summarise, a minority of mostly single adults in this study were sexually active with new partners whilst on holiday. This activity may have placed them at some increased risk of preventable infection with sexually transmitted disease, including HIV. The following section seeks to characterise those in this study who were likely to have sexual intercourse with new and unknown partners abroad and to discuss the extent and context of preventive behaviours, such as condom use.

Characterising the 'performers'

Those most likely to have had sex abroad (see Table 7.3):

- were male rather than female;

- were single and/or travelling without a partner;
- were under 20 years of age;
- had had two or more sexual partners at home in the past two years;
- had at some time (not necessarily while on holiday) tried illegal drugs; and
- had got very drunk at least once while on holiday.

It is perhaps too easy from this type of data to generate 'risk profiles' of individuals for whom constellations of 'risk factors', such as drinking and drug-taking, are associated with sexual activity. By so doing it would be easy to take the next step and promulgate the notion that there is a 'type' of person who engages in sex on holiday who can be readily targeted and whose 'risky' behaviour readily altered. One cannot in any case adduce cause and effect from factors that are merely associated with sexual activity. Prospective studies designed to identify factors that independently predict sexual behaviour are required to achieve this. The evidence from such studies is equivocal regarding the nature of the relationship between, for example, alcohol and casual sex or alcohol use and unsafe sexual practices in studies of gay men (Ekstrand and Coates 1990; Ostrow et al. 1990; Weatherburn et al. 1993).

Concentration upon risk behaviours in risky individuals also focuses attention squarely upon the individual. It can lead us to forget that sexual decision-making is not necessarily a rational process (Hunt and Martin 1988). It can also lead us away from close examination of the context within which sexual behaviour occurs. Yet there is now an impressive body of evidence which demonstrates ways in which socio-economic and cultural context shape people's experience of sexual life. Thus the system of labour and production in South African mining locations in which migrant labourers are forced to leave their families to secure employment and live in unwelcoming hostels, without any privacy and surrounded by security fences, sets the scene for men to seek comfort and company with prostitutes (Jochelson et al. 1991). In Nigeria, the working and social life of long-distance truck drivers coupled with the economic vicissitudes of female hawkers en route, who provide the drivers with sexual and domestic services for money, influences the pattern of sexual experience and networks of contacts made (Orubuloye et al. 1993).

Studies across cultures have also demonstrated how the shape of sexual roles may shift in time and place; by relationship and social class (Coxon *et al.* 1993; Tan 1994). Thus sexual identity and sexual role-playing may not be inherently individualistic characteristics of self. Such propositions challenge the essentialist idea that sexuality has an entirely biological basis and highlight the influence of the 'social' in sexual experience.

Sexual culture, norms and values have also been found to influence the meaning of certain sexual acts for individuals, to fashion desire and erotic significance as in the case of the importance of transgression *vis-à-vis* anal sex in Brazil described earlier (Parker 1992). In addition, sexual language and understandings of sexual categories have been found to vary considerably across cultures (Gillies and Parker 1993), as does the normatively proscribed power that women have in a sexual interaction (Holland *et al.* 1990).

These few examples demonstrate ways in which the context of sexual activity influences the nature of experience. Holidays abroad thrust individual tourists into unfamiliar environments governed by unfamiliar norms and values. Whilst this study could not explore the context of behaviour further, the importance of context cannot be over-emphasised: it is crucial to interpretation of the limited findings available thus far on preventive behaviours during sexual intercourse with strangers on holiday.

Condoms and conundrums

In this study, of the seventeen people who had had sexual intercourse abroad, twelve said they had been carrying condoms at the time. Nine said they had used condoms at some point during their new sexual encounter; however, twelve reported that they had had intercourse at least once with their new partner without using a condom for protection against sexually transmitted disease or unwanted pregnancy. Thus people will still have sexual intercourse with strangers without using condoms even when condoms are in their possession. The youth hostel study from Copenhagen reported data resulting in broadly similar conclusions (Worm and Lillelund 1989). These data have extremely important implications for the outcomes one should expect from investment in mass-media health education aimed at travellers abroad.

One might expect media blitzes exhorting tourists to pack condoms in their suitcases to increase awareness sufficiently to encourage people to carry condoms. The slim evidence available from the Nottingham study would support this view. However, it does appear that such messages may not be translated into action when individuals are faced with a new sexual situation abroad. This limited study could not answer the crucial question of why individuals chose not to protect themselves against sexually transmitted disease, including HIV, when having sex in strange places with strangers, but the findings do underscore the notion that sexual decision-making is probably not always a rational process.

Interestingly, condom use is not particularly prevalent in sexual encounters between new partners at home in the UK. The national sexual survey found that 34 per cent of men and 41 per cent of women who had sex with one new partner in the previous month used a condom. Among those who had two or more partners in the previous month, the proportion using condoms fell to 18 per cent for men and 10 per cent for women (Johnson *et al.* 1994).

There have been surprisingly few investigations aiming to explore sexual experience and the meaning of sexuality in any reasonable depth in a way which might, for example, help explain lack of condom use in potentially 'risky' sexual situations. We do know, however, from the few qualitative studies in the field, that at least the first sexual encounter between young people is generally mute, with the activity proceeding through coded physical messages (Ingham *et al.* 1991). This would limit discussion or negotiation of condom use, particularly in holiday destinations where, in addition, real language barriers and cultural differences in sexual symbols and codes prevail.

Gender is also a powerful factor that needs to be considered. Women tend to believe that men are more knowledgeable sexually and wait for them to take the lead in talking about sexual matters (Holland *et al.* 1991). This is unfortunate since men report a dislike of 'sex talk' which they equate with having somehow failed to provide physical pleasure for women (Waldby *et al.* 1993). Men still, however, like to be 'on top' in sexual dealings with women, to take the initiative and be in control (Waldby *et al.* 1993). This is coupled with a reluctance among young women especially, to accept and express their sexual feelings and to fear that the use of condoms may have a negative effect on their personal reputations (Holland *et al.* 1990). Thus women are concerned about being labelled as sexually promiscuous if they use condoms and report that they acquiesce to men's desire for penetrative sex as part of a complex contract which signifies a relationship involving love and romance, as well as unspoken trust in the chosen partner to protect a woman's sexual reputation within a given social set or group. The social nature of sexual relationships is only just beginning to be unravelled. These insights into the positive benefits of not using condoms, for both men and women, stress the need for further work from the perspective of the social context of sex – if sexuality which embraces not only intercourse, but values, beliefs, norms, comfort, desire and fantasy, is to be properly understood.

CONCLUSION

The findings from this exploratory study, when taken with the limited available data from other studies of travellers abroad, would suggest that whilst the holiday destination represents a completely new and different context for most tourists, only a minority of these are engaging in casual sex with relatively unknown partners. Most of these individuals, however, do not use condoms and consequently place themselves at risk of sexually transmitted disease or unwanted pregnancy. The experience of sexual encounters abroad requires further qualitative investigation, although it seems unlikely that funding agencies will be persuaded to fund an ethnography of 'our nation on holiday', which might none the less attract serious attention from able researchers in the field (Hawkes and Hart 1993). There is, however, little doubt that qualitative work does need to be undertaken 'at home' to provide further insights into the social as well as sociable nature of our sexual world.

At our present level of understanding, there seems little more that local health and travel agencies can do for holidaymakers other than offer the information they currently provide on prevention of ill-health and mishap whilst abroad.

REFERENCES

Baty, B. and Templeton, R. (1991) 'Tourism and the tourism industry in 1990', *Employment Gazette*, 99: 491–502.
Behrens, R. H. and Porter, J. D. H. (1990) 'HIV infection and foreign travel', *British Medical Journal*, 301: 1217.

Catania, J. A., Coates, T. J. and Stall, R. (1992) 'Prevalence of risk related factors and condom use in the United States', *Science*, 258: 1001–6.

Conway, S., Gillies, P. A. and Slack, R. (1990) 'The health of travellers. A report on a study of people in Nottingham, concentrating upon sexual behaviour whilst travelling abroad and risk-taking in the context of STD and HIV transmission', unpublished, Department of Public Health, Medicine and Epidemiology, University of Nottingham.

Coxon, A. P. M., Coxon, N. H., Weatherburn, P., Hunt, A. J., Hickson, F., Davies, P. M. and McManus, F. J. (1993) 'Sex role separation in sexual diaries of homosexual men', *AIDS* 7: 877–82.

Dare, O. O. and Cleland, J. (1993) 'Reliability and validity of survey data on sexual behaviour', *Proceedings of the IUSSP Working Group on AIDS, Conference: AIDS Impact in the Developing World: the Contribution of Demography and Social Science*, 5–9 December, Annecy.

De Schryver, A. and Meheus, A. (1989) 'International travel and sexually transmitted diseases', *World Health Statistics* 42: 90–9.

Department of Health and Social Security and the Welsh Office (1987) *AIDS Monitoring Responses to the Public Education Campaign February 1986–February 1987*, London: HMSO.

Ekstrand, M. and Coates, T. J. (1990) 'Maintenance of safer sexual behaviours and predictors of risky sex: the San Francisco men's health study', *American Journal of Public Health* 80: 973–7.

Ellis, C. J. (1990) 'HIV infection and foreign travel', *British Medical Journal* 301: 984–8.

Feachem, R. G. and Phillips-Howard, P. A. (1988) 'Risk to UK homosexuals of contracting AIDS abroad', *Lancet* ii: 394–5.

Galt, M., Gillies, P. A. and Wilson, K. (1989) 'Surveying knowledge and attitudes towards AIDS in young adults – Just 19', *Health Education Journal* 48: 162–6.

Gillies, P. A. and Parker, R. G. (1993) 'Cross cultural perspectives on sexual behaviour and prostitution', *Proceedings of the IUSSP Working Group on AIDS Conference: AIDS Impact in the Developing World: the Contribution of Demography and Social Science*, 5–9 December, Annecy.

Hawkes, S. J. and Hart, G. J. (1993) 'Travel, migration and HIV', *AIDS Care* 5: 207–14.

Herold, E. and Way, L. (1988) 'Sexual self disclosure among university women', *Journal of Sex Research* 24: 1–4.

Holland, J., Ramazanoglu, C., Scott, S., Sharpe, S. and Thomson, R. (1990) 'Sex, gender and power: young women's sexuality in the shadow of AIDS', *Sociology of Health and Illness* 12: 336–50.

Holland, J., Ramazanoglu, C., Scott, S., Sharpe, S. and Thomson, R. (1991) 'Between embarrassment and trust: young women and the diversity of condom use', in P. Aggleton, P. Davies and G. Hart (eds) *AIDS: Responses, Intervention and Care*, Basingstoke: Falmer Press.

Hunt, S. J. and Martin, C. J. (1988) 'Health-related behavioural change – a test of a new model', *Psychology and Health* 2: 207–30.

Ingham, R., Woodcock, A. and Stenner, K. (1991) 'Getting to know you . . . young people's knowledge of their partners at first intercourse', *Journal of Community and Applied Psychology* 1: 117–32.

Jacoby, A. (1991) 'Possible factors affecting response to postal questionnaires: findings from a study of general practitioner services', *Journal of Public Health Medicine* 12: 131–5.

James, N. J., Bignell, C. J. and Gillies, P. A. (1991) 'The reliability of self-reported sexual behaviour', *AIDS* 5: 333–6.

Jochelson, K., Mothibeli, M. and Leger, J. P. (1991) 'HIV and migrant labour in South Africa', *International Journal of Health Services* 21: 157–73.

Johnson, A. M., Wadsworth, J., Wellings, K. and Field, J. (1994) *Sexual Attitudes and Lifestyles*, Oxford: Blackwell Scientific Publications.

Kinnersley, S. (1991) 'Magaluf Madness', *Sunday Mirror*, July 14: 4–5.

Leigh, B. C., Temple, M. T. and Trocki, K. F. (1993) 'The sexual behaviour of US adults: results from a national survey', *American Journal of Public Health* 83: 1400–8.

Maddox, J. (1989) 'Sexual behaviour unsurveyed', *Nature* 341: 181.

Muhondwa, E. P. Y. (1988) 'Impertinent interviewers and lying respondents: a critique of survey research method for heterosexual HIV transmission research in Africa', *Abstracts of the Fourth International Conference on AIDS*, Reid 12–16 June, in Stockholm, Abstract number 5092, 1: 337.

Orubuloye, I. O., Caldwell, P. and Caldwell, J. C. (1993) 'The role of high risk occupations in the spread of AIDS: truck drivers and itinerant market women in Nigeria', *International Family Planning Perspectives* 2: 43–8.

Ostrow, D. G., Van Raden, M. J., Fox, R., Kingsley, L. A., Dudley, J. and Kascow, R. A. (1990) 'Recreational drug use and sexual behaviour change in a cohort of homosexual men', *AIDS* 4: 759–65.

Parker, R. G. (1991) *Bodies, Pleasures and Passions: Sexual Culture in Contemporary Brazil*, Boston MA: Beacon Press.

—— (1992) 'Sexual diversity, cultural analysis and AIDS education in Brazil', in G. Herdt and S. Lindenbaum, (eds) *The Time of AIDS: Social Analyses, Theory and Method*, Newbury Park, CA: Sage Publications.

Raffaelli, M., Campos, R., Merritt, A. P., Siqueira, E., Antunes, C. M., Parker, R., Greco, M., Greco, D. and Halsey, N. (1994) 'Sexual practices and attitudes of street youth in Belo Horizonte, Brazil', *Social Science and Medicine* 37: 661–70.

Roberts, H. and Magowan R. (1992) *Lifestyle Results – 1992 Trent Lifestyle Survey*, Sheffield: Trent Health.

Roberts, H., Pearson, J. C. G. and Dengler, R. (1993) 'Impact of a postcard versus a questionnaire as a first reminder in a postal survey', *Journal of Epidemiology and Community Health* 47: 334–5.

Smith, C. and Nutbeam, D. (1990) 'Assessing non-response bias: a case study from the 1985 Welsh Heart Health Survey', *Health Education Research* 5: 381–6.

Sonne-Holme, S., Sorenson, T. I. A., Jansen, G. and Schmohr, S. (1989) 'Influence of fatness, intelligence, education and sociodemographic factors on response rates in a health survey', *Journal of Epidemiology and Community Health* 43: 369–74.

Spira, A., Bajos, N. and ACSF Investigators (1993) *Les comportements sexuels en France*, Paris: La Documentation Française.

Tan, M. (1994) 'From Bakla to Gay: Shifting gender identities and sexuality among Filipino men who have sex with men' in R. G. Parker and Gagnon (eds) *Conceiving Sexuality: Sex Research in a Postmodern World*, New York: Routledge.

Van Landingham, M., Kmodel, J., Saengtienchai, D. and Pramualratana, A. (1994) 'Aren't sexual issues supposed to be sensitive?', *Health Transition Review* 4: 85–90.

Waldby, C., Kippax, S. and Crawford, J. (1993) 'Research note: Heterosexual men and "safe sex" practice', *Sociology of Health and Illness* 15: 246–56.

Weatherburn, P., Davies, P. M. and Hickson, F. (1993) 'No connection between alcohol use and unsafe sex among gay and bisexual men', *AIDS* 7: 115–19.

Worm, A. M. and Lillelund, H. (1989) 'Condoms and sexual behaviour of young tourists in Copenhagen', *AIDS Care* 1: 93–6.

Chapter 8

Risk and liminality
The HIV-related socio-sexual interaction of young tourists

Nicholas Ford and J. Richard Eiser

INTRODUCTION

As a movement, in both social as well as geographical space, tourism affords opportunities for new and potentially life-enhancing social interactions. Whether or not such interaction has an adverse impact upon HIV transmission or more general sexual health depends specifically upon how far it follows 'safer' practices which prevent the exchange of body fluids which can transmit HIV. One specific tourist market which has a particular potential for new socio-sexual interaction on holiday is the young (defined for instance from mid-teens to late twenties) and 'sexually unattached'. Young people comprise one of the fastest-growing components of national and international mobility. According to the World Tourist Organisation, in 1989 there were some 50 million crossings of European frontiers by young people aged 15–24, 80 per cent of whom originated from within Europe itself (Youth Mobility and Health Working Group 1990). If the present proportion of young travellers' visits is maintained, this 50 million figure will become 78 million by the end of this century. With the democratisation and removal of travel restrictions from Eastern Europe and the growing integration within the European Community, there are strong grounds for predicting that the mobility of Europeans will continue to increase (Youth Mobility and Health Working Group 1990). These trends highlight the importance of addressing the issue of youth mobility in HIV risk-reduction strategies.

This chapter reports on a study which sought to investigate the socio-sexual interaction of young tourists in Torbay, in South-West England (Figure 8.1). In particular, the study examined the

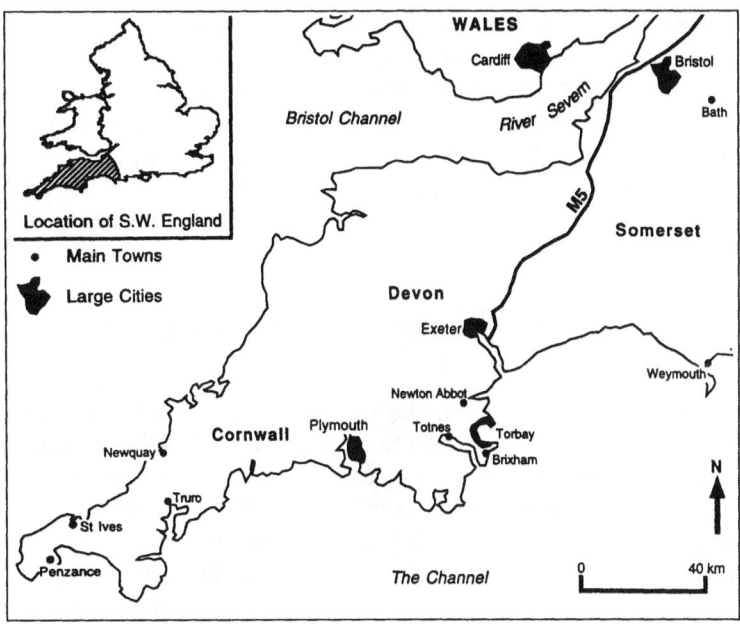

Figure 8.1 South-West England: location and the Torbay district

tourists' socio-sexual interaction as a specific form of situated behaviour, seeking to understand the links between the holiday environments, attitudes and propensities (for instance, pertaining to change and disinhibition) and actual sexual contact. The rationale for this research focus is that in order to influence patterns of sexual behaviour (for instance, through health promotion activities) it is necessary to understand the underlying cognitive beliefs, attitudes and values. The study developed out of the earlier collaborative research between the Institute of Population Studies, University of Exeter and Torbay Health Authority. This prior research into residents (16–24 years of age) in Torbay and district (Ford 1990a) and tourism workers (16–24 years of age in Cornwall and Devon (Ford 1990b)) indicated substantial levels of sexual interaction with tourists.

This chapter commences with a discussion of recent research on young people's mobility, followed by a discussion of a conceptual framework and methodology of the Torbay survey. Then a review of key findings is presented. The survey findings are outlined by reference to a profile of the respondents' socio-demographic characteristics, sexual and drug-using behaviour on holiday, and the social characteristics and socio-sexual propensities of the sexually active tourists. The chapter concludes with a preliminary theoretical interpretation and a discussion of the findings' implications for HIV harm-minimisation/risk-reduction and sexual-health promotion strategies.

YOUNG PEOPLE, MOBILITY AND TOURISM: CONCEPTUAL ISSUES

To place this study within the context of the broader literature of tourism studies, the definition of the term 'tourist' is briefly examined, then the social impacts of tourism, and behavioural and motivational studies of tourism are also reviewed, together with the special characteristics of the tourist resort environment, focusing in particular on the concept of 'liminality' and the emerging field of tourist health. A useful definition of a 'tourist' is a voluntary, temporary traveller, travelling in the expectation of pleasure from the novelty and change experienced in a relatively long and non-recurrent round-trip (Cohen 1974: 533). The key theme in this definition is the purpose of the trip, which Cohen characterises as travelling for non-instrumental purposes with the specific expectation of pleasure. In his review of the social psychology of tourist behaviour, Pearce (1982, 1993) has stressed two key aspects of the academic treatment of the subject: first, the tendency for a somewhat disparaging and critical stance towards tourists, viewed as either nuisance or environmental despoilers (Turner and Ash 1975); and second, the paucity of behavioural and motivational studies relative to the scale of the tourist phenomenon and number of economically related studies. One response to this derisive attitude to the concept of the tourist has been the attempt by some commentators to imbue tourism with cultural significance (MacCannell 1976, 1992; Crick 1989). MacCannell has described tourism as the quest of modern (post-industrial) men and women responding to an experientially fragmenting division of labour, in a search for authenticity supposedly to be found in other, more exotic cultures. These notions may seem somewhat distant from the experience of British tourists sunbathing in Torbay.

In considering the motivational aspects of tourism, it is useful to relate it to the two broad theories of leisure: the 'compensatory leisure hypothesis' (that people seek the opposite kinds of stimulation in their leisure environment to that at work) and the 'spillover leisure hypothesis' (that people seek the same kinds of stimulation in their leisure as in their work) (Pearce 1982). Mannell and Iso-Ahola (1987) have argued that the psychological benefits of the tourist experience derive from the interplay of two motivational forces: to escape from routine and stressful environments, and to seek recreational opportunities. Dann (1981) has further reviewed the 'push' and 'pull' factors implied in these conceptualisations, stressing that tourist satisfaction is inherently related to expectations that are based on motivation.

Within the broad area of tourism studies, the concern with social impact is also of interest (see Mathieson and Wall 1982). Research into the social impacts of tourism is concerned with the three aspects of: the tourist, the host, and the tourist–host interrelationship. More specifically, such work seeks to assess the social impact of tourism in changing the quality of life of the residents at tourist destinations. The major part of the literature concerning the social impact of tourism focuses upon international travel, highlighting the effects of cross-cultural interaction. Furthermore, most of this research examines the effects of the interaction between affluent tourists from 'Western' countries and the poorer residents of host countries in the Less Developed World. One of the themes of the social impact studies has been that tourism can have an undesirable effect on the moral standards of the host population, including the growth of prostitution, crime and gambling (Mathieson and Wall 1982). Indeed, the main sexual focus of tourism studies has been upon prostitution, interpreted in terms of tourist–host economic inequality and exploitation. Recent writing has highlighted the implications of 'sex tourism' for the international transmission of HIV from, and to, such countries as Kenya, Thailand and the Philippines (Panos 1990; see also Hall in Chapter 9 of this volume). Pre-AIDS writing tended to focus more directly on the sexual exploitation of (mainly) women in the host countries (Wereld 1979). Cohen (1987) has outlined the cross-cultural confusions and misunderstandings inherent to the Western tourist – Thai 'bar girl' sexual encounters and relationships. However, much of the writing on tourism and prostitution has tended to be speculative, offering little evidence of the connections between tourism, prostitution and the spread of STDs (Mathieson and Wall 1982).

There have been a few ethnographic studies of non-pecuniary, socio-sexual interaction between tourist and host populations, for instance in Gozo (Boissevain 1979) and Israel (Cohen 1971). These studies have identified the desire by young members of host populations for connections and friendship with visitors. One quantitative study of tourists' 'safe sex' behaviour surveyed young tourists staying in a youth hostel in Copenhagen (Worm and Lillelund 1988). This survey focused upon (a) whether visitors carried condoms in their luggage when travelling and (b) use of condoms in sexual encounters with Danish residents. Five per cent of male visitors and 1 per cent of female visitors had in fact engaged in sexual intercourse with Danes. In general, however, despite the implication inherent to typologies of tourists that youths comprise a highly differentiated population, there is an extreme paucity of tourism studies focusing specifically upon the behaviour of young people.

Returning to the themes of motivation and the basic feature of tourism as a change in environment, one of the most interesting contributions has been the socio-cultural exploration of the seaside resort by Shields (1990). His review of the cultural positioning of the seaside resort has especial pertinence to this Torbay study. It is therefore worth outlining his notions in some detail and in particular his application of the concept of 'liminality'. Shields considers the seaside resort, epitomised by Brighton, as occupying a position constructed within the broader framework of the spatialisation of sites of British culture. The very concept of the seaside resort has been associated with the pursuit of pleasure. Shields argues that the seaside or beach has become a socially defined zone which is appropriate for specific behaviours and patterns of interaction which are outside the norms of everyday behaviour, dress and activity. In contrast to routine everyday life, behaviours in the resort are perceived as casual, pleasure-seeking and hedonistic.

Shields uses the concept of 'liminality' to account for this special status of the beach. The concept of the liminal is derived from the work of van Gennep (1908) on 'rites of passage' via Turner (1979). The essential feature of the liminal is the designation of moments of discontinuity in the social fabric – an 'in-betweenness' involving a temporary loss of social bearings. Van Gennep developed the concept with respect to the spiritual transitions in the 'rites of passage' of adolescents in ritualistic traditional societies. The 'limen' or 'margin' is a threshold through which the subject passes from one social status to another, in which social rights and obligations may be temporarily suspended. Turner (1979) uses the term liminoid to characterise the nature of leisure in modern societies. Paralleling Iso-Ahola's (1984) concept of tourist motivations of escaping routine and seeking recreation, Turner emphasised leisure as 'freedom from' obligations and regulation and 'freedom to' enter new symbolic worlds of entertainment. A further aspect of leisure is the 'freedom to' engage in new friendships and social interactions. Shields relates the concept of liminality to the rowdy fun of the holidaymakers, who can revel in the anonymity and pleasure-seeking atmosphere of the resort (Bourdieu 1985). Within the highly regulated modern industrial society, the pubs, bars and nightclubs of the seaside resort may be viewed as permanently liminoid settings and spaces. Indeed, psycho-active drug use (primarily alcohol) may seem to justify and facilitate entry into the liminoid states of mind and social interaction (Crowe and George 1989). These explanatory concepts contributed to the formulation of the conceptual framework of this Torbay survey.

A final area of research of relevance to this study is the growing interest in tourist health (Pasini 1990). This fast-growing field reflects the public health response to the global expansion of tourism. Tourist health encompasses concerns with communicable and non-communicable diseases; environmental health; food safety; accidents; visitor lifestyles and their quality of life; climate and health; and the management of tourist health. This particular chapter seeks to redress the strong medical bias and lack of a coherent psycho-social input which has characterised much of the early work into tourist health. The potential transmission of HIV is one of the most emotive problems confronting tourist health. This study is firmly placed within this field and is seeking to strengthen the behavioural basis of research into tourist health and provide guidance for tourism-related, HIV risk-reduction strategies.

There have been relatively few behavioural and psycho-social studies of tourists and an extreme paucity of such studies pertaining to young people and their socio-sexual interaction on holiday. In terms of the social impact of tourism, there has been a preponderant focus upon international tourism to less developed countries, with most of the writing concerning sex and tourism focusing on prostitution. The conceptual literature on tourist motivations and more specifically the liminality of the tourist resort social environment provides sound bases for the elaboration of a conceptual framework that examines young tourists' sexual behaviour in relation to holiday motivations, leisure activities, social interaction, attitudes and propensities pertaining to the holiday experience. The survey described below sought to generate quantitative survey data from which to examine these notions and their implications for HIV risk-reduction strategies

TOURISM IN DEVON AND TORBAY: A YOUNG PEOPLE'S RESORT

The West Country has a primary position in England's tourism industry (Williams *et al.* 1991), receiving one-fifth of all domestic tourism trips made by British tourists in England (Devon County Council Property Department 1990), although it has been in competition with overseas destinations (Shaw *et al.* 1991). Of the one-third of these visits which are to Devon, Torbay is by far the most popular destination, attracting around one-third of the total. Not only does Torbay receive in excess of 1 million visitors per year, but it also has a reputation as a young people's resort and a centre of nightlife. The tourist period is highly seasonal with nearly 70 per cent of all tourist nights in Devon being spent in the four summer months of June to September (Devon County Council Property Department 1990). Whilst the majority of young visitors to Torbay are British, there is also an increasing proportion of young people from abroad, many of whom come to Torbay to attend courses in English language instruction and form a significant international tourist presence (British Tourist Authority 1990).

At the outset of the research it is important to stress that whilst this study is concerned with certain potentially negative consequences of youth mobility, it is also important to note its beneficial aspects. These positive aspects include not only the crucial importance of tourism to Torbay's economy, but also the more intrinsic benefits of tourism as a recreational activity for visitors (Ryan 1991). International tourism also provides an opportunity to enhance understanding of, and respect for, different cultures. Indeed, these positive attributes of tourism provide the starting point for the study's consideration of young tourists' socio-sexual interaction. The challenge for tourist resorts such as Torbay is to meet these tasks in a way that both enhances the tourist 'holiday experience' and minimises the potential health risks.

OBJECTIVES, CONCEPTUAL FRAMEWORK AND METHODOLOGY

The immediate objective of this study was to undertake a survey into the HIV-related behaviours and attitudes of young (16–29 years of age), 'sexually unattached', English-speaking tourists visiting Torbay. The survey was undertaken in summer 1990 among 1,033 young people visiting Torbay.

The ultimate objective of the study is to provide information which can help contain the transmission of HIV by contributing to the HIV risk-reduction strategy being implemented by Torbay Health Authority. It was decided not to interview visitors under the age of 16 because of the sensitivity of some of the questions on sexual activity and the legal requirement for parental consent to interview under-16 year olds. The 14 year age range allows analysis to assess changes in tourists' socio-sexual behaviour spanning important phases in maturation. 'Sexually unattached' tourists refer to those who are on holiday in Torbay unaccompanied by a sexual partner. It was felt that for those young people who go on holiday with their sexual partner, sexual interaction with a new partner on holiday is somewhat less likely. Thus the behaviour of 'sexually attached' tourists has less relevance to the health authority's HIV risk-reduction strategy. The study focuses on English-speaking tourists for two reasons: first, British visitors comprise a large majority of visitors to Torbay; and second, it would be particularly difficult to undertake a detailed interview on these issues with visitors who may not be fully fluent or conversant with the English language. The survey does nevertheless address the question of the socio-sexual interaction of tourists with visitors from overseas in Torbay.

The conceptual framework is structured in terms of three sets of variables; background variables (A, B), independent/intermediate variables (C, D, E, F, G, H) and dependent variables (I, J). The analysis of the data is undertaken at three levels;

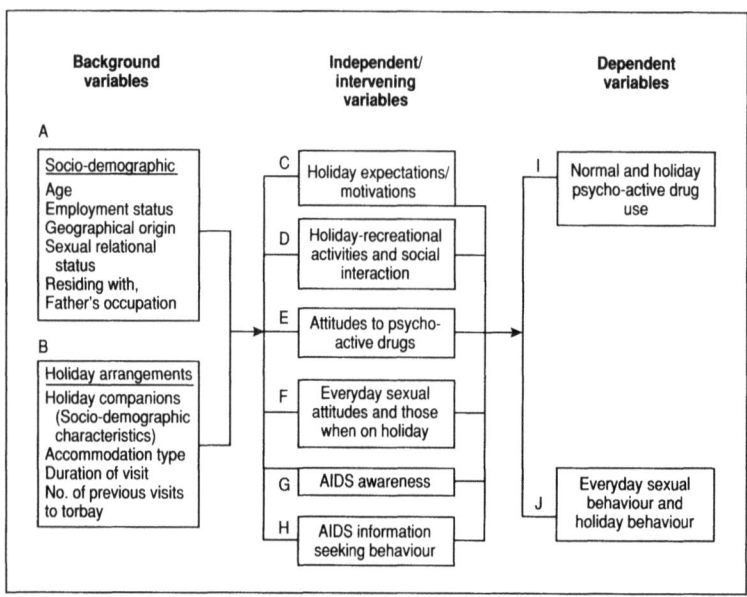

Figure 8.2 Conceptual framework of the Torbay survey of young tourists' sexual behaviour

description (frequencies and patterns), explanation (cross-tabulation and correlation) and interpretation (which includes implications of findings for practical initiatives and further research) (Figure 8.2).

The survey was undertaken during the months of July, August and early September 1990 among 1,033 young tourists visiting Torbay. Twenty-one areas were identified in Torbay (by the Torbay Health Promotion Service) as the major areas where tourists could be found by day (including Torquay, Paignton and Brixham) (see Figure 8.1). By undertaking interviewing at the end of the week, it was hoped the respondents would have been in Torbay for some time. Twenty-eight interviewers worked on the survey over the summer months; interchanging as they themselves went on holiday. The majority of the interviewers were students from the local South Devon College who were studying Tourism. It was felt having interviewers who were of similar ages to the respondents would help the respondents to feel at ease and enhance open response to the questions.

Interviewers chose a random start point within their allocated sampling area and approached respondents who appeared to be in the sampling quota. Each respondent was asked five questions which they had to fulfil before the interview continued. The respondent had to be English-speaking, aged between 16 and 29 years, on holiday in Torbay, have been in Torbay for more than two days, single and *not* on holiday with a girlfriend or boyfriend. In any single group of people who were eligible for interview no more than three were to be interviewed. It was not feasible to apply a strict quota sampling methodology because the age and sex composition of Torbay tourists was not known. Each interviewer aimed to do ten interviews per week, seeking to interview the same number of males and females and at least one 26–29 year old each week (to make sure the sample included an adequate number of respondents from the older age range). An ongoing record of sex and age was kept to monitor the pattern. As the survey progressed it became evident that there was no need to modify the sampling strategy. Detailed briefing concerning the interview schedule was undertaken by the staff of the Institute of Population Studies prior to the undertaking of the survey.

The data collection instrument (schedule-structured questionnaire) comprised two parts. The first part (covering questions on socio-demographic characteristics, AIDS awareness, holiday motivations, leisure behaviours, sexual attitudes, etc.) involved the interviewers asking questions of the respondent and recording his/her answers. The interviewer tried to do this out of earshot of anyone else, leading the respondent away from any group. The second part (covering questions on sexual and drug-injecting behaviour) was given to the respondent for his/her self-completion. The second part was completed in the interviewer's presence but he/she did not see the answers, since once completed, the respondent placed it in the envelope provided and sealed it, before handing the envelope back to the interviewer.

The questionnaire was well received by the respondents who seemed to recognise the pertinence of the survey, 83 per cent stating that they felt the survey to be 'worthwhile' or 'very worthwhile'. The interview took between twenty and thirty minutes to administer. The questionnaire included predominantly fixed format questions. In order to enhance the reliability of the responses to some of the more complex questions, for instance concerning attitudes to sexual behaviour, such questions were approached from different angles within the structured formats. At the end of the interview, respondents were thanked for their co-operation in the survey and given two HIV/STD prevention leaflets (the Health Education Authority's *Your Guide to Safer Sex and the Condom* and *Guide to a Healthy Sex Life*). In this way, it was intended that the survey would not only collect information but also attempt to 'raise consciousness' of HIV/STD-related issues among tourists.

FINDINGS FROM THE SURVEY

The full detail of the survey is contained in the report 'Sex on holiday' (Ford 1991a). The survey findings are summarised here in terms of:

- a brief review of the contextual sets of variables including the respondents' (usual) non-holiday sexual and drug-using (including alcohol) behaviour, holiday motivations and broad types of leisure activities on holiday;
- a description of the levels of drug use and sexual activity on holiday; and
- a discussion of the social characteristics of the most sexually active tourists, and the influence of the tourist environment and experience upon socio-sexual propensities and attitudes.

Contextual findings

The respondents were fairly evenly divided by sex (males 53 per cent; females 47 per cent) and were drawn from a wide range of ages within the 16–29 age band (16 = 15%, 17–18 = 24%, 19–22 = 33%, 23–26 = 15%, 27–29 = 9%). The numbers in the older age groups progressively declined, reflecting the increasing proportion in these age groups who would have been on holiday with a sexual partner. Nevertheless, the sample contained sufficient numbers within the older (mid- and late-twenties) age groups for meaningful statistical analysis and comparison to be made. The respondents were from a wide range of geographical regions in the UK, in proportions which could be expected to reflect the overall pattern of origins of tourists to Torbay.

The concern with the sexual behaviour of tourists is primarily twofold. First, it is possible that the holiday experience may involve an increased frequency of sexual interaction with new sexual partners. Second, mobility, of whatever form, is implicated in STD transmission and tourism comprises a specific form of mobility.

This survey is essentially concerned with young tourists' patterns of socio-sexual interaction with new partners on holiday. It was emphasised at the outset that the survey was only addressing 'sexually unattached' tourists, that is, tourists who were not on holiday with a sexual partner. The obvious logic of this sample selection is that those tourists who are on holiday with a sexual partner are unlikely (or at least, very much less likely) to engage in sexual activity with a new partner while on holiday. The first question to be asked is whether and how far sexually unattached tourists differ from the general population of their cohort. The main social difference is that the sample contains a higher proportion who are not currently in a steady relationship (by comparison with the prior socio-sexual lifestyle surveys of residents in the South-West of England (Ford 1991b, 1993). However, despite this difference (taking into account age and sex), the tourist sample strikingly replicated the residents' survey findings in terms of experience of psycho-active drugs, non-holiday alcohol consumption, sexual attitudes and experience, perceived vulnerability to HIV infection and knowledge about AIDS. This replication is interesting in that it may point towards not only a regional, but also a national pattern in young people's socio-sexual lifestyles. The important starting point for this study is that the sample of tourists was sufficiently large and obtained in such a way as to be broadly representative of young people in terms of sexual and drug-using behaviours.

It was considered useful to consider tourists' sexual interaction on holiday within the context of the broad types of holiday characteristics including accommodation, company, leisure activities and overall holiday motivations. Respondents' accommodation types ranged from guest houses (26 per cent) to caravans (21 per cent), self-catering apartments and hotels (18 per cent), with small numbers camping or staying with friends or relatives. The majority (58 per cent) of respondents had come on holiday with friends of their own sex, while smaller numbers had come with their family (24 per cent), with friends of both sexes (10 per cent) or alone (9 per cent). The youngest (16 year old) respondents tended to be on holiday with their parents.

The main motivations expressed by respondents for the holiday in Torbay were to escape their usual situation and seek freedom from inhibitions in a different environment. The wish to meet and make new friends on holiday was also seen to be basic. Consequently, for this particular group of tourists, nightlife was commonly the most important holiday activity. The beaches seemed largely to comprise only a backdrop in the day for the enjoyment of socialising in pubs and nightclubs in the evening.

DRUG-USING AND SEXUAL BEHAVIOUR

The findings concerning behaviour on holiday are reviewed primarily in terms of levels of illegal drug use, alcohol consumption, social interaction with new friends, and sexual activity. Given that the study sought to investigate the holiday experience as a form of situational influence upon sexual behaviour, particular attention was given to psycho-active drug use (including alcohol) on holiday. Psycho-active drugs are viewed as having a situational influence upon patterns of behaviour in interaction with psychological expectancies of their effects, and the social and place setting. Sixteen per cent of males and 8 per cent of females had taken illegal drugs (mainly cannabis) during their holiday, although only six respondents had injected (three of them sharing needles/syringes). The potential overlap between injecting drug use and sexual activity was examined by reference to the eighteen respondents who had ever (i.e. not necessarily on holiday) injected illegal drugs. It was noted that as a category these respondents were particularly sexually active on holiday, with twelve of them engaging in intercourse with new partners while on holiday. Furthermore, seven of these had not taken the precaution of using a condom and six of these had engaged in intercourse with Torbay locals.

The majority of illegal drug use on holiday took place along with alcohol consumption. This raises the issue of the 'potentiating' effects of the one drug upon the effects of the other. However, the main point is that by far the most common psychoactive drug taken on holiday is alcohol. Indeed, given the almost universal increase in young tourists' levels of alcohol consumption on holiday, it could be suggested that alcohol is almost basic to the holiday experience of most young tourists. The level of alcohol consumption on holiday stands out as a health issue in its own right, irrespective of the association with patterns of sexual interaction. Thirty-six per cent of male and 19 per cent of female respondents, consumed levels of alcohol (over 36 units and over 21 units, within the holiday week, respectively) at which the Health Education Authority suggests damage to health is likely. The potential health risk of excessive alcohol consumption is generally believed to arise following sustained consumption at such levels over an extended period of time. Thus given that, for each individual, the holiday takes place over only a limited time period, it would appear that the health risk is low for these young tourists, particularly if the holiday 'binge' is followed by a period of 'drying out' after the holiday. Thus the major implications of these levels of alcohol consumption are in terms of the social effects on patterns of behaviour. The association between levels of alcohol consumption and sexual activity are noted below, and interpreted by reference to relevant theory. The surveys of residents in the South-West of England (Ford 1991b, 1993) had detailed sections on AIDS awareness. Key AIDS knowledge variables and perceived vulnerability to HIV infection (in the next two years) were included in this survey of young tourists. There was a striking replication of the residents' survey findings in the tourist survey. For instance, with regard to chances of HIV infection, 44 per cent of both tourists and residents felt that they had '*no* chance' of being infected, with a very similar percentage (46 per cent of tourists and 45 per cent of residents) admitting to a '*slight* chance' of becoming infected. This congruence of findings suggests that both groups derive from the same underlying culture which has a very low personally perceived vulnerability to HIV infection.

One of the main objectives of this survey was to generate quantitative data from which to assess levels of sexual activity with new partners among tourists in Torbay. The findings reveal a high level of social interaction with 51 per cent (equal numbers of males and females) of respondents reporting meeting a new boy/girlfriend during their holiday. Fifty-seven per cent of this interaction was with other visitors (including 9 per cent with visitors from overseas) and 43 per cent was with Torbay locals. The nature of this interaction tended to be highly transient with little emotional involvement or expectation for relationship development. Indeed, emotional involvement (as measured by perceived likelihood of keeping in contact after the holiday) in encounters was also seen to be inversely related to the level of sexual activity taking place.

Table 8.1 Sexual behaviour among young tourists in Torbay by sex and age group (%)

	No sexual contact	Sexual contact but no intercourse	Intercourse with		p
			One partner	Two or more partners	
Total sample	66	10	17	7	
Sex					
Male	61	8	20	11	p < 0.005
Female	72	11	13	4	
Age group					
16	73	17	5	5	
17–18	69	15	11	5	
19–22	65	7	22	6	p < 0.005
23–26	59	4	24	13	
27–29	70	8	9	13	

One-third (34 per cent) of respondents reported engaging in some form of physical sexual contact with a new partner on holiday, with one-quarter (24 per cent) engaging in sexual intercourse (Table 8.1). Thus it appears that for most of these tourists (and especially those in the older age groups) any physical sexual interaction on holiday tends to involve (penetrative) sexual intercourse. The disparity in the proportion of males (31 per cent) and females (17 per cent) who reported engaging in intercourse during the holiday may be explained in three ways:

- greater interaction of males with non-tourists, i.e. more of their sexual partners would not have appeared in the survey;
- a possible measure of over-reporting on the part of males; and
- the possibility that a relatively small number of females would have engaged in intercourse with numerous partners, and that these being a very small proportion would have a low probability of appearing in the sample survey.

The key finding here is evidence of substantial levels of sexual interaction with new partners on holiday, which compared with respondents' total numbers of partners in the last year (Ford 1993), indicates substantially higher frequency of new sexual partners on holiday than when at home.

The risk of HIV or other STD infection from sexual interaction depends very much upon whether or not protective measures (e.g. condom use) are taken. Given that the major part of the sexual contact involved (penetrative) sexual intercourse, a key concern is level of condom use. Only a minority (41 per cent) of respondents engaging in sexual intercourse reported taking the precaution of using a condom, and 32 per cent reported using no contraceptive at all during intercourse on holiday. As found in the Torbay residents' socio-sexual lifestyle surveys (Ford 1990a), a higher proportion of males than females reported not using any form of contraception, probably indicating that a proportion of males were not aware (and more disturbingly, not concerned) that their female partners were taking some precaution, presumably hormonal contraception. A progressive decline in level of condom use by age of respondents was also noted, with condoms being used in intercourse by 52 per cent of the 17–18 year olds but only 36 per cent of the 23–26 year olds. The problem of promoting the consistent practice of 'safe(r) sex' is particularly acute concerning those tourists in their mid-twenties. Of particular concern for STD transmission is the finding that the level of condom use is lowest for those tourists who engaged in intercourse with more new sexual partners on holiday, with condoms being used by 46 per cent of those who had one new partner, but by only 32 per cent of those who had two or more partners. This most sexually active category thus multiplies their risk of receiving or transmitting STD infection.

CHARACTERISTICS OF THE SEXUALLY ACTIVE TOURISTS

The social characteristics of those tourists who were most sexually active on holiday are of particular interest, given the potential implications for the targeting of HIV-prevention initiatives. However, there is relatively little variation in socio-demographic characteristics between the sexually active and non-sexually active respondents, except that the former were more likely to be from the 19–26 age range and to be in a steady or 'engaged' relationship (but not on holiday with their partner). The relatively high levels of sexual contact with new partners on holiday among those in steady relationships is an interesting indicator of levels of infidelity. The sexually active tourists were also similar to the rest of the sample in tourist leisure activities, except that they exhibited higher levels of alcohol consumption and illegal drug use, both at home and on holiday. Indeed, for both males and females higher levels of alcohol consumption were associated with higher numbers of sexual partners. However, a decline in level of condom use with level of alcohol consumption was found only for males.

However, the sexually active category differed most significantly from the others in terms of their sexual attitudes, both in general and on holiday. Members of this category hold a 'casual-recreational' sexual philosophy (wherein intercourse outside of a sexual relationship is considered admissible) with positive attitudes to casual sex. Thus, not surprisingly, their general sexual attitudes predispose them to casual sexual interaction on holiday. Furthermore, the perceived effect of the holiday environment and experience upon tourists' sexual propensities was seen to vary dramatically according to level of sexual activity on holiday (see Table 8.2 on pp. 170–1).

The sexually active category was much more likely than others to feel that on holiday they are more confident with members of the opposite sex, less concerned about social sanctions or constraints, less particular about who they interact with sexually, and more likely to engage in casual sex. Furthermore they were more likely than others to hold the expectation that other males and females on holiday were also seeking casual sex. The ways in which the holiday environment and experience act differentially as a situational influence upon behaviour for different tourists is thus important.

INTERPRETATION, IMPLICATIONS AND THEORETICAL ISSUES

The overall holiday situation for young people in Torbay is one in which there is a high level of social interaction, including a substantial level of sexual contact. Much of this sexual interaction falls outside the requirements of 'safe(r) sex', thus posing a potential STD/HIV public health threat. The holiday resort is essentially an environment of some measure of sexual and emotional transience.

The tourist resort was referred to above as occupying a special 'liminal' place within our national socio-cultural space (Shields

1990). 'Liminality' refers to an 'in-between-ness' involving a temporary loss of social bearings. Within the holiday environment such liminality may include a greater openness to socio-sexual contact with new friends, a removal of norms and constraints on personal behaviour, and possibly an enhanced recklessness within passing sexual encounters. For the majority of the tourists in the survey (who did not engage in sexual intercourse during their holiday), the sense of being personally influenced by the liminal qualities of the resort was equivocal. However, one of the most interesting findings was that for the particular minority of tourists who are predisposed towards, and engage in, sexual intercourse on holiday, the resort environment is strongly imbued with the qualities of the 'limen', that marginal environment in which casual sexual interaction is relatively available and takes place. In seeking to understand this differential perception and experience of the resort's liminality, it is necessary to consider tourists' expectations, social context and leisure lifestyles. For the most sexually active tourists' casual sexual interaction on holiday is clearly part of the desired holiday experience. They have an expectation that other (both male and female) tourists hold the same expectation. In social terms, these attitudes and propensities are not held by isolated individuals, but are comprised of shared orientations and tendencies within, and reinforced by, the social group. The reinforcing social group can be viewed on two levels: first, the small, usually single-sex group of friends with whom the individual is on holiday; second, the wider socio-cultural cohort who share the same sexual philosophy. The implication here is that health promotion is addressing not only the individual, but more gainfully the group. Indeed, the small holiday group probably positively reinforces, by means of social rewards, 'prestigious success' in the sexual sphere.

Casual sexual interaction for the most sexually active tourists is not an isolated activity which occurs unintentionally but is positively desired and is related to a pattern of tourist leisure activities. There is an overlap between casual sex, frequent visiting of pubs and nightclubs, and high levels of alcohol consumption. Positive attitudes to both casual sex and alcoholic intoxication probably relate to an underlying dimension of 'permissiveness' which contributes to the sense of what makes up a good holiday.

The link between alcohol consumption and sexual behaviour is of course complex and only partly pharmacological in nature

Table 8.2 Sexual propensities and attitudes of young tourists in Torbay by sexual behaviour on holiday (%)

Attitudes	No sexual contact on holiday	Sexual contact on holiday but not intercourse	Intercourse with:		p
		(% agree)	One partner	Two or more partners	
1 When on holiday I mostly just like to rest in the day, so that I have lots of energy to go out at night.	30	44	36	25	<0.0005
2 On holiday I may like to flirt with new friends but that's as far as it goes.	39	41	26	21	<0.0005
3 I feel more confident with members of the opposite sex when I am on holiday.	41	64	62	70	<0.0005
4 Relationships you make on holiday don't need to carry on afterwards.	51	59	64	73	<0.0005
5 If I fell in love on holiday I would want to continue the relationship afterwards.	45	40	40	39	NS
6 I am a different person on holiday.	33	27	43	64	<0.0005
7 It is easier to make contact with new friends of the opposite sex when on holiday than when at home.	51	69	67	78	<0.0005

Table 8.2 continued

Attitudes	No sexual contact on holiday	Sexual contact on holiday but not intercourse	Intercourse with:		p
			One partner	Two or more partners	
8 Most (unattached) males on holiday are looking for casual sex (meaning sexual intercourse outside a steady relationship).	47	64	70	85	<0.0005
9 Most (unattached) females on holiday are looking for casual sex.	20	33	45	66	<0.0005
10 I am more likely to engage in casual sex when on holiday than when I am at home.	25	35	65	74	<0.0005
11 I am not so worried about what other people think of me when I am on holiday.	40	58	61	74	<0.0005
12 You don't have to be so bothered about who you go out with when you are on holiday because you are probably never going to see them again.	35	46	61	80	<0.0005
13 I feel that going to bed with someone has to involve a lasting commitment.	39	32	8	11	<0.0005
14 I would never go to bed with someone unless I had had time to really get to know them.	56	49	14	12	<0.0005

Note: n = 1,033

(Crowe and George 1989; Ford 1990c). Even at low concentrations, alcohol acts as a physiological depressant on sexual behaviour (Price and Price 1983). The changes in sexual behaviour attributed to alcohol occur despite the alcohol-induced lessening of physiological arousal (Reinarman and Leigh 1987). Both psychological experiments (Schachter, 1964) and cross-cultural anthropological analysis (MacAndrew and Edgerton 1969) stress that the main influence of alcohol upon sexual propensities is related to socially learned expectancies of the likely effects. Furthermore, the specific effects of intoxication are seen to depend upon the particular meanings attached to drunkenness in a given culture, i.e. cultural beliefs that alcohol promotes sexual disinhibition will give rise to such behaviour patterns ('drunken comportment') within the given culture (MacAndrew and Edgerton 1969). Indeed, 'being drunk' is thus understood as 'socially allowing' certain behaviours within a cultural setting. This, in turn, relates to the powerful 'excuse utility' function of alcohol, whereby a cultural belief in the disinhibiting effects of alcohol allows blame for certain deviant, reckless or anti-social behaviours to be attributed to the drug rather than to the individual (Critchlow 1983). A further crucial factor relating to the behavioural 'effects' of alcohol is 'situational specificity', whereby the impact of psycho-active drug use is conditioned by the situational and social environment within which it is consumed (Critchlow 1986). Thus alcohol may have different 'effects' depending upon whether it is consumed at home or in a nightclub setting.

The survey findings clearly indicate that the holiday experience entails increased levels of alcohol consumption for most respondents, especially for those who engage in the highest levels of sexual activity on holiday. For this group in particular, alcohol is ascribed the classic 'excuse utility' of enhancing the likelihood of engaging in casual sex. Key findings of pertinent social research were briefly outlined above in order to emphasise that the link between alcohol consumption and sexual behaviour is not a simple pharmacological relationship. It seems highly likely that for the most sexually active group of young tourists, the consumption of alcohol (and its anticipated effects) is viewed not only as a leisure activity in its own right but also one conducive to the fostering of casual sexual interaction, which for them is an integral part of the holiday experience. Such expectancies and attitudes are shaped and reinforced by the peer group context. In seeking to foster 'safe(r)' sexual behaviour on holiday, public health and health promotion departments face the problem not only of raising awareness of potential risks but also, more subtly, of unravelling the underlying expectancies. Part of the problem faced by HIV prevention workers is that they are seeking to influence behaviours which are positively sought and socially reinforced by certain groups of young tourists.

Implications for HIV risk-reduction strategies

The foregoing sections have identified and highlighted the nature of HIV-related public health problems related to the socio-sexual activities of young tourists visiting Torbay. Given that the most sexually active tourists are particularly influenced by the resort environment in their sexual behaviour, HIV prevention messages conveyed in the home area before the holiday are not likely to have a significant impact. National mass media messages designed to stimulate forethought and planning will be largely irrelevant to the most sexually active tourists, for whom the 'liminal' qualities of the holiday experience entail some suspension of the usual norms and constraints that regulate behaviour. It is therefore especially important to develop HIV risk-reduction initiatives that engage the attention of this group when they are actually in the resort.

Influencing sexual behaviour is a highly complex process, ideally involving a multi-faceted, interactive strategy which relates to different stages of maturational development (Abramson 1983). Tourist-oriented HIV prevention initiatives have little scope to be part of a long-term process. The emphasis of such initiatives in tourist resorts should essentially be concerned with raising mindfulness of potential risk within a 'liminal' environment. The information and messages conveyed in such a strategy should seek to have different effects upon different tourists according to their personal intentions to practise 'safe(r) sex'. For instance, to reinforce the resolve of those individuals who are confident in their capability to take protective precautions consistently; to provide encouragement for those who intend to follow such precautions, but are uncertain about their ability to put such intentions into practice; and for those who are sexually active and do not intend to use condoms, to help them to recognise their behaviour as risky, and to encourage them to take precautions against infection. The survey findings indicate that the main focus of tourist-related HIV prevention strategies should be this third category of tourists.

The objective of such tourist-related sexual health promotion is to influence holiday behaviour in ways that will reduce STD/HIV infection. This objective can be approached in a number of ways, for instance, heightening awareness of risk-taking behaviours, attempting to reduce 'unrealistic optimism' (van der Velde et al. 1992), imparting information (e.g. the prevalence and persistence of STDs), and appealing to values (e.g. look after your own health, be responsible/caring towards others, such as potential sexual partners). Given that most sexual contacts made on holiday in Torbay are made in pubs and nightclubs, such venues provide pertinent settings for HIV prevention initiatives. HIV-related initiatives in such venues are likely to have the dual benefit of reaching relevant groups of both tourists and locals. Such nightlife-based initiatives need to pursue a fun approach to informing and motivating, and are probably best met by peer facilitation strategies. There may be some concern that by highlighting or increasing awareness of HIV-related risk, a resort could possibly harm its appeal to potential holidaymakers. It is thus important for Torbay Health Authority to stress that it is simply taking a caring attitude to a serious potential public health problem. Furthermore, should tourists and locals take note of the messages, then the risk of HIV transmission in the resort will be reduced.

It is important to stress that not all young tourists are predisposed towards casual sex on holiday. Care should be taken in tourism-related, risk-reduction messages and initiatives not to reinforce the expectation of casual sex on holiday. Those who are predisposed towards casual sex could perhaps be made aware that not all tourists have the same expectations.

Most of the sexually active tourists multiply their potential risk of infection by not using condoms. Part of the reason for this is that they do not consider that their behaviour makes them vulnerable to HIV infection. Thus HIV risk-reduction initiatives should at least seek to make this group aware that their sexual behaviour involves a real risk of infection. General media messages about the need to use condoms on holiday are most likely to be reinforcing to those young tourists who already intend to take such precautions, but are not so likely to influence those tourists who do not wish to follow protective practices on holiday.

If this key group of tourists feels that they behave differently when in the holiday resort, then HIV prevention messages in metropolitan or non-tourist areas will be of very limited relevance to their practice or non-practice of 'safe(r) sex' on holiday. Thus HIV risk-reduction initiatives have to be implemented in the tourist resort to stand any chance of influencing behaviour. To be potentially effective, resort-based HIV prevention initiatives should actively reach and engage the attention of the particular group that is most sexually active. Health promotion could well stress that HIV can be transmitted via only one sexual encounter and thus the fleeting holiday experience entails no lessening of risk. The social peer group has the capacity to either both inhibit or promote protective sexual practices on holiday by providing peer support or sanctions for particular behaviour. Health promotion could seek to interact with these processes by highlighting concern about friends' sexual behaviour.

If tourists (in particular the most sexually active) have greater awareness of the more prevalent STDs (e.g. chlamydia, HPV (genital warts), HSV2 (genital herpes), this may alter the calculus of risk in favour of higher condom usage. Health promotion could gainfully focus upon the 'persistent' nature of such infections. Virological persistence could be contrasted to the fleeting temporary nature of the holiday sexual encounter.

Health promotion could highlight the potential effects of holiday sexual interaction for sexual partners. The notion of 'safe(r) sex' can include an element of concern/responsibility for sexual partners. In this sense, condom use on holiday could be promoted as an aspect of caring (by not risking undesirable consequences such as infection or pregnancy) for a partner, including of course one met on holiday. The translation of some of these foregoing implications into a practical strategy are discussed below in Chapter 14.

ACKNOWLEDGEMENTS

The authors would like to acknowledge with gratitude the research assistance of Elspeth Mathie, the feedback from Marlene Inman, and funding support from Torbay Health Authority.

REFERENCES

Abramson, P. R. (1983) 'Implications of the sexual system', in D. Byrne and W. A. Fisher (eds) *Adolescence, Sex and Contraception*, New Jersey: Lawrence Erlbaum Associates, 49–64.
Boissevain, J. (1979) 'Impact of tourism on a dependent island: Gozo, Malta', *Annals of Tourism Research* 6: 76–90.
Bourdieu, P. (1985) 'The social space and the genesis of groups', *Theory, Culture and Society* 14: 723–44.
British Tourist Authority (1990) *English Language Course Visitors to the UK 1990*, London: British Tourist Authority.
Cohen, E. (1971) 'Arab boys and tourist girls in a mixed Jewish–Arab community', *International Journal of Comparative Sociology* 14: 89–103.
—— (1974) 'Who is a Tourist? A conceptual clarification', *Sociological Review* 22: 527–55.
—— (1987) 'Sensuality and venality in Bangkok: The dynamics of cross-cultural mapping of prostitution', *Deviant Behaviour* 8: 223–4.
Crick, M. (1989) 'Representations of international tourism in the social sciences: sun, sex, sights, savings and servility', *Annual Review of Anthropology* 18: 307–44.
Critchlow, B. (1983) 'Blaming the booze: the attribution of responsibility in drunken behaviour', *Personality and Social Psychology Bulletin*, 9: 451–73.
—— (1986) 'The powers of John Barleycorn: beliefs about the effects of alcohol on social behaviour', *American Psychologist* 41: 751–64.
Crowe, L. C. and George, W. H. (1989) 'Alcohol and human sexuality: review and integration,' *Psychological Bulletin* 105, 3: 374–86.
Dann, G. M. S. (1981) 'Tourist motivation: an appraisal', *Annals of Tourism Research* 8, 2: 187–219.
Devon County Council Property Department (1990) *Devon Tourist Review, 1989*, Exeter: Devon County Council.
Ford, N. J. (1990a) *AIDS Awareness and Socio-Sexual Lifestyles of Young People in Torbay and District*, Exeter: Institute of Population Studies, University of Exeter.
—— (1990b) *A Comparative Analysis of The Socio-Sexual Lifestyles of Workers in the Tourism Industry with Other Young Residents in Devon and Cornwall*, Exeter: Institute of Population Studies, University of Exeter.
—— (1990c) *Psycho-Active Drug Use, Sexual Activity and AIDS Awareness of Young People in Bristol*, Exeter: Institute of Population Studies, University of Exeter.
—— (1991a) *Sex on Holiday: The HIV-Related Sexual Interaction of Young Tourists Visiting Torbay*, Exeter: Institute of Population Studies, University of Exeter.
—— (1991b) *The Socio-Sexual Lifestyles of Young People in the South-West of England*, Bristol: South Western Regional Health Authority.
—— (1993) 'The AIDS awareness and sexual behaviour of young people in the South-West of England', *Journal of Adolescence* 15: 393–413.

Ford, N. J. and Inman, M. (1992) 'Safer sex in tourist resorts', *World Health Forum* 13: 77–80.
Gennep, A. van (1960) [first published 1908] *The Rites of Passage*, London: Routledge and Kegan Paul.
Health Education Authority (1989) *Guide to a Healthy Sex Life*, London: Health Education Authority.
Iso-Ahola, S. E. (1984) 'Social psychological foundations of leisure and resultant implications for leisure counselling', in E. T. Dowd (ed.) *Leisure Counselling*, Springfield, Illinois: Charles C. Thomas, 97–125.
MacAndrew, C. and Edgerton, R. B. (1969) *Drunken Comportment*, Chicago: Aldine.
MacCannell, D. (1976) *The Tourist: A New Theory of the Leisure Class*, New York: Shocken Books.
—— (1992) *Empty Meeting Grounds: The Tourist Papers*, London: Routledge.
Mannell, R. C. and Iso-Ahola, S. E. (1987) 'Psychological nature of leisure and tourist experience', *Annals of Tourism Research* 14: 314–31.
Mathieson, A. and Wall, G. (1982) *Tourism: Economic, Physical and Social Impacts*, Harlow: Longman.
Panos (1990) *AIDS, The Third Epidemic*, London: Panos.
Pasini, W. (ed.) (1990) *Tourist Health: Proceedings of the Second International Conference on Tourist Health*, Rimini: WHO Collaborating Centre for Tourist Health.
Pearce, P. L. (1982) *The Social Psychology of Tourist Behaviour*, Oxford: Pergamon Press.
—— (1993) 'Fundamentals of tourist motivation', in D. G. Pearce and R. Butler (eds) *Tourism Research: Critiques and Challenges*, London: Routledge, 113–34.
Price, J. A. and Price, J. H. (1983) 'Alcohol and sexual functioning: a review', *Advances in Alcohol and Substance Abuse* 2: 43–56.
Reinarman, C. and Leigh, B. C. (1987) 'Culture, cognition, and disinhibition: notes on sexuality and alcohol in the age of AIDS', *Contemporary Drug Problems*, Fall: 387–91.
Ryan, C. (1991) *Recreational Tourism*, London: Routledge.
Schachter, S. (1964) 'The interaction of cognitive and physiological determinants of emotional states', in L. Berkowitz (ed.) *Advances in Experimental Social Psychology*, New York: Academic Press.
Shaw, G., Greenwood, J. and Williams, A. (1991) 'The United Kingdom: market responses and public policy', in A. Williams and G. Shaw (eds) *Tourism and Economic Development: Western European Experiences*, London: Belhaven 2nd edn.
Shields, R. (1990) 'The system of pleasure: liminality and the carnivalesque at Brighton,' *Theory, Culture and Society* 7: 39–72.
Turner, L. and Ash, J. (1975) *The Golden Hordes: International Tourism and the Leisure Periphery*, London: Constable.
Turner, V. (1979) *Process Performance and Pilgrimage: a Study in Comparative Symbology*, New Delhi: Concept.

Van der Velde, F. W., Hooykas, C. and Pligt, J. van der (1992) 'Risk perception and behaviour: pessimism, realism and optimism and AIDS-related health behaviour', *Psychology and Health* 6: 23–38.

Wereld, O. (1979) 'Sex tourism in Thailand', *ISIS International Bulletin*, 13: 9–12.

Williams, A., Greenwood, J. and Shaw, G. (1991) *Cornwall Tourist Visitor Survey 1990*, Exeter: Tourism Research Group, University of Exeter.

Worm, A.-M., and Lillelund, H. (1988) 'Use of condoms and sexual behaviour of young tourists in Copenhagen', *Ugeskr Laeger*, 150: 1156–8.

Youth Mobility and Health Working Group (1990) *Youth Mobility and Health*, Rimini: WHO Collaborating Centre for Tourist Health.

Chapter 9

Tourism prostitution
The control and health implications of sex tourism in South-East Asia and Australia

C. Michael Hall

INTRODUCTION

People's behaviour is often different when they are away from home and despite the threat of HIV/AIDS, some people are likely to relax their normal codes of sexual or drug using behaviour while travelling.
(Commonwealth Department of Health, Housing, Local Government and Community Services 1992: 2)

Sex tourism is one of the most emotive issues in the study of tourism and health. Sex tourism, otherwise known as tourism prostitution, is tourism where the main purpose or motivation is to consummate commercial sexual relations (Hall 1992). Sex tourism has been given increasing media exposure in recent years, with reports usually focusing on tourism prostitution in Thailand or the Philippines. Although the campaign against child prostitution by the Bangkok-based End Child Prostitution in Asian Tourism (ECPAT) has started to influence public opinion, much of the recent attention given by commercial media to sex tourism has not arisen because of any new-found concern for the disempowering nature of tourism prostitution, but because of the spread of AIDS and the potential for international HIV transmission through the interregional movements of sex-oriented tourists (Karel and Robey 1988; Wood 1988; De Schryver and Meheus 1989; Ford and Koetsawang 1991; Hall 1994). It is currently estimated that there are 2.5 million people in the South and South-East Asian region who are HIV positive. This figure is expected to increase by 1 million a year by the end of the decade (*Canberra Times* 1993a).

Sex tourism comprises a series of linkages that 'can be conceptualised as one between a legally marginalised form of commoditisation (sexual services) within a national industry (entertainment), essentially dependent on, but with a dynamic function in, an international industry (travel)' (Thanh-Dam 1983: 544). In South-East Asia the institutionalisation of sex tourism commenced with American and Japanese militarism and has since become systematised into a major item of inbound travel to the region by recreational tourists. Prostitution is technically illegal in many South-East Asian countries, but the law is poorly enforced, because of official corruption, entrenched cultural values, organised crime, and the income and foreign exchange it generates.

Sex tourism is a major component of international travel to South-East Asia and is a significant source of foreign exchange for countries such as the Philippines and Thailand. Although exact figures are impossible to obtain, one estimate in 1985 was that 'between 70 and 80 per cent of male tourists who travel from Japan, the United States, Australia, and Western Europe to Asia do so solely for the purpose of sexual entertainment' (Gay 1985: 34). While such an estimate is almost certainly on the high side, especially given contemporary concerns over AIDS, it is likely that sexual entertainment is still a major motivating factor for many male travellers to a number of destinations within South-East Asia.

The chapter is divided into three main sections. The first provides a brief account of sex tourism in South-East Asia. It will be argued that government concerns surrounding sex tourism have only grown because of the health implications rather than social or moral concerns. It will further be noted that the vast majority of research lies on the supply of the sex tourism product rather than the demand. However, an attempt will be made to account for some of the demand for sex tourism. This first section will therefore illustrate the nature, trends and health impacts of sex tourism and the risk-taking behaviour of travellers. The second section will discuss attempts to control sex tourism in terms of the demand and supply side of tourism prostitution. Specific reference will be made to the attempts of governments to control tourism prostitution through health checks and formal legal procedures. Thailand will be used to illustrate the difficulties of controlling the supply side. From the demand side, the utility of educative programmes on AIDS and STDs and legislative action will be discussed, with a specific case study of the Australian efforts to promote safe sex for tourists. The final section will attempt to integrate the various dimensions and issues which surround sex tourism and health. It will be argued that moral and religious concerns have made education campaigns of travellers and prostitutes extremely difficult in many areas where sex tourism exists. However, unless educational campaigns are supported by government in conjunction with a corresponding legalisation of prostitution activities, it would seem likely that the spread of STDs and HIV infection will be extremely difficult to prevent, with corresponding major health, social and economic problems in host and guest countries alike.

SEX TOURISM IN SOUTH-EAST ASIA

Sex has long been recognised as a component of travel motivations. Romantic images fill many tourist brochures, and as Matthews (1978: 51) has observed: 'metropolitan tourists leave their morals and manners at home when visiting sun spots abroad. They seek exotic and erotic vacations far away from the social constrictions of home.' The psychological changes that many tourists undergo during the various stages of the travel process undoubtedly influence tourist behaviour in many locations. Many tourists behave differently than they would otherwise do at home, with such behaviour being an essential element of the recreational aspects of the tourist experience and the promotion of certain tourist products. Although such changes of behaviour may help explain 'casual' encounters between tourists and members of the local community (Ford 1991), including sex workers, it does not explain the large amount of organised travel to South-East Asia specifically for sexual purposes.

No single reason can explain why tourists travel explicitly for sex with prostitutes. However, a number of related reasons can be offered. First, the promotional images associated with tourism which portray Asian women as sensual and submissive may act to reinforce the tourist's complete control over the prostitute's body obtained by purchase (Hall 1994). For example, Filipino women are represented in the literature of penpal clubs and mail-order bride businesses as 'meek, docile, submissive, home oriented and having tremendous capacities in bed' (Philippine Women's Research Collective 1985: 19) and many Australian males have sought Filipino women through these routes. Similarly, in a defiant letter to the *Bangkok Post* in 1992 'from an Englishman who signed himself "Sex-tourist", the man explained that he came to Thailand, and would continue to come, because the girls are prettier here, more amenable, and less aggressive than their Western counterparts' (Hillmore 1992: 17). A second reason is a search for sexual novelty, which may include the desire for sex with a person of a different race, child sex, or sex away from the domestic environment. Third, is the value placed in some cultures on the taking of virginity. Fourth, in the case of the 'growing preference for children [is] the fatally mistaken belief that they are less likely to be carrying sexually transmitted diseases, particularly AIDS' (Ansley 1993a: 3). Fifth, is a desire for sex and a 'good time' away from the bounds of conventional behaviour. Most fundamentally, however, the motivations for sex tourism are an outcome of a desire on the part of a tourist for self-gratifying erotic power through the control of another's body. Therefore, sex tourism is not simply about sex, but is a response to the complex interaction of gender, class, cultural, sexual and power relations in both the tourist's and the sex worker's society which sanctions the commodification of certain human relationships.

While an understanding of the motivations of sex tourists is important for analysing the demand side of the sex tourism equation, it is clearly also important to realise that a certain set of social, economic, gender and power relations must also exist in the host country to allow tourism prostitution to flourish. Sex tourism in South-East Asia can be characterised as having developed through four distinct stages (Hall 1992). The first stage is that of indigenous prostitution within a patriarchal society in which women are already subject to concubinage and bonded prostitution. For example, in the case of Thailand, Phongpaichit (1982) traced the historical origins of prostitution to a culture of male dominance in which polygamy and concubinage played a significant role. The second stage is that of economic colonialism and militarisation, in which prostitution is a formalised mechanism of dominance and a means of meeting the sexual needs of occupation forces: for example, the American presence in Taiwan and Korea following the Korean War and in the Philippines and Thailand during and following the Vietnamese War. The commoditisation of sexual relations is marked in the third stage by the gradual substitution of overseas military forces by international tourists. Hall (1992) argued that during this third stage, sex tourism may become a formal mechanism by which authoritarian governments can further national economic goals. The fourth, and current, stage for most of the nations of South-East Asia is that of newly industrialised nation status. Despite the increased material standard of living in many areas, sex tourism is still widespread. Indeed, prostitutes tend to originate in economically marginal areas where incomes and standards of living are lowest. Therefore, the economic relationship between the newly industrialised nations of South-East Asia and the developed world may find itself replicated in the economic power differential between the buyer and the seller of tourism prostitution (Graburn 1983).

CONTROLLING THE SUPPLY OF TOURISM PROSTITUTION: THE SITUATION IN THAILAND

> Thailand's main campaigner against AIDS, Government Minister Mechai Viravaidhya, has developed a showman's technique to emphasise the problem facing his country. He points to a beautiful young dancer and sings her praises and beauty. Then he tells his audience that there is a good chance she will die of AIDS.
>
> (Hillmore 1992: 17)

In few other countries around the world has tourist motivation been so linked with sex as it has been with travel to Thailand. Although concubinage and a patriarchal society have led to a situation in which prostitution is an integral part of Thai sexual culture, tourism has been inextricably linked to its growth since the early 1960s. Although exact numbers of prostitutes are virtually impossible to ascertain, it has been estimated that in 1957 there were 20,000 prostitutes, 400,000 by 1964, and 500,000 to 1 million prostitutes in the early 1980s (Phongpaichit 1982; Taylor 1984; Hong 1985). Richter placed the number of prostitutes in Thailand ...

> at one million, which would mean that at any given time almost 4 per cent of Thailand's female population is involved. That does not include all those women who have been prostitutes and have left this short-lived career, nor does it number all the men and boys now a part of the industry.
>
> (Richter 1989: 86)

The majority of Thai commercial sex workers come from the economically marginal north and north-east of the country and are often from ethnic minorities (Phongpaichit 1982). At both an individual and a family level, involvement in the commercial sex industry by young girls is typically a result of its economic attraction. However, it should be noted that whereas some individuals freely engage in the sex industry in order to meet specific financial needs, there is a growing body of evidence that in some northern villages 'involvement in the commercial sex industry is perceived as a legitimate means of addressing the rural family's deepening indebtedness and where saving can actually occur, offers opportunities for economic advancement' (Ford and Koetsawang 1991: 409).

Despite much of the publicity surrounding Thailand's sex industry, it must be recognised that the many Thai prostitutes service local clientele rather than the traveller. Even so, sex tourism has been a major income generator for Thailand, although in recent years the economic benefits have become increasingly questioned because of the damage that sex tourism has done to Thailand's image, its social impacts on the sex workers and their families, and the potential spread of STDs and AIDS (Cohen 1988; Richter 1989; Hall 1992).

In 1989 the Thai Public Health Ministry actively started campaigning against prostitution and the promotion of Thailand as a sex tour destination (Hall 1994). The primary reason for the campaign was the recognition that sexually transmitted diseases such as AIDS could pose major problems for Thailand's rapidly growing tourism industry and for the Thai economy in general. For example, the Asian Development Bank has calculated that:

> through the death and disablement of AIDS sufferers – usually from the economically productive 20–40 age group – Thailand ... had lost almost $3 billion so far and by 2000 this would rise to $3.5 billion a year if the disease went unchecked.
>
> (*Canberra Times* 1993a: 8).

A Thai Health Ministry survey of HIV/AIDS in Thailand's sex industry indicated that about 3,000 sex workers were infected with HIV, while a World Health Organisation report estimated that the number of infected people in Thailand was between 45,000 and 50,000, compared with the official figure of 14,000 (Corben 1990). As of 15 November 1990, official figures indicated that there had been 24,141 cases of AIDS, AIDS-related complex and HIV reported in Thailand (Ford and Koetsawang 1991). In tourist centres such as Chiang Mai, tests have suggested that one of every two prostitutes in the region carries the virus (Robinson 1989), while it has also been estimated that as many as 70 per cent of female commercial sex workers in Thailand have some form of STD (Ford and Koetsawang 1991).

The concern for the manner in which the AIDS dimension of sex tourism was seen to be harming the country's tourism industry is well indicated in the comments of the Thai Deputy Public Health Minister, Suthas Ngernmuen:

> Thailand's profitable tourism industry has been an inhibiting factor in promoting AIDS awareness ... More than two-thirds of the overseas visitors entering Thailand are single men, and medical officials avoided publicising the appalling AIDS statistics for fear of damaging the country's healthy tourist business ... But it is long past time for the government to change Thailand's image as a sexual paradise. We should promote tourism in more appropriate ways, and campaign more against AIDS.
>
> (cited in Robinson 1989: 11)

The Thai government has considered a number of options to curb the spread of AIDS, including operating testing programmes for certain visitors, and distributing condoms in hotels or at the airport (Hall 1994). Part of the AIDS programme includes 'rehabilitating' and skilling prostitutes, while the Defence Ministry is providing an AIDS education programme for servicemen. The Public Health Ministry has proposed the issuing of health cards to brothel workers, which would indicate the holder's personal background and the results of tests conducted for sexually transmitted diseases, including AIDS (Corben 1990). The issuance of three-monthly health cards is only an indirect measure of controlling AIDS and does relatively little to deter the sex tourist. Instead health cards may only further attract visitors to certain brothels or locations and may also allow the possibility of corruption in order to obtain cards which give workers in the sex industry clean bills of health. In addition, such measures may fail to control the more informal elements of the Thai sex industry. Therefore, in the longer-term, if the Thai government is serious about controlling AIDS, major emphasis has to be given to replacing Thailand's image as a sex tour destination and in providing alternative economic and social support mechanisms for those who use prostitution as a means of employment (Hall 1994). However, as Corben (1990: 9) reported: 'tourism authorities in Thailand are extremely sensitive to reports about sex activities and the rising incidence of AIDS and other sexually transmitted diseases in Thailand'. For example, after a damning examination of the sex trade and the major role it plays in Thailand's tourism industry by the *Far Eastern Economic Review*, the Governor of the Tourism Authority of Thailand (TAT), Dharmnoon Prachuabmoh, attacked the *Review* and argued that 'Any effective measures adopted by the Thai government to curb the spread of AIDS would be fine with us. It is the welfare of the Thais, not the tourist dollar, that must come first' (Corben 1990: 9).

The AIDS scare has already had an impact on some Thai tourist destinations. Visitor arrivals by road from Malaysia were estimated to have dropped by over half for most of 1989 at the southern town of Hat Yai, renowned for its bars and massage parlours (Asia Travel Trade 1989, 1990). Similarly, AIDS has tarnished the image of Pattaya and this, associated with environmental problems, is believed to have contributed to a sharp decline in the number of visitors to the resort area (Hillmore 1992; Hall 1994). According to Panga Wattanakul, the President of the Pattaya Hotels Association: 'although there had been a 13 per cent increase last year in the number of tourists coming to Thailand, there had been a decrease of 30 per cent in each of the past two years [in visitors to Pattaya]' (cited in *Asia Travel Trade* 1990: 56).

In order to attract more female tourists and counteract Thailand's image of sex tourism and AIDS, the Chairman of the Tourism Authority of Thailand and a leading anti-AIDS campaigner, Minister Mechai Viravaidhya, planned a Women's Visit Thailand year campaign in 1992. According to the Minister:

> We want women to come particularly from countries where some of their men have come here on sex tours'. . . . We want them to see what their men get up to and how they have exploited uneducated women and children. We want their women to come and see the good Thai women and encourage Thai women to stand up to the brutality and disrespect they have suffered. More action must come from Thai women them-

selves, otherwise the country will still be seen as the brothel of the world.

(Kelly 1991: 44)

The Minister's stance has led him to be severely criticised by some members of the tourism industry and to an accusation of a conflict of roles (Hail 1992). It is readily apparent that some sections of Thailand's tourism industry are still keen to promote sex tourism because of its financial benefits. Indeed, authorities are aware that they will be unable to curb AIDS by closing down the sex industry as it an integral component of Thai economy and society. Therefore, Minister Viravaidhya has embarked on the twin policy of education and control. Education is encouraged by the Minister, who has adopted a high public profile on AIDS issues and the importance of condom use. Control has been maintained by the Minister's targeting of brothel owners in order to ensure that they force clients to use condoms: 'The owners being warned that if one of their girls receives medical treatment for a sexually transmitted disease, the brothel will be closed for a day. The second offence will close the establishment for a week' (Hillmore 1992: 17). Nevertheless, while such efforts are laudable, the use of condoms does not appear to be widespread among prostitutes who are working in lower-class brothels or who are freelancing in order to supplement their incomes. Many of the prostitutes are illiterate and cannot read the AIDS-prevention brochures. In addition, many of the sex workers appear somewhat philosophical about catching AIDS. The Buddhist belief in reincarnation has meant that workers believe that if they die of AIDS they will be born again, and may have a better working life (Hillmore 1992). Indeed, Ford and Koetsawang (1991: 407) observe that 'perception of the potential risk of HIV infection may be influenced by the folk belief in "*siang duang*", which translates as "taking your fate"'.

The long-term health implications, through the spread of AIDS and other STDs, and the social impacts of sex tourism are enormous and represent a potentially severe threat to Thailand's development programme. In order to meet the challenge of AIDS to the Thai society and economy, the government is faced with having to overcome official corruption and deep-rooted cultural attitudes towards sex and the role of women. Such a task will not be easy, but unless the government takes firm and decisive action not only will the broader tourism industry be damaged, particularly that geared towards the family market, but also the human base of Thai economic development.

CONTROLLING THE DEMAND FOR TOURISM PROSTITUTION: THE SITUATION IN AUSTRALIA

As in the supply side of sex services to tourists, education is a key element in controlling demand. Education has been a key component of Australia's national HIV/AIDS strategy, which has been highly regarded internationally as a model HIV/AIDS campaign (Commonwealth Department of Health, Housing, Local Government and Community Services [DHHCS] 1993). The major goals of the National Strategy are to eliminate transmission of HIV and to minimise the personal and social impacts of HIV/AIDS.

In 1991–2 the DHHCS implemented a campaign aimed at Australians travelling overseas, domestic travellers, and tourists visiting Australia, with Aus.$1,313 million (or 2.21 per cent of total Commonwealth programmes) and matched funding programme expenditure on travellers as a primary target group in the national HIV/AIDS strategy (National Evaluation Steering Committee 1992: 29). The campaign arose because of:

> the increasing incidence of STDs amongst heterosexual men returning from South-East Asia and the discovery of HIV infection amongst travellers returning to Australia . . . travellers need targeting to reinforce the risks of unprotected sex and needle use, as well as risks of infection through other means such as unsecured blood supplies or high levels of infection amongst sex workers in some countries.
> (Commonwealth Department of Health, Housing, Local Government and Community Services 1993: 28)

The campaign has utilised a series of widely distributed brochures and posters, a video, the inclusion of HIV information on airline tickets, and advertising in airport toilets. According to the National Evaluation Steering Committee (1992: 57), 'The preliminary evaluation indicates that the campaign has been well received, with reasonably high levels of recall by travellers.'

The national campaign is not primarily targeted at those travellers who are normally categorised as sex tourists (i.e. those who participate in formally organised sex tours to South-East Asia).

Instead the campaign is geared towards the recreational traveller. The necessity for such a campaign is illustrated by the results of a study of planned sexual behaviour of young Australian visitors to Thailand (Mulhall et al. 1993). In a sample of 213 participants who were travelling to Thailand without a spouse or partner, only 34 per cent said they had no plans to have sex, while 57 per cent said they would 'definitely' have sex or would do so 'depending on who they met'. The type of partner likely to be chosen included: fellow Australians (58 per cent), fellow travellers of other nationalities (70 per cent), Thai nationals (46 per cent), 'bar girls' (14 per cent) and others (15 per cent). There was a significant difference in the intentions of men and women to have sex: 17 per cent more men than women reported planning or hoping to have sex whereas 34 per cent more women than men answered 'no' to planning or hoping to have sex. Eighteen per cent more men than women answered 'depends' on planning or hoping to have sex. Of the 194 participants who answered the question on condom use, 82 per cent said they would use condoms 100 per cent of the time (Mulhall et al. 1993).

More worrying findings have emerged from studies of German tourists in the company of Thai prostitutes (Kleiber 1991) and a study of returning male travellers from South-East Asia who visited an STD clinic in Melbourne, Australia (Rowbottom 1991). In the German study only 28 per cent of all subjects (152) used condoms regularly, while in the Australian study there was also a low frequency of condom use (28 per cent). In addition, both studies found the number of sex partners in Thailand to be reasonably high with 25 per cent of the Australians and 12 per cent of the Germans having more than five partners during their stay in Thailand. The results from these studies reinforce the need for a broad educational campaign in the effort to reduce the spread of HIV/AIDS by travellers. As Mulhall et al. (1993: 535) observed:

> It is probable that the distinction between a person who has sex while travelling, and a 'sex tourist', is not only difficult and arbitrary, but also potentially misleading. Certainly, men do travel to Thailand specifically for the purpose of sex, but they are a difficult group to identify ... since 'sex tours' are usually officially banned by tourist organisations.
>
> (*Bangkok Post* 1989)

Given the sexual risk-taking behaviour by tourists to Thailand and other regions of South-East Asia, traveller education campaigns are an essential element in reducing the spread of HIV/AIDS and other STDs. Nevertheless, concerns have arisen in some quarters that 'the Government must not be seen to be condoning sex tourism in its educative approach to safe sex practices of tourists' (McMenamin 1993: 20). Therefore, it is perhaps not surprising that legislative means are also being considered in an attempt to reduce the impacts of organised sex tourism, and child sex tourism in particular.

Legislative control of child sex tourism

Child prostitution is gravest where poverty is most profound.
(Symanski 1981: 61)

Child prostitution is a major social and health problem in South-East Asia. Tourism is intimately related with child prostitution, with children being proffered for tourists from Europe, Australia, New Zealand, the United States and wealthier Asian countries such as Japan. According to the *New Zealand Herald*:

> large numbers of Australian paedophiles were travelling to Asia for sex with children so that they could avoid the risks of being identified and charged at home. In many cases the men were on well-organised package tours aimed specifically at paedophiles.
> (*New Zealand Herald* 1993a: 12)

Although exact numbers of paedophiles travelling for reasons of child sex are extremely difficult to quantify, Nick Smith, a member of the New Zealand parliament, has reported that about 200 New Zealanders a week were involved in child sex in Asia, with many New Zealanders participating in Australian tours (*New Zealand Herald* 1993b).

Australian Federal and State Attorneys-General agreed in June 1993 to frame new laws to enable prosecution of Australians who travel abroad to have sex with children, and those Australians who encourage or arrange for that to happen (Ansley 1993a). According to the Attorney-General of New South Wales, Mr John Hannaford,

If they [Australian tourists] are convicted on these sex tours they could lose their passports and not be allowed to travel ... All of the states will be moving to introduce mutually consistent legislation to make sure this field is completely covered and appropriate criminal sanctions will be introduced.

(*Canberra Times* 1993b: 16)

Germany and Sweden are also attempting to use legislative means to curb child sex tourism. Nevertheless, there are major difficulties in implementing national legislation on child sex in terms of extraterritorial jurisdiction and the obtaining of evidence from minors abroad. However, according to the Australian Attorney-General, Mr Michael Lavarch, 'Proof is the difficulty but the Australian Federal Police does have its presence in a number of these countries – we have co-operation, for instance, in drug cases already' (*Canberra Times* 1993b: 16).

This legislation, the Crimes (Child Sex Tourism) Amendment Bill, is due to be presented to federal parliament early in 1994. The bill is designed to dissuade Australians from participating in child sex tourism. Once enacted, the law will make it an offence in Australia for an Australian citizen to have sex with a child overseas, and the organisation of sex tours will be actionable. The law will provide for jail terms of up to seventeen years for having sex with a child under 12, and up to fourteen years' jail for sex with a child between 12 and 16. Australians convicted of doing indecencies upon, or in the presence of, children outside Australia will face jail terms of up to twelve years. Any Australian convicted of inciting, organising or profiting from child sex tourism inside or outside Australia could be jailed for up to ten years. The same week that legislation appears, a special mutual-assistance treaty between Australia and the Philippines will come into effect to enable the exchange of information between the two countries on Australian paedophiles. A similar treaty together with an extradition treaty is currently being negotiated between Australia and Thailand (Cook 1993; *New Zealand Herald* 1993a).

The New Zealand government announced in July 1993 that it would consider new laws to prosecute New Zealand paedophiles who travel to Asia to have sex with children. The government acted in response to a series of reports on child prostitution at the first World Congress on Family Law and Children's Rights, held in Sydney. The New Zealand Minister for Justice, Mr Doug Graham, after previously

> informing the Bangkok-based organisation End Child Prostitution in Asian Tourism that such laws were 'impossible', apparently changed his view after the Australian Attorneys-General agreed to new legislation that will create a federal offence of initiating, organising or profiting from child sex tourism or other forms of sexual exploitation of children.
> (Ansley 1993b: 1)

In addition to legislation, New Zealand was also requested to tie foreign aid to compliance with the United Nations' Convention on the Rights of the Child, to support a new international protocol on the sexual exploitation and abuse of children, and to support calls for sex tourism to be declared an international crime on the same level as hijacking and piracy (Ansley 1993c).

A campaign against child sex tourism organised by ECPAT was launched in New Zealand on 20 November 1993. However, according to *New Zealand Travel Trade* (1993: 1), 'outbound tourism interests appear to be turning their backs' on the national campaign, probably for fear of creating further negative images of the tourism industry.

Despite the Department of Justice's interest in the Australian laws on making it a crime for Australian citizens to have sex with children overseas, New Zealand has held off introducing legislation in order to witness the Australian experience, although they have commenced collecting information on paedophiles who travel overseas for sex with children (*New Zealand Herald* 1993b). As the New Zealand Commissioner for Police stated: 'I think most countries believe this sort of behaviour should not be allowed ... The question is, how do you stop it?' (*New Zealand Herald* 1993c: 4).

CONCLUSION

> The rapid global spread of the AIDS virus (HIV) can be directly linked to the mobility and behaviour of modern travellers.
> (Commonwealth Department of Health, Housing, Local Government and Community Services 1992: 2)

As this chapter has demonstrated, control of the possibility of HIV transmission to and from tourists travelling specifically for sexual relationships must be undertaken by dealing with both the supply and demand elements of the sex tourism equation. In the case of Thailand, control is best undertaken in the short-term through educative programmes, while in the longer-term prostitution can only adequately be managed if consideration is given to the cultural, economic and gendered nature of tourism prostitution. An understanding of issues of economic marginalisation and economic development are critical to 'solving' the issue of why women and, increasingly, children and some young men turn to, or are forced into, prostitution. In addition, despite some opposition from vested interests within the Thai tourism industry, firmer measures are being undertaken by government to control and regulate sex tourism (Richter 1989). However, while such measures are valuable, the problem remains that much of the sex tourism 'industry' is informal and casual in nature, which by definition makes government regulation extremely difficult. Therefore, an educational campaign on the transmission of HIV/AIDS to all sections of the Thai community is essential to control the spread of AIDS.

A broad-based educational campaign is also an essential element of the Australian response to the health challenges posed by HIV/AIDS. As part of the national HIV/AIDS strategy, Australian health authorities have specifically targeted inbound and outbound travellers with AIDS information. Given the evidence of the current risk-taking behaviour of Australian tourists while in Thailand, such measures appear vital in reducing the risk of HIV/AIDS transmission. As Mulhall *et al.* concluded:

> while 'sex tourists' should be specifically targeted if possible, particularly as they may act as 'core-transmitters' of STDs and HIV, they are usually difficult to identify. Therefore, it is vital that all sexually active persons should be specifically advised of the dangers of casual sex and encouraged to take and use condoms.
>
> (Mulhall *et al.* 1993: 535)

Australia is also seeking to apply legislative measures to control child sex tourism. Nevertheless, the difficulties in applying Australian laws overseas may mean that legal measures will only be a last resort in curbing sex tourism. However, the passing of such measures and accompanying agreements with the Thai and Philippine governments will at least mean that the previous logic, found in the intersection of social values and economic interests for pursuing the sex worker rather than the clients, is at last starting to be overcome (Kaplan 1977).

International travel and the spread of HIV/AIDS are inseparable. Control of HIV/AIDS transmission can only be effective if management regimes take into account the supply and demand aspects of 'sex tourism' and its international dimensions. Most fundamentally, however, control requires, in the short-term, effective education programmes that encourage appropriate safe-sex practices and, in the longer-term, both educative campaigns that promote attitudinal change and economic development programmes which can change the material basis for tourism prostitution. Such a task will not be easy. It was ironic that on the day this chapter was completed the *Canberra Times* (1993a) ran an editorial on the enormous impact that AIDS has had on Australia and the Asia–Pacific region and noting the need for a co-ordinated attack on AIDS. The travel pages of the same newspaper featured a story on the attractions of Bangkok, highlighting the attractions of Patpong Road, 'where you can choose any vice' (Uhlmann 1993: 25). Education, as they say, begins at home.

ACKNOWLEDGEMENTS

The author would like to acknowledge with gratitude the assistance of Sandra Haywood, Alison de Kleuver of the Commonwealth Department of Health, Housing, Local Government and Community Services, Ron James and Brenda Rudkin in the preparation of this chapter.

REFERENCES

Ansley, G. (1993a) 'The child sex trade: grappling a monster', *New Zealand Herald*, 10 July, Section 2: 3.
—— (1993b) 'NZ law likely on child sex tours', *New Zealand Herald*, 6 July, Section 1: 1.
—— (1993c) 'NZ urged to act on child sex trade', *New Zealand Herald*, 9 July, Section 1: 5.
Asia Travel Trade (1989) 'Tourism still top earner although mid-year growth off,' 21, October: 51–3.
—— (1990) 'AIDS problem menaces tourism', 22 November: 56–7.
Bangkok Post (1989) 'TAT [Tourism Authority of Thailand] to ban support for UK "sex tour" operators', 18 August: 24.

Canberra Times (1993a) 'Regional attack on AIDS commendable', 5 December: 8.
—— (1993b) 'Sex tourists targeted', 5 November: 16.
Cohen, E. (1988) 'Tourism and AIDS in Thailand', *Annals of Tourism Research* 15: 467–88.
Commonwealth Department of Health, Housing, Local Government and Community Services (1992) *Travel Safe: An HIV/AIDS Education Campaign for Travellers*, Canberra: AIDS/Communicable Diseases Unit, Department of Health, Housing, Local Government and Community Services.
—— (1993) *National AIDS Campaign 1986–1992*, Canberra: Submission by AIDS/Communicable Diseases Branch for the Evaluation Panel Review of National HIV/AIDS Programs, Department of Health, Housing, Local Government and Community Services.
Cook, M. (1993) 'Cry freedom', *Good Weekend: The Sydney Morning Herald Magazine*, 7 November: 12–20.
Corben, R. (1990) 'Thailand takes another step to curb AIDS', *Asia Travel Trade*, 22, June: 7–9.
De Schryver, A. and Meheus, A. (1989) 'International travel and sexually transmitted diseases', *World Health Statistics Quarterly* 42: 90–9.
Ford, N. (1991) *Sex on Holiday: The HIV-Related Sexual Interaction of Young Tourists Visiting Torbay*, Exeter: Institute of Population Studies, University of Exeter.
Ford, N. and Koetsawang, S. (1991) 'The socio-cultural context of the transmission of HIV in Thailand', *Social Science and Medicine* 33, 4: 405–14.
Gay, J. (1985) 'The patriotic prostitute', *The Progressive* 49, 3: 34–6.
Graburn, N. (1983) 'Tourism and prostitution', *Annals of Tourism Research* 10: 437–56.
Hail, J. (1992) 'Thailand: a new approach', *Asia Travel Trade* 23, May: 24–31.
Hall, C. M. (1992) 'Sex tourism in South-East Asia', in D. Harrison (ed.) *Tourism and the Less Developed Countries*, London: Bellhaven, 64–74.
—— (1994) 'Nature and implications of sex tourism in South-East Asia', in V. Kinnaird and D. R. Hall (eds) *Tourism and Gender* Chichester: Wiley, 142–63.
Hillmore, P. (1992) 'Thailand tries to clean up its sex image', *The Press*, 1 April: 17.
Hong, E. (1985) *See the Third World While it Lasts*, Penang: Consumers Association of Penang.
Kaplan, J. (1977) 'The Edward G. Donley Memorial Lecture: non-victim crime and the regulation of prostitution', *West Virginia Law Review* 79: 593–606.
Karel, S. G. and Robey, B. (1988) 'AIDS in Asia and the Pacific', *Asian Pacific Population Forum* 2: 1–14 and 18–29.
Kelly, N. (1991) 'Counting the cost', *Far Eastern Economic Review*, 18 July: 44.

Kleiber, D. (1991) 'AIDS und (sex-)tourismus', in *AIDS und tourismus*, Niedersächsisches Sozialministerium, Edition AIDS 11, Hannover: 1–28.

Matthews, H. G. (1978) *International Tourism: a Political and Social Analysis*, Cambridge: Schenkman Publishing Company.

McMenamin, B. (1993) 'Sex tours of Asia breed corruption (Letter to the editor from national coordinator, End Child Prostitution in Asian Tourism (ECPAT) Australia)', *The Age*, 23 October: 20.

Mulhall, B. P., Hu, M., Thompson, M., Lil, F., Lupton, D., Mills, D., Maund, M., Cass, R. and Millar, D. (1993) 'Planned sexual behaviour of young Australian visitors to Thailand', *Medical Journal of Australia* 158, 8: 530–5.

National Evaluation Steering Committee (1992) *Report of the Evaluation of the National HIV/AIDS Strategy*, Canberra: Report to the Minister for Health, Housing and Community Services and the Intergovernmental Committee on AIDS by the National Evaluation Steering Committee, Australian Government Publishing Service.

New Zealand Herald (1993a) 'Child-sex trips will soon earn jail terms', 29 November, Section 1: 12.

—— (1993b) 'Police eyes on child sex travellers', 23 November, Section 1: 26.

—— (1993c) 'Quick law unlikely on child sex tourism', 16 November, Section 1: 4.

New Zealand Travel Trade (1993) 'Industry ignores child sex tourism', 21, 20: 1.

Philippine Women's Research Collective (1985) *Filipinas for Sale: an Alternative Philippine Report on Women and Tourism*, Quezan City: Philippine Women's Research Collective.

Phongpaichit, P. (1982) *From Peasant Girls to Bangkok Masseuses*, Geneva: International Labour Organisation.

Richter, L. K. (1989) *The Politics of Tourism in Asia*, Honolulu: University of Hawaii Press.

Robinson, G. (1989) 'AIDS fear triggers Thai action', *Asia Travel Trade* 21, September: 11.

Rowbottom, J. (1991) 'Risks taken by Australian men having sex in South-East Asia, *Venereology* 4: 56–9.

Symanski, R. (1981) *The Immoral Landscape: Female Prostitution in Western Societies*, Toronto: Butterworths.

Taylor, D. (1984) 'Cheap thrills', *New Internationalist* 142: 14.

Thanh-Dam, T. (1983) 'The dynamics of sex-tourism: the cases of South-East Asia', *Development and Change* 14, 4: 533–53.

Uhlmann, A. (1993) 'You need at least three nights to see Bangkok', *Canberra Times*, 5 December: 25.

Wood, W. B. (1988) 'AIDS North and South: Diffusion patterns of a global epidemic and a research agenda for geographers', *Professional Geographer* 40: 266–79.

Part III

Tourism and health promotion

Chapter 10
Health tourism
A business opportunity approach
Eric Laws

INTRODUCTION

Health tourism is the term which has been applied to the industry catering for combined health and tourism motivations. The precursor of the World Tourist Organisation, the International Union of Tourist Organisations, identified it as the 'provision of health facilities utilising the natural resources of a country, in particular water and climate' (IUOTO 1973: 7). Hall (1992) regarded health tourism as the primary motivator for specific forms of special-interest tourism. Goodrich and Goodrich (1987) have defined health tourism as the promotion by a tourist destination of its health care facilities and services. Underpinning the proliferation of health tourism services offered by public and commercial organisations are two social concerns. One is a recognition of the personal significance to clients of their health, and their wish to present an attractive appearance (Featherstone 1982). The second factor is the growing recognition that many people are excluded from tourism and leisure facilities resulting from their disabilities (Baker 1989).

This chapter adopts a broad view of health tourism, defining it as leisure taken away from home, where one of the objectives is to improve one's state of health. The chapter reviews the literature concerning the basis of health tourism purchases, and illustrates the opportunities presented by careful market segmentation and product development based on health-related criteria. Attention is then focused on those members of society whose access to tourism is limited by their disability or age. In conclusion, this chapter identifies the need for further research in the field of health tourism at both practical and conceptual levels.

HEALTH AND TOURISM INTERACTIONS: A BUSINESS TYPOLOGY

Health is often a motivational factor in individuals' decisions to purchase holidays, but its significance varies in intensity. In the extreme case it is the determining factor, an example is travel to obtain specialised surgery. Other people wish to improve their fitness during a vacation through diet or activities such as swimming, and in such cases the type of health facilities available is a factor in choosing among competing destinations. Many destinations promote their general health-enhancing features, such as a stimulating climate or environment, while the range of health facilities available can also be a specific way in which destinations promote themselves as distinctive.

Frechtling (1993) has argued that health and tourism should be seen as partners in market development. Two main tasks for marketing managers are to identify discrete groups or segments in the market, and to develop appropriate products for each segment. Marketing experts have shown that products offer their purchasers a 'complex cluster of value satisfactions' (Levitt 1986). The generic or core features of a product or service can be augmented in varied ways to meet the needs of different market segments. The generic holiday product consists of accommodation and transport: these are sold as basic tourism packages which are enhanced with additional services (Laws 1991), such as sporting facilities or health care programmes. This process of differentiation is undertaken both to meet the requirements of specific groups of clients, and to distinguish one tourism supplier from others in the marketplace.

Individuals in Western society enjoy freedom of choice amongst the entire range of products and services affordable to them, while in aggregate their choices are a context for producers' decisions, which also reflect the underlying (and changing) technologies of production and distribution. Together, these factors result in changes to the marketplace conditions of demand and supply. Economists have long noted that the decision to spend money on a specific product can be understood as reducing one's ability to buy other goods and services. However, factors perceived as likely to influence one's health may have a higher order of priority than most consumption decisions. Good health is an important form of personal capital (Heggenhougen 1987), thus health-related

Health tourism 201

	Primary service	Service enhancement facilities	Environment	Improved access	Advertising
Example discussed in text	Israeli spas	Cruises	Hawaii	English tourist board	Attractive people & places
Travellers' health motivation				✓	✓
Social access					✓
Climate		✓	✓		✓
Physical activities			✓		✓
Improved fitness		✓			✓
Recuperation	✓	✓			✓
Cure	✓				

(Vertical axis: Increasing Market Potential; Horizontal axis: Increasing General Relevance of Health Focus)

Figure 10.1 Tourism organisation's focus on health

decisions have the significance of an investment in one's well-being, and holiday offers which combine health advantages with standard vacation features such as attractive scenery, climate and cultural environments may represent a spending priority.

Figure 10.1 presents a conceptual model illustrating the main interactions between tourism and health which are examined in this chapter. The vertical axis records the increasing size (market potential) of various health motivations in tourism purchases – travel for the purposes of cure being assumed to be a small segment compared to the large numbers of people interested in improving their health, undertaking physical activities, or improving their access to leisure facilities because of an infirmity. On the left of the horizontal axis, specialised facilities such as spa treatments represent the primary service of certain destinations (Israel being an example discussed in this chapter). The increasingly general appeal of exercise and diet facilities (cruise lines), health environments (Hawaii) and improved access to leisure (Britain) are shown towards the right. The horizontal axis also shows that advertising based on health appeals can be targeted at all potential clients.

INFLUENCING CONSUMERS' HEALTH TOURISM PURCHASES

Consumerism is a key to understanding many aspects of modern society (McCracken 1990). Consumers' decisions are influenced by the specific messages and images employed to stimulate purchases, which are intended to channel demand towards particular products or brands. Advertising imagery reflects society's current values, and at the same time their vividness and frequent repetition give advertisers a leading role in the development of consumers' preferences. The images used in marketing frequently emphasise the beauty of female and male human bodies, portraying them as vehicles of pleasure and self-expression in leisure settings associated with hedonism and display. While the use of these emotional appeals is not restricted to tourism (Rothschild 1987), many travel brochures feature sexual images which emphasise the importance of personal appearance. At the same time, a wide range of other consumer products including cars and fashion products are advertised by displaying physically attractive people against the exotic attractions of distant beaches, mountains or great cities, thereby reinforcing the multiple connections between health, tourism and consumption decisions.

These advertising messages promote the view that one's body qualities are 'plastic and moldable' in Featherstone's (1982) memorable phrase. Similarly, the publicity for dietary and exercise programmes emphasises the individual's ability to influence and control his or her appearance. People's state of health is also used in advertising by most sectors of the tourism industry, for example destination and tour operator promotions frequently portray images of slim, bronzed and fit people enjoying an active and outgoing social life. Featherstone has shown how Douglas Fairbanks and Hollywood helped to popularise the suntan during the 1930s, which had up until then been regarded mainly as a form of treatment for tuberculosis.

Going against the established wisdom which held that the fashionable body must avoid the effects of the sun, lest it be associated with the tanned labouring body, he allowed his darkened face to appear in films and the popular press. Featherstone also argues that, as a result, the beach became transformed

> into a place where one gained a suntan – the hallmark of a successful holiday. For the first time sunbathing on the beach brought together large numbers of people in varying degrees of undress, legitimating the public display of the body.
>
> (Featherstone 1982: 180–1)

HEALTH TOURISM AS SERVICE ENHANCEMENTS

Hawaii

Tourists heading south from the industrial and winter-frost regions of both the European and American continents are a major feature of the tourism industry. Hawaii ranks as one of America's most successful sunbelt tourist destinations, receiving a total of 6.5 million visitors in 1992 (Hawaii Visitors Bureau 1993). Its core tourism product consists of an ideal tropical climate, volcanic and verdant Pacific islands, a choice of high-quality accommodation, and a wide range of leisure and sporting amenities. The enhancements currently being promoted emphasise Hawaii's attributes as a healthy destination, including opportunities for sports participation at all levels, and a wide range of medical and recuperative services.

> Hawaii is and looks to be a healthy place. The fortunes of geography and climate have spared it many of the indignities of industrial and post industrial development. Its three major industries, tourism, government employment and agriculture are clean endeavours when compared with smokestack environments. And, whereas complex environmental issues continue to be associated with all three economic endeavours, such as continued high use of pesticides and herbicides in pineapple and sugar production, their visibility is minor compared with those associated with traditional industrial development.
>
> (Neubauer 1992: 148)

The Hawaiian government actively attracts major sporting events, believing that it benefits from the attendant publicity for the healthy outdoor lifestyle of its visitors and residents. The annual Aloha Games feature forty-five sports from arm-wrestling to canoeing, and a decathlon, providing opportunities for mass participation by specialists and amateurs. The Games are featured by the media across the American states.

Cruises

The core product of cruise lines is the high level of luxury and the lavish catering they offer as they cruise between the ports where passengers may disembark for brief guided excursions. Kerstetter (1986) has shown how they reacted to slow growth in the industry by introducing a number of service enhancements, including health-related facilities.

> To combat slow growth in passenger volume, cruise lines are resorting to a number of different strategies: some are offering 24 hour, long weekend, and one week cruises. Royal Viking Lines is adding casinos, lengthening each ship some ninety feet, building health spas, adding golf and tennis pros to their staffs, and offering special menus to dieters.
>
> (Kerstetter 1986: 434)

Other lines have enhanced their core product with a range of themed cruises.

> Cunard Lines' *QE2* was recently remodelled to include a branch of California's Golden Door Spa. It boasts a pool, a mirrored exercise room, jogging track, juicebar and par course. Two of Cunard's other ships have full time instructors leading passengers in the Vitality Shipshape Program that includes elementary yoga, pool exercises, and aerobics at three levels of intensity ... travel agents have even bought into the fitness craze by specialising in health and fitness cruises. Agencies such as 'Timeless Travels' have already offered a cruise entitled 'Lets Get Physical' complete with a chiropractor and a body builder.
>
> (Kerstetter 1986: 434–5)

Similar opportunities exist in other tourism sectors, many airlines are conscious of their clients' health concerns, and are providing a higher quality of travel environment including more frequent changes of air in the cabin, and catering and seating facilities on board which reflect passengers' health concerns. Some airlines now offer simple exercise advice, or massage services to passengers.

TOURISM FOR MEDICAL REASONS

Heggenhougen (1987: 47) has suggested that 'most people have specific beliefs about the causation of illness ... and linked to those beliefs are specific ideas about appropriate therapy'. Shillitoe and Christie (1989) argue that many people distrust modern technical medicine based on diagnosis resulting in treatment regimes which are expertly planned in terms of optimal biomedical considerations. The distrust stems in part from the patient's isolation and lack of scientific understanding resulting in his or her perceived inability to participate in decisions about the programme of treatment. Clients undertaking health tourism for medical reasons often benefit from the social support of staff and other patients in attractive settings where they can also anticipate informed and sympathetic discussion of their condition, with a consequent gain in understanding and knowledge about the disease and the course of treatment. This social process reinforces self-efficacy, the belief that individuals themselves carry out the expert's health recommendations.

Some countries have a reputation for exceptional medical provision: patients from many countries are attracted to centres of medical excellence such as Harley Street in London. Other people travel to countries where particular treatments can be obtained which are unavailable from their own health services for technical, resource or religious-dogmatic reasons. One example is the flow of women from the Irish Republic seeking abortion in Britain. This international mobility of people seeking health treatments sometimes creates tensions between residents and the visitors who are able to obtain free or discounted treatment under the terms of local social insurance, or who can afford to bypass local waiting lists. A recent case was discussed in the *Los Angeles Times* under the headline 'Health visitors manipulate system'. More than half of the 7,000 people excluded from Medi-Cal annually in the area because answers on their application proved false were found to be residents of other countries (Wielawski 1993).

Spa tourism in Israel

Tourist destinations vary in the relative emphasis they place on their health and leisure facilities. Becheri (1989) has distinguished spa resorts catering for a broad social base of clients where health care such as massage or dietary therapies are a secondary benefit of the stay, from other centres which are insulated from the general resort atmosphere, and offer special health services such as douching or physiotherapy.

The Israeli government has identified health tourism as a segment of the industry meriting special development. Modern treatments are offered for rheumatic, arthritic and dermatological conditions at spas in the Sea of Galilee and the Dead Sea, and for respiratory ailments in the desert town of Arad. The National Tourism Plan now provides zoning legislation designed to protect its spas from nearby developments, and from pollution (Niv 1989). The marketing task is to focus attention on Israel's health care facilities for overseas visitors and the Ministry of Tourism promotes health tourism in the following terms: 'Legend holds that King Solomon partook of the health-giving properties of the hot springs in his realm ... For centuries Bedouin poetry has celebrated the curative powers of the Hamme Zohar hot springs at the Dead Sea' (Israeli Ministry of Tourism 1986).

The publicity material distributed by both the Israeli authority and commercial operators emphasises that the specialist treatment centres are all located within a couple of hours' journey of the country's classical sites and its major cities. These features are promoted as positive complements to the health care regime, as the following quotation shows: 'A relaxing atmosphere is seen to be a major contributing factor in the alleviation of many conditions together with a solid infrastructure of top quality hotels, restaurants, and entertainment facilities' (Israeli Ministry of Tourism 1986).

Spa tourism is an alternative to medical treatment for certain conditions. Countries such as Denmark, Germany and Austria pay or refund the medical elements of a spa treatment, and may pay for a companion to accompany patients, particularly children. BarOn (1989) has developed a formula by which the costs of medical and spa treatments may be compared. The patient's costs include travel, accommodation and meals, but the total expenditure can be offset by reduced household expenses during absence. He argues that the expense of spa treatment should be compared with the cost of alternative treatment such as hospitalisation, day clinics or treatment at home. The analysis continues with a fuller comparison of medical and spa treatment, which includes consideration of the quality of life, the value of feeling well to the individual and his family, and the holiday benefits gained during a stay at the spa. In contrast to medical treatments which can have side-effects for some patients, 'the "natural" spa treatments provide positive benefits including relaxation and enjoyment in new site and activities, with new friends, novel food and drink, and escape from a European winter' (BarOn 1989: 12).

The Israeli National Tourist Office in London lists forty-three British tour operators featuring holidays to Israel, of whom ten provide specialised health tours. Clients of one company, VIP Health Holidays, are offered a package at a Dead Sea spa specialising in the treatment of psoriasis and other skin and breathing disorders. The company's brochure promotes this package as an alternative to treatment in the UK. 'Special youth instructors supervise children during free time programmes when they are not receiving treatment, making the Dead Sea suitable for both adults and children alike' (VIP Tours 1993). The blueprint for medical attention includes a check-up on arrival by the dermatologist, daily nurse treatment, ointment up to $20 per week, and unlimited entrance and use of the nature solarium. After their final check-up, clients are given a medical report signed by the attending dermatologist. The effectiveness of spa treatment has been investigated for suffers of psoriasis.

> 60% responded completely during their stay of up to 4 weeks, i.e. there were no signs or symptoms by the end of their treatment. A further 13% showed 90–99% improvement as measured by the total residual skin area still effected ... a total of 93% had an improvement of at least 70%.
> (Abels, Rose and Bearman 1987, cited in BarOn 1989: 14)

BENEFITS OF IMPROVING SOCIAL ACCESS TO HOLIDAYS

Tourism provides a change of scene, as by definition it entails travel away from home (Burkhart and Medlik 1981). A second characteristic with consequences for health is the social opportunities afforded by tourism. Many tour companies use their clients' age as a primary way of segmenting their markets. They offer separate programmes for elderly people or youths, with an explicit emphasis on the opportunity to make new contacts. Mahon, Yarcheski and Yarcheski (1993) assert that loneliness is more prevalent among adolescents, and 'negatively influences the individual's perceived health status'. Tourism may therefore have an important role in mitigating loneliness and the psychological distress which results from isolation by bringing together people of similar backgrounds in the relaxed social context of a holiday.

However, taking a holiday is difficult or impossible for a large number of people. Mobility barriers are encountered by elderly or disabled people. Impaired hearing or sight, or mental handicap, are circumstances which restrict the tourism opportunities open to others. Table 10.1 summarises the findings of a survey by the English Tourist Board (1985), which shows that although cost is the major factor inhibiting the general population from taking a vacation, some 29 per cent of the respondents who had not taken a vacation in the previous year gave disability, age-infirmity or illness as the reason.

From the point of view of the tourism industry, these findings point to a significant market which could potentially be served, while the advantages of improved access at a personal level include enhanced leisure opportunities and an improved quality of life. The English Tourist Board has advocated a 'positive attitude to what have become known as "special needs"'. Many of the problems encountered by elderly and disabled people (and those who accompany them) stem from the insensitive design of tourist spaces. Stairs, narrow doors, and bathrooms equipped

Table 10.1 Reasons for not taking a holiday (English Tourist Board Survey 1985)

Reason	%
Cost	48
Time	11
Personal disability	14
Ill	10
Infirm/elderly	5

only for fit people all present real barriers to wheelchair users, those with poor sight, or the elderly. Although it is very difficult to adapt the medieval buildings which are a major part of Britain's heritage attractions (Westwood 1989), the modern hotels, restaurants and transport termini which are being added to the tourist infrastructure should be designed and equipped for easy use by disabled visitors.

Inability to participate in holidays is a serious matter, for the disadvantaged individual, those who care for him or her, and for society generally. Baker points out that being unable to travel or to stay temporarily away from one's routine surroundings,

> is an isolating factor, which can also undermine health. ... Holidays, far from being a frivolous activity, are part of living the fullest life possible ... they can give the carer the strength to carry on or the opportunity to meet new friends. They can give the frail and elderly or those with mobility problems a welcome change from a perhaps restrictive or isolated routine.
>
> (Baker 1989: 13)

The positive benefit gained from holiday-taking extends beyond the time spent away from home. The involvement and enjoyment start with planning and anticipating the break, continue with the enjoyment of holidays, and persist after returning home. 'Recollecting even a modest holiday has long-term beneficial effects' (Baker 1989: 13). Planning and arranging holidays for disabled people requires reliable, detailed information, and ease in making the arrangements. Since elderly and disabled people often travel with companions, selling a holiday to one disabled person typically results in several clients; conversely, an organisation unable to accommodate disabled visitors loses the business of the entire group. Baker's report to the English Tourist Board recommends that access information should be included in hotel brochures and activity or attraction leaflets, and that group organisers should be encouraged to contact a venue to specify the requirements of disabled clients prior to the visit.

Holiday access for elderly people

The potential British market of additional holidaytakers for whom access is difficult includes 10.3 million pensioners. Baker (1989) argues that this segment is particularly important to the domestic holiday industry because retired people are more likely than the general population to take two or more holidays. They are less likely to go abroad, and more likely to take off-peak breaks. Their average stay is six nights, one longer than average, and they tend to use the more profitable serviced accommodation in preference to self-catering arrangements.

An American study of the mature traveller market (Loverseed 1993) reported that mature people often holiday in warmer climate zones prior to considering house purchase there. In addition to price and comfort, the availability of features such as grab bars in bathrooms, night lights, medical facilities and dietary menus influences their choice of holiday accommodation. While on holiday they wish to be active both mentally and physically. A popular programme combines language classes in the mornings with hiking in the afternoon.

Many European and American tour operators target elderly travellers with exclusive programmes contained in separate brochures. However, Loverseed has warned that people do not like to be thought of as 'old'. Using stereotypical words on promotional material, such as 'golden years' is off-putting to them. A more subtle and acceptable approach is to use older-looking models to promote tours or cruises and 'to show them engaged in interesting activities – playing tennis, hiking in the mountains or eating a dinner by candlelight in a romantic inn' (Loverseed 1993: 64).

Holiday access for disabled people

Disabled people form a second major segment for whom access to holidays is restricted. Baker (1989) found that in Britain, there were 6.2 million registered disabled people in 1985; 5.8 million lived in private households, two-thirds were over 60, and 500,000 were wheelchair users. Brown (1991) states that there are 50 million disabled people in Europe, and reports that the potential tourism segment, including family, carers and friends is therefore at least 150 million people.

Three main purposes for travel have been identified amongst the general population: vacation, visiting friends and relatives, and travelling on business (Holloway 1986). Business travellers typically pay full rates for both hotels and transport, while the other two market segments are more likely to be price-sensitive, and to buy inclusive packages or discounted services whose marginal pricing basis does not yield the operator maximum unit revenue. Similarly, disabled people also travel for varied reasons, and as a result of more open employment policies, an increasing number of people with disabilities are travelling on business. Improved access and facilities for disabled clients therefore represent a business opportunity for hotel groups, conference and exhibition centres, and transport operators.

Improving social access to tourism

Many tourism organisations are concerned about the practical problems when disabled, elderly or ill people mix with the healthy (Baker 1989). A common strategic response has been to segregate elderly or disabled people, providing separate group tours, transportation or accommodation for them. The stigma created by purposeful segregation can generate a feeling of inferiority, and has been criticised because 'one's rights and privileges for a normal life include the opportunities to recreate in a normal environment' (Bedini 1989: 43).

The argument is two-fold: people should be free to take whatever holiday they like, but any problem encountered by those with disabilities is likely to reduce their propensity for future leisure participation, with detrimental effects on their quality of life. However, the elimination of discriminatory provision, policies and attitudes depends on better understanding. Baker (1989) has advocated an objective assessment of accessibility and the

- integration not segregation;
- increased marketing and information;
- improvements in transport;
- training for architects to cater for the wider average;
- consultation with organisations representing disabled people when planning
- objective assessments of accessibility;
- the development of internationally agreed standards.

Figure 10.2 Key factors in improving holiday access for disabled people
Source: Based on Baker (1989) and Brown (1991)

development of marketing standards for disabled people: 'Drawing up international minimum standards is one solution, but design solutions to improve access to buildings and leisure or sporting amenities is a better way forward than legislating for ramp access' (Baker 1989: 30). Figure 10.2 summarises the key points in improving access to tourism.

CONCLUSION

This chapter has discussed some of the links between two major interrelated human issues: health and tourism. It has shown how destinations such as Hawaii and Israel, and tourism businesses such as cruise lines and tour operators, have successfully expanded their core features, providing additional services focused on the needs of people seeking a health element as part of their recreation. Improvements to leisure access for disabled people have been shown to represent both an enhancement to personal wellbeing and an opportunity to increase business activity.

The link between health and tourism, and the repercussions of one on the other, have been introduced here, but further research is needed if their significance is to be clarified. This chapter has drawn on a wide range of published research, but the health sectors of tourism have not yet received any systematic analysis. There is inadequate data on health tourism, stemming in part from the lack of an internationally agreed definition. Operational issues which remain to be evaluated include the relative costs and effectiveness of different forms of treatment in competing locations. Assessment is also needed of the individual, family and community quality of life benefits to be gained by a widening access to tourism, or of combining health care with holidays. The issues raised in this chapter highlight the need for further research. One area of interest is the potential for new business opportunities offered by a fuller understanding of the health tourism sectors. A second field of enquiry is the development of appropriate conceptual and analytical approaches whereby the significance and nature of health tourism may be better understood.

With a more informed approach to product development, and promotion of the positive benefits of health tourism, the health sectors of tourism could offer significant potential to specialist destinations and tour operators as the third millennium approaches.

REFERENCES

Abels, D. J., Rose, T. and Bearman, J. E. (1987) *The Treatment of Psoriasis*, Ben Gurion University, mimeograph.
Baker, M. (1989) *Tourism for All*, London: English Tourist Board.
BarOn, R. (1989) 'Cost benefit consideration for spa treatments, illustrated by the Dead Sea and Arad, Israel', *Revue de Tourisme* 4: 12–15.
Becheri, E. (1989) 'From thermalism to health tourism', *Revue de Tourisme* 4: 15–19.
Bedini, L. (1989) 'Separate but equal, segregated programming for people with disabilities', *Leisure Today*: 40–4.
Brown, F. (1991) 'Tourism for all', conference report, *Tourism Management* 12, 3: 198–9.
Burkhart, A. and Medlik, S. (1981) *Tourism, Past, Present and Future*, London: Heinemann.
English Tourist Board (1985) *Holiday Motivations*, London: English Tourist Board.
Featherstone, M. (1982) 'The body in consumer culture', *Theory, Culture and Society* 1: 18–33.
Frechtling, D. (1993) 'Health and tourism, partners in market development', Presentation to the TTRA 24th Annual Conference, reported in C. Di Persio, C. Goeldner, G. Hayden, 'Highlights of the 24th Annual TTRA Conference', *Journal of Travel Research* 32, 1: 52–63.
Goodrich, J. and Goodrich, G. (1987) 'Health care tourism, an exploratory study', *Tourism Management* 8, 3: 217–22.
Hall, C. M. (1992) 'Adventure, sport and health tourism', in B. Weiler and C. M. Hall (eds) *Special-Interest Tourism*, London: Bellhaven Press.
Hawaii Visitors Bureau (1993) *Trends and Segments*, Honolulu: Hawaii Visitors Bureau.
Heggenhougen, H. (1987) 'Traditional medicine (in developing countries): intrinsic value and relevance for holistic health care', *Holistic Medicine* 2: 47–56.
Holloway, C. (1986) *The Business of Tourism*, (1st edn), London: Pitman.
Israeli Ministry of Tourism (1986) *Health Tourism*, Jerusalem: Israeli Ministry of Tourism.
IUOTO (1973) *Health Tourism*, Geneva: United Nations.
Kerstetter, D. (1986) 'Cruise ships', in A. Epperson (ed.) *Private and Commercial Recreation*, Pennsylvania: Venture Publishing.
Laws, E. (1991) *Tourism Marketing, Service and Quality Management Perspectives*, Cheltenham: Stanley Thornes.
Levitt, T. (1986) *The Marketing Imagination*, New York: Free Press.
Loverseed, H. (1993) 'US mature travellers market', *Travel and Tourism Analyst* 1: 51–64.
McCracken, G. (1990) *Culture and Consumption*, Bloomington: Indiana University Press.
Mahon, N., Yarcheski, A. and Yarcheski, T. (1993) 'Health consequences of loneliness in adolescents', *Research in Nursing and Health* 16: 23–31.

Neubauer, D. (1992) 'Hawaii the health state', in H. E. Leichter (ed.) *Health Policy Reform in America: Innovations from the States*, New York: M. E. Sharpe Inc., Armonk.
Niv, A. (1989) 'Health tourism in Israel: A developing industry', *Tourism Review* 4: 30–2
Rothschild, M. (1987) *Marketing Communications*, Lexington: Health and Co.
Shillitoe, R. and Christie, M. (1989) 'Determinants of self care: the health belief model', *Holistic Medicine*, 4: 3–17.
VIP Tours (1993) *Health Holidays at the Dead Sea*, London.
Westwood, M. (1989) 'Warwick Castle, safeguarding for the future through service', in D. Uzzell (ed.) *Heritage Interpretation*, London: Belhaven Press.
Wielawski, I. (1993) 'Health: visitors manipulate system', *Los Angeles Times*, pages A1 & A14, 1 September.

Chapter 11

Travel health promotion: advances and alliances

David Stears

INTRODUCTION

A visit to the high-street travel agent to book a holiday or make arrangements for a business trip quickly reveals the sophistication and highly organised structure of modern travel. The vast array of travel packages, permutations of routes and levels of accommodation are examples of the kind of information stored on comprehensive databases, which are instantly accessible via the travel agent's desktop computer. This impressive high-tech front to the travel industry is only a component of advanced transportation systems and world-wide communication networks, all of which serve to add glamour and excitement to travel and tourism. However, this might well be a deceptive representation of modern travel and tourism. The reality is often a less glamorous image of travel being associated with a growing list of potential health risks. For many would-be travellers, these are often 'hidden' health risks obscured by the more positive images presented through colourful mass-media advertising and careful marketing of exotic holiday destinations and luxury travel facilities.

It is of course important to appreciate the useful public service role played by travel agents, and at the same time acknowledge the vested interests of the whole travel industry. Travel agents and tour operators are, after all, in the business of making travel and tourism as attractive as possible and selling travel packages and holidays to potential clients. The additional activity of promoting the health of travellers presents a definite challenge for the travel industry and those concerned with the health of the public. Even though European legislation has been introduced, which places a responsibility on the part of tour operators to give health information about various destinations to their clients (CEC 1992), health promotion still remains a relatively 'uncharted area' for the vast majority of those involved in the travel industry.

Consideration should also be given to the relative freedom of individual travellers to adopt particular health behaviours with respect to travel and tourism. Indeed, this raises the ethical question of whether travel health promotion should or can ignore the autonomy of the individual traveller. As travel and tourism continue to increase in popularity, so associated health hazards are identified. Therefore serious attention has to be paid to the health and safety of travellers and the environment of their destinations.

Travel and tourism are recognised as components of a major international industry, with a reported 480 million international tourists per year and international tourist receipts estimated at over US $209 billion per annum in the late 1980s (Alleyne 1991). The industry is equally important to the economies of less developed and developed countries. Set in this context, travel health promotion represents important strategic activities and public policies which, if properly instigated, can contribute significantly to the maintenance and growth of international economies. Mann and Mantel (1991) and Alleyne (1991) draw attention to the objectives of travel medicine and travel health promotion in meeting the health needs of travellers. Reference is also made by the same authors to the importance of developing objectives to protect the public health interests of countries being visited by travellers and tourists. Health promotion therefore has an important part to play in the travel and tourism industry of the 1990s.

Development of travel health promotion presents both health services and the travel industry with major challenges. These need serious consideration if a comprehensive and effective health promotion service is to be created for travellers nationally and internationally. The key challenges are:

- acceptance of responsibility for providing travel health promotion to travellers;
- establishing realistic objectives for promoting the health of travellers;
- development of strategies to educate travellers about their own personal health risks, and the problems they may pose as visitors to the public health of different environments;

- development of an informed approach to travel health promotion through effective intersectoral collaboration and healthy alliances;
- development of thorough evaluation procedures to monitor the effectiveness of health promotion strategies offered to travellers.

DEFINITION OF TRAVEL HEALTH PROMOTION

There are many definitions of health promotion and a full discussion of these is beyond the scope of this chapter. However, recent additions to the ranks of theoretical models and perspectives (Bunton and MacDonald 1992; Downie *et al.* 1993; Tones and Tilford 1994) have helped to clarify the meaning of the term sufficiently to provide an understanding of 'travel health promotion'. In very general terms, health promotion is concerned with strategies to advance, in some positive way, the holistic well-being of individuals or populations. Bunton and MacDonald (1992) have further emphasised two key elements of health promotion: first, the *individual* (lifestyle) element and, second, the *structural* (fiscal/ecological) element. Both, it is suggested, play critical parts in any health promotion strategy. Tannahill (1985) has developed a model which is perhaps most widely accepted by practitioners and is readily adapted to a notion of 'travel health promotion'. This model is based on three overlapping areas of activity: Health Education, Prevention, and Health Protection.

Using a recent interpretation of Tannahill's model of health promotion (Downie *et al.* 1993), it is possible to explain how health promotion can be applied to the health of travellers and tourists. The three overlapping areas in Tannahill's model generate seven 'domains', all of which correspond to existing and potential travel health promotion activities. These are:

1 *Preventive services*: immunisation for travellers against diseases such as yellow fever, typhoid and hepatitis A, and medication (e.g. anti-malarials).
2 *Preventive health education*: educational activities directed at influencing lifestyle in order to prevent ill-health. For example, health education directed at the lifestyles of 'at risk' travellers (i.e. use of condoms to prevent sexually transmitted diseases in sexually active individuals; use of sun blocks to prevent skin

burning/skin cancer; use of a particular diet to reduce risks of diarrhoea and sickness).

3 *Preventive health protection*: health protection is associated with legal or fiscal controls, regulatory guidelines, policies and voluntary codes of practice – all of which make healthy choices easier choices. At one level such controls may apply to the travel industry and at another to the traveller. With respect to travel health, this might include insurance and driving regulations for tourists when driving hire cars abroad, or drug laws and drinking age limits enforced in certain countries.

4 *Health education for preventive health protection*: this domain highlights activities that stimulate a social environment conducive to the success of preventive health protection. In terms of the health of travellers, this is a key area where work is still required and perhaps is only being undertaken by a limited number of researchers and through aspects of the mass media. Recent TV documentaries in the United Kingdom have highlighted holiday accidents, health issues and lack of health facilities overseas, and teenage prostitution. These are examples of the kind of agenda-setting that is required to stimulate preventive health protection. Intensive lobbying for legislation is necessary as health education alone is not always effective in securing preventive health protection for travellers.

5 *Positive health education*: there are two aspects to this domain – the first corresponds to health education directed at influencing the behaviour of travellers (e.g. changing sexual behaviour to reduce risk of STDs; reducing exposure to the sun; changing dietary habits to prevent gastrointestinal illness). The second aspect of this domain refers to those activities that help individuals, groups and populations to develop positive health attributes (e.g. health-related skills, decision-making and self-esteem). This latter aspect of health education could feature as part of school, college or community health promotion programmes which focus primarily on travel health issues.

6 *Positive health protection*: this is the deliberate application of 'healthy public policy' to the prevention of ill-health and disease. An example of positive health protection is the introduction of the British government's white paper *The Health of the Nation* (Department of Health 1992) and its implications for the health protection of travellers. A further example

is in Spain (Costa Brava), where public funds have been used together with a policy of developing resorts for elderly people in order to promote the positive health of this age group.

7 *Health education aimed at positive health protection*: this domain involves the raising of public awareness and support for health protection measures, particularly among policymakers (Commission for the European Community (CEC), government departments and international health agencies).

When applied specifically to the health of travellers and tourists, health promotion can be categorised by the activities of their respective practitioners. Broadly speaking, preventive services are the remit of qualified medical and paramedical personnel whereas the health education domains are the provinces of a range of different agencies who currently provide pre-travel information, education, guidance and counselling for travellers.

It is appropriate in the context of this chapter to refer to health promotion in a rather general sense, that is, an activity that includes health education, prevention and health protection. Since 1984 the World Health Organisation has supported the adoption of the all-embracing term 'health promotion' in preference to highlighting more specific activities or domains such as health education and health protection (World Health Organisation 1985). The use of this umbrella term recognises the importance of a multi-dimensional approach to improving health. Health is neither solely advanced by, nor the responsibility of, a single discipline or professional group. Therefore it would seem appropriate to approach the development of travel health promotion through an interdisciplinary framework. The implications of this for intersectoral collaboration are clear. However, it is necessary to relate this multidisciplinary approach to what might constitute effective practice.

PRINCIPLES OF EFFECTIVE HEALTH PROMOTION

Tones (1992) has described seven key principles which underpin effective practice in health promotion. These are:

- equity;
- empowerment;
- healthy public policy;

- reorientation of health services;
- intersectoral collaboration;
- development of empowering personal and social skills; and
- internationalism.

These seven principles provide a useful framework for clarifying and enhancing the aims and objectives of travel health promotion.

Equity

Inequalities have long been identified as a major barrier to good health (Townsend and Davidson 1982; Whitehead 1987). In order to provide positive health promotion for travellers, inequalities experienced by certain groups need to be identified and remedied at national and international levels. The implications of inequalities in health care among international travellers cast a new perspective on an old issue: an issue which health promotion professionals have been struggling with at a national level for over ten years. Ethnicity, class, gender and sexuality are sources of difference within a broad category of travellers and provide potential bases for differential provision of health advice and inequalities in health care. It is significant, for instance, that very few anti-malarial campaigns have been organised – although many travellers to the African and Asian sub-continents are at risk, particularly those from ethnic minority groups; and vaccination against hepatitis B is not recommended in connection with travel abroad – despite the risk associated with sexual activity, particularly among gay men.

Empowerment

Positive health is difficult to attain without an empowered and involved public, and travellers are no exception. Health promotion strategies aimed at the traveller should therefore focus on encouraging participation, developing self-empowerment, and sharing responsibility for health status. This is particularly important with respect to decisions individuals make about their health behaviour before, during and after travelling to various destinations.

Healthy public policy

Wider appreciation of health promotion for travellers can only be achieved through the creation of a public policy that recognises the relationship between travel and health issues. Such a policy must reflect supportive structures which can make healthy choices, easier choices, for travellers and tourists. The government's white paper *The Health of the Nation* (Department of Health 1992) provides a useful blueprint for developing travel health policy in the United Kingdom. The white paper emphasises the use of health education and health promotion as a means of meeting clear public health targets, many of which are associated with the behaviour and lifestyles of travellers (e.g. sexual health implications of sexual behaviour abroad and skin cancer risks associated with short-term, intense exposure to the sun in hotter climates).

Reorientation of health services

The continued good health of travellers is clearly dependent on the provision of sound medical services: immunisation and medical certification for entry into certain countries being the responsibility of the medical profession. However, sound health promotion for travellers demands a health service supportive of broader health promotion objectives rather than singular concern with medical intervention. Travel clinics as established in some primary health settings in the United Kingdom could be focused on such objectives. It is recognised, however, that such initiatives are currently under threat because of changes in the government's arrangements for funding general practitioners' activities.

Intersectoral collaboration

The provision of effective health promotion will rest upon the collaboration between different institutions and organisations. Public health departments, medical centres, health promotion units, higher education research units, travel agents, tour operators, tourist boards, local authorities and regional and district health authorities are examples of relevant institutions/organisations which need to be mobilised into collaborative networks. Such networks are necessary if an effective health promotion service for travellers is to be realised.

Development of empowering personal and social skills

Preventive health action on the part of the traveller is dependent on the acquisition of a range of health, life and social skills. These skills are a key factor in making empowered choices about health and lifestyles when travelling at home or abroad. A question mark hangs over this particular key principle of travel health promotion: in practice, whose responsibility is it to aid the development of such skills? Is it those providing basic education, the medical/paramedical professionals, travel agents, the media or a combination of all who have a role in educating travellers?

Internationalism

An international perspective is central to the development of effective health promotion for travellers. International networks for travel medicine have been established to provide an exchange of research findings and practices related to travel health promotion (e.g the International Society of Travel Medicine). The CEC has developed international health programmes which are associated with travel health issues; these include health promotion research and campaigns (e.g. the Europe against Cancer programme (research/health promotion on skin cancer) and Europe against AIDS (summer campaign on sexual health and young people)). Similar initiatives are now required to maximise the effects of health promotion for travellers within countries and across international borders.

HEALTH NEEDS ASSESSMENT AS A FUNCTION OF HEALTH PROMOTION

Needs assessment is an essential element of health promotion. Bradshaw (1972) suggested that 'felt', 'expressed', 'normative' and 'comparative' needs should be examined as part of planning health promotion programmes. Felt health needs of travellers are by definition difficult to assess. Expressed needs, however, are those needs that are revealed by the traveller. Felt needs can be expressed needs if a traveller wishes to communicate his/her needs to others voluntarily or in response to some form of enquiry. Normative needs are those identified by professional people such as health care personnel who have an involvement in a traveller's health care. Those involved in the health promotion of travellers are likely to be directed by, or respond to, normative needs. Such needs are satisfied only by the successful transmission of advice based on epidemiological evidence and may be far removed from the expressed needs or felt needs of the traveller.

The degree of control over the health promotion process governs the extent to which the normative needs will override felt and expressed needs of travellers. For example, normative travel needs are of paramount importance within the military forces, where quick deployment of troops and maintenance of good physical health status are a priority. It has been revealed that the positive health status of US Navy and Marine Corps personnel during Operations Desert Shield and Desert Storm was maintained due to accurate non-combat health-risk assessment and early preventive medical interventions (Sharp et al. 1991). The judgements made about normative needs by those controlling military troops are understood and justified on strategic grounds. However, compared with military personnel, the civilian traveller/tourist is not always young, healthy and informed about health risks associated with travel and the new environments in which they might find themselves.

DELIVERY AND ACQUISITION OF TRAVEL HEALTH INFORMATION

Fundamental questions can be raised about the responsibility for delivery and acquisition of travel health information. Zacek (1991: 323) asks:

> Who bears the responsibility for informing travellers about health risks and assuring that they have adequate health information? What part should be played by travel professionals? By health-care providers? And by the travellers themselves?

The answers to such questions, she suggests, are dependent on such variables as: the type of traveller (business, leisure or immigrant); the destination to be visited (home or abroad); and how the travel arrangements are made (through airline, travel agent, or corporate business travel department). As many travellers do not seek medical or health advice, Zacek recommends that those specialising in travel medicine should provide better information on health issues for the public through existing travel industry networks. Included within these networks would be educational institutions, trade associations and travel trade publications. The call for intersectoral collaboration regarding travel health information for the public is already well documented (Reid *et al.* 1986; Cossar 1992; Schiff 1991).

Travel agents have been cited both in the United States of America and the United Kingdom as good potential sources of health promotion (Patterson *et al.* 1991; Cossar *et al.* 1993). Cossar *et al.* state that most international travel in the United Kingdom is booked through travel agents. Holiday visits account for 68 per cent of the total of international travellers, and package tours account for 36 per cent. Attention is also drawn to the fact that although inclusive package tours have decreased over the last twelve years, the European Community directive has since December 1992 placed a legal obligation on all operators of package travel, package holidays and package tours in member states to provide adequate health information for their customers (CEC 1992). The implications of this legislation for operators of package travel have been discussed at length (Downes 1993). Operators are posed with the dilemma of providing enough health information in their literature to satisfy legal requirements, yet will be conscious of business implications of creating a negative impression of health risks associated with certain destinations. A further concern might well be the potential litigation associated with information or health advice (or the lack of it) which endangers clients' health or lives. It is therefore expected that operators will provide the minimum of health information in their literature in order to comply with the law.

Research undertaken in Scotland has provided useful data on the provision of health promotion information found in travel brochures. Reid *et al.* found that in sixty-four travel brochures collected from public display at an established independent travel agent in Glasgow, one-third carried no health advice. It was further established that winter travellers and travellers to Europe were likely to receive less health advice than world-wide travellers. However, even brochures for world-wide travellers provided limited specific advice (only four out of the fifteen brochures in this category contained specific health advice). In a later and more comprehensive study of brochures from two travel agents in Edinburgh, Cossar *et al.* (1993) found an increase in the number of brochures covering world-wide travel and a higher proportion of those covering specific health information. Specific health advice continues to be inconsistent and some travellers are at risk of contracting a preventible disease while others may develop a false sense of security.

There is a clear case for further development of health promotion for travellers. Such development requires a sound theoretical framework reflecting congruence with current health promotion strategies. The practical objectives for effective travel health promotion should therefore reflect the expressed needs of travellers and not just the normative needs assessment of health professionals. Research has indicated that tour operators have started to provide health information for travellers in travel brochures. However, this information is likely to be of limited benefit if it is not supported by a wider network of health promotion. There is real potential for intersectoral collaboration in the production and distribution of specialist health promotion materials, the training of health educators, and the expansion of comprehensive preventive services.

NATIONAL SURVEYS OF TRAVEL HEALTH PROMOTION IN DISTRICT HEALTH PROMOTION/ EDUCATION UNITS

Two surveys have been conducted that investigate the travel health promotion undertaken by district health promotion units in the United Kingdom (Stears 1993; Clift and Coakley 1994). These units have a potential role in the development of intersectoral collaboration in relation to travel and health. The earlier survey was of 207 units throughout England, Wales and Northern Ireland, undertaken in the summer of 1992, whereas the later survey involved 170 units in England alone, during the spring of 1994. This work was undertaken as part of the Travel, Lifestyles and Health project (Clift and Page 1994).

The surveys shared the same objectives, that is to:

- examine the different types of travel health promotion undertaken within district health authorities/health trusts;
- examine the extent to which intersectoral collaboration has been developed at the delivery stage of travel health promotion initiatives; and

- establish the range of local health promotion campaigns, projects and resources that have been developed for travellers in England.

Postal questionnaires were used in both surveys to establish whether units were undertaking travel health promotion work and to elicit information about the kind of travel health promotion initiatives units were pursuing. The 1992 survey revealed that 43 per cent of all units questioned were undertaking some kind of travel health promotion work. However, the 1994 survey showed that 71 per cent of English units were now involved in some form of travel health promotion.

Tables 11.1, 11.2 and 11.3 show comparative data from the two surveys. Table 11.1 indicates the main travel health issues being focused upon by units. The increase in health promotion activities on skin cancer and sexual health issues between 1992 and

Table 11.1 Main travel health issues addressed by District Health Promotion Units in the UK

Travel health issues	1992 survey		1994 survey	
Skin cancer	23 units	36%	57 units	79%
Sexual health	38 units	59%	56 units	78%
Immunisation	14 units	22%	13 units	18%
Alcohol abuse	–	–	7 units	10%

Table 11.2 Resources used in travel health promotion by District Health Promotion Units in the UK

Travel health resources	1992 survey		1994 survey	
Leaflets	29 units	45%	39 units	54%
Posters	7 units	12%	23 units	32%

Table 11.3 Settings where local travel health promotion has been developed in the UK

Settings	1992 survey		1994 survey	
Travel agents	8 units	12%	26 units	36%
Primary health care	4 units	6%	22 units	31%
Education establish.	2 units	3%	19 units	26%
Pharmacists	2 units	3%	15 units	21%

1994 is probably due to the introduction of specific targets for improving health in these areas as part of the British government's white paper, *The Health of the Nation* (Department of Health 1992). Table 11.2 shows the main type of resources used by units to inform the public about travel health issues. Leaflets and posters have consistently formed the mainstay of resources used and the latter survey indicates an increase in the use of such materials. Two-thirds of those units responding to the 1994 survey suggested that they would appreciate nationally produced travel health promotion materials and a quarter of the respondents welcomed more information on local campaigns and examples of good practice from other units (see Figures 11.1 and 11.2 for examples of health promotion material focusing on care for the skin and on sexual health in the context of holidays/travel).

Table 11.3 indicates the main agencies with which the health promotion units are working to promote the positive health of travellers. Intersectoral collaboration has increased in key areas (i.e. with travel agents and primary health care centres) and interesting developments have taken place with education establishments and pharmacists.

Primary health care centres and pharmacists are important agencies for developing travel health promotion. Useful advice has appeared in professional journals to encourage practice nurses to develop specific skills in the area of travel health promotion (Howells 1993b). Of particular interest is the suggestion that health professionals should develop 'travel related protocols' (Howells 1993a) in order to give positive guidance to travellers, identify professional roles and responsibilities, and provide uniformity of information for all those involved in travel health.

The two national surveys further identified the need to develop staff training in order to work with travel agents and primary health care staff. The latter survey also identified that nearly two thirds of units working in the area of travel health had no plans to evaluate their work or had not yet formulated evaluation procedures.

Surprisingly, only 10 per cent of units in the latter survey referred to aspects of their locality as a reason for developing travel health promotion work (e.g. a particular district might have within its catchment area a major international airport, sea port or high population of tourists). Such centres of tourism provide

Figure 11.1 Health promotion materials produced in the UK on health risks associated with exposure to the sun

captive audiences for travel health promotion. Airport departure lounges, for example, have been shown to be ideal locations for conveying travel health messages. Gruer *et al.* (1993) describe a successful four-week safer-sex campaign held at Glasgow International Airport, where an estimated 66,000 people passed through the airport lounge during the campaign and 10,500 people actively took part in the campaign. Evaluation of this kind of campaign showed that the public thought that such a venue was entirely appropriate for promoting the health of travellers, with only 6 per cent of passengers failing to see the relevance of the campaign.

A comprehensive campaign was launched in Torbay during 1993 by the District HIV Prevention Co-ordinator and jointly monitored/evaluated by the University of Exeter. The campaign,

Are you thinking of bringing anything back from your holiday?

SUN, SEA, SANGRIA AND SEX!

Every year 36 million Britons travel abroad. Of course not all of them have sex with new partners while they are away.

But a recent study of Nottinghamshire travellers found that 5% did have sex with people they met on holiday.

The rate of HIV infection in most European countries is higher than in Britain.

Travellers to popular summer destinations like Spain, France and Italy, who have unprotected sex, are currently three times more likely to become infected with HIV than at home.

Checklist:
Sun Cream
Sun Glasses
First Aid Kit
Insect Repellent
CONDOMS

DON'T FORGET

Using a condom will protect you from HIV and other infections such as syphilis and gonorrhea as well as unplanned pregnancies.

It's much easier nowadays to ask for condoms at chemists, supermarkets, garages, even record stores.

It may not be so simple to find the right words in Spanish or Greek.

So take some with you.

I fancy you

HIV is the virus which can lead to AIDS.

The two main ways of catching HIV are

- having sexual intercourse without using a condom
- sharing injecting drug equipment

Many of the people now infected in Britain acquired the virus abroad

DON'T FORGET
THE KITEMARK

Figure 11.2 Safer sex on holiday leaflet produced by the Gloucestershire Department of Health Promotion, UK

which is in its second year, was established to 'raise public awareness of the dangers of unprotected sexual intercourse in a resort in which during the holiday season, there is a highly mobile cosmopolitan population'. This is a further example of a local campaign which focuses on a catchment group. It would appear from both the 1992 and 1994 surveys of health promotion/education units that there is both scope and a need for units to establish similar captive audiences for travel health promotion campaigns.

Sexual health, skin cancer and accidents are health issues that relate to potential risk factors associated with travel and tourism. All three are also *Health of the Nation* targets and therefore worthy of development as the focus for local travel health promotion campaigns. Further examples of such local campaigns and examples of good practice can be found in Clift (1994). However, it would appear there is scope and a demand for further sharing of information on, and updates of, travel health promotion practice.

A NATIONAL TRAVEL AND HIV PREVENTION CAMPAIGN

Further developments in travel health promotion have occurred at a national level in Britain. For example, the Department of Health launched a national 'Travel Safe' campaign in early June 1993. This was 'part of their ongoing communication programme to educate members of the public about HIV/AIDS'. This HIV prevention campaign warned travellers of the risks of contracting HIV and gave information on how to reduce the risks of infection (see Figure 11.3 for campaign materials). The campaign was targeted at business travellers who were sexually active, young (17–30 age group) 'backpackers', executives seconded overseas, and holidaymakers and those people visiting relations/friends abroad. In order to distribute the campaign message, professional sectors which had direct contact with the target audience were identified: i.e., medical/health-related organisations; chemists; ABTA travel agents; personnel managers in companies having frequent business travellers to Asia, Eastern Europe and Africa; student unions in universities; youth hostels and other similar organisations.

In early June, 31,000 separate communications were made with potential distributors of the Travel Safe campaign materials (which

Figure 11.3
Department of Health's Travel Safe campaign materials produced in the UK, 1993/4

consisted of a Freepost order form for the Travel Safe leaflets/ Travel Safe Code card, posters and display dispenser). One-third of this group responded and requested campaign materials. Simultaneously, a media advertising campaign was mounted through the quality and medical press. The campaign also advertised the Health Literature Line, which provided a back-up service for companies and individual travellers.

Evaluation of the 1993 campaign (BJM Research and Consultancy 1993) highlighted the general acceptance of the materials by women and young males who were inexperienced travellers but questioned its success in meeting the needs of the business traveller. These findings are consistent with wider research, which acknowledges the business traveller as a difficult group on which to target travel health promotion, especially in the area of sexual health. Elliott et al. (1993) found among a sample of large oil companies in Scotland, that the companies are more likely to provide advice on malaria and tetanus than sexually transmitted diseases. The recommendation from this research was the development of programmes specifically designed for businessmen who work overseas on how to prevent sexually transmitted diseases. This again focuses on the need to develop intersectoral collaboration in order to provide comprehensive advice for all travellers.

CONCLUSION

There is no doubt that 'travel and health' represents a new, dynamic and significant field of interest for health promotion professionals. The health issues facing international travellers, and their needs for information, education and sound advice, should be of interest to all those involved in the practice of health promotion and with an involvement in training and research. Recent developments in the theory of health promotion serve to clarify the aims of health promotion work in the area of travel and provide valuable guidance on the construction of effective interventions. To date, in the United Kingdom some interesting examples of practical work have been pursued in this field by health promotion specialists, and this has clearly been stimulated by health policy and targets set nationally. There is clearly substantial room for further developments, however – both in practice and research.

REFERENCES

Alleyne, G. (1991) 'Health and tourism: the intersectoral linkages', in H. Lobel, R. Steffen and P. E. Kozarsky (eds) *Travel Medicine 2, Proceedings of the Second Conference on International Travel Medicine*, Atlanta: ISTM.

BJM Research and Consultancy (1993) *An Assessment of the Travel Safe Leaflet and its Distribution: a Combined Qualitative and Quantitative Report*, London: Central Office of Information, prepared by Context Research and BJM Research Consultants Ltd.

Bradshaw, J. (1972) 'The concept of social need', *New Society* 19: 640–3.

Bunton, R. and MacDonald, G. (1992) *Health Promotion: Disciplines and Diversity*, London: Routledge.

CEC (1992) 'Council directive on package travel, package holidays and package tours', *Official Journal of the European Communities* 158: 59–63.

Clift, S. (1994) 'Going on holiday? Have a healthy time', *Healthlines* July/August: 17–19.

Clift, S. and Coakley, L. (1994) *Survey of Travel Health Work in English Health Promotion Units*, Centre for Health Education and Research, Canterbury, Christ Church College.

Clift, S. and Page, S. (1994) 'Travel, lifestyles and health', *Tourism Management* 15, 1: 69–70.

Cossar, J. H. (1992) 'Traveller's health – a time for rationalisation?', *Scottish Medicine* 12, 1: 3.

Cossar, J. H., McEachran, J. and Reid, D. (1993) 'Holiday companies improve their health advice', *British Medical Journal* 306: 1069–70.

Department of Health (1992) *The Health of the Nation: a Strategy for Health in England*, London: HMSO.

Downes, J. J. (1993) 'Legal liabilities and the travel trade: the EC package travel directive, part II', *Travel and Tourism Analyst* 2: 69–87.

Downie, R., Fyfe, C. and Tannahill, A. (1993) *Health Promotion: Models and Values*, Oxford: Oxford University Press.

Elliott, L., Cowan, L., Gruer, L. and Hardie, A. (1993) 'Business travel and sexually transmitted diseases', *British Medical Journal* 306: 586.

Gruer, L., Cowan, L., Elliott, L. and Farrow, K. (1993) 'In response to a call for travellers to receive appropriate information on safer sexual behaviour', *British Medical Journal* 306: 394.

Howell, K. (1993a) 'Travel health: a case for health promotion', *Practice Nursing*, 16 February–1 March 1993.

Howell, K. (1993b) 'Accident prevention for holidaymakers', *Practice Nursing*, Clinical Supplement on Travel Health, 14–17 May 1993.

Mann, J. M. and Mantel, C. F. (1991) 'Travel and health: a global agenda', in H. O. Lobel, R. Steffen and P. E. Kozarsky (eds) *Travel Medicine 2, Proceedings of the Second Conference on International Travel Medicine*, Atlanta: ISTM.

Patterson, S. C., Niolu, R. B., McMullen, R. and Jong, E. C. (1991) 'Travel agents and travel medicine clinics: the potential for co-operative efforts to inform the public on health care issues', in H. O. Lobel, R. Steffen and P. E. Kozarsky (eds) *Travel Medicine 2, Proceedings of the Second Conference on International Travel Medicine*, Atlanta: ISTM.

Reid, D., Cossar, J. H., Ako, T. I. and Dewar, R. D. (1986) 'Do travel brochures give adequate advice on avoiding illness?', *British Medical Journal* 293: 1472.

Schiff, A. L. (1991) 'Informing travellers of health risks', in H. O. Lobel, R. Steffen and P. E. Kozarsky (eds) *Travel Medicine 2, Proceedings of the Second Conference on International Travel Medicine*, Atlanta: ISTM.

Sharp, T. W., Daniell, F. D., Berg, S. W. and Trump, D. H. (1991) 'Travel and preventive medicine in the US Navy and Marine Corps: the Navy preventive medicine information system', in H. O. Lobel, R. Steffen and P. E. Kozarsky (eds) *Travel Medicine 2, Proceedings of the Second Conference on International Travel Medicine*, Atlanta: ISTM.

Stears, D. F. (1993) *Travel Health Promotion: a Survey of the Work of District Health Promotion Units in the UK*, Travel, Lifestyles and Health

Working Paper No. 2, Canterbury Christ Church College.
Tannahill, A. (1985) 'What is health promotion?', *Health Education Journal* 44: 167–8.
Tones, K. (1992) 'Empowerment and the promotion of health', *Journal of the Institute of Health Education* 30, 4: 133–7.
Tones, K. and Tilford, S. (1994) *Health Education: Effectiveness, Efficiency and Equity*, London: Chapman Hall.
Townsend, P. and Davidson, N. (1982) *Inequalities in Health*, Harmondsworth: Penguin.
Whitehead, M. (1987) *The Health Divide*, London: Health Education Council.
World Health Organisation (1985) 'Health promotion: a WHO discussion document based on the summary report of the Working Group on Concept and Principles of Health Promotion, Copenhagen, July 9–13, 1984', *Journal of the Institute of Health Education* 23, 1.
Zacek, J. C. (1991) 'Informing travellers about health risks, health and tourism: the intersectoral linkages', in H. O. Lobel, R. Steffen and P. E. Kozarsky (eds) *Travel Medicine 2, Proceedings of the Second Conference on International Travel Medicine*, Atlanta: ISTM.

Chapter 12
Have fun in the sun: protect yourself from skin damage
Ros Weston

INTRODUCTION

Over the last century increased affluence for some socio-economic groups in the UK and Europe has meant an increase in travel both at home and internationally with the resulting boom in the holiday industry (Alleyne 1991; Youell 1994). As working hours have shortened, so leisure time has increased. This has resulted in behaviour change related to leisure and how people choose to spend their free time. This chapter will consider the important health issues involved in encouraging safe leisure time in the sun both within the UK and abroad. Emphasis is placed on outbound travel from the UK, domestic and international tourism as a context for encouraging safe leisure time in the sun.

Increasingly, health promoters are encouraged to collaborate with a range of agencies to form 'Healthy Alliances' to educate, protect and prevent ill-health (Department of Health 1992). This includes reducing risk-taking behaviour which may lead to increased early morbidity and reduced life expectancy. They seek to promote positive health and healthy lifestyles and to offer individuals the opportunity to take responsibility for their own health, even when the wider political, economic or environmental conditions are less than propitious. To reduce risk in the sun and encourage behaviour change, collaborative action is required from personnel in the travel industry, health promoters, primary care professionals, teachers, pharmacists, the cosmetics industry, the media and dermatologists to ensure that campaigns and specifically targeted information and education reaches the consumers (Newton 1994).

Health promotion in relation to sun exposure is not an easy

task for those involved as the issues are complex. Sunbathing is an enjoyable activity related to leisure time; it is often associated with increased feelings of health and well-being (albeit perhaps more psychological than actual), and is also associated with self-esteem, fashion and sexuality. Current messages about sun protection follow a plethora of lifestyle messages and have been criticised recently by Ingrams (1994):

> As the summer progresses we must become used to the bossy voices on the BBC telling us not to spend too long in the sunshine (what little there is of it) for fear of succumbing to skin cancer. Weathermen have been instructed to include the measurement of the ozone layer in their daily forecasts. Without wishing to deny the risk of melanoma I have a strong feeling that these well meaning warnings will do more harm than good in that they will simply make people alarmed about sitting in the sun, a practice I will persist in thinking is highly beneficial healthwise ... these people [government funded health educators] have only themselves to blame if the majority of people take no notice of such health warnings. These people have cried wolf too often in the past and people have become cynical.
>
> (*Observer*, May 1994)

If the general public do adhere to the same view, then the task of encouraging safe-sun behaviour is further complicated by these juxtaposed views and by the contradiction of having to alter something that is believed to be beneficial to health. Along with other personally enjoyable habits and addictions, already the focus of health promotion and the efforts of personal behaviour change, one has to change something that makes us feel good! Health promoters need to be highly skilled in communication, understanding and empathy if they are to be successful in promoting the safe-sun message (Newton 1994).

THE TASKS FOR HEALTH PROMOTION

In addressing the risks posed by exposure to the sun, the principal tasks for health promotion professionals and collaborating partners are:

- to promote a consistent, simple and clear message which is economical and practical for everyone (Newton 1994);

- to promote specific messages to specifically targeted groups (Newton 1994);
- to interpret the epidemiological evidence in ways that will help individuals to understand their own personal risk;
- to carry out needs assessment and research to clarify perceptions of knowledge, beliefs, attitudes, behaviour, misconceptions and myths of each target group to whom they intend to promote a message or for whom they are to develop a campaign (Green and Kreuter 1991);
- to be clear about what people already know and have achieved in lifestyle change and build on that using planned and measurable interventions (Prochaska 1992);
- to be aware of the wider political, economic and environmental constraints operating at a given point in time or geographically, for individuals or populations (Green and Kreuter 1991);
- to remind travellers about specific climatic conditions in the country they are travelling to or in their own country, e.g. when sailing or skiing;
- to understand that behaviour change takes time (sometimes as many as five attempts in seven years, sometimes more) and therefore there is a need for follow-up interventions to keep the message in the public mind and to reinforce and maintain protective behaviour in the sun (Prochaska 1992);
- to understand the fear and anxiety such a message may cause and the increased load on the health services this may bring;
- to understand that for both professionals and the lay public, fear of cancer can block the message being communicated and change is therefore resisted (Weston 1994);
- to be vigilant about the process for developing interventions using an accepted research model which includes integral evaluation and, in the case of behaviour change, evaluation which can measure efficacy and effectiveness of the intervention (Green and Kreuter 1992).

To implement health promotion messages successfully, all partners need to be clear that there is not one public mind about cancer, but many public minds. It is just as likely that there are many public minds about the risk of skin cancers associated with sunbathing habits. The first task is to understand how each target group perceives the issue. This will ensure that the basis of an intervention is sound and the message more likely to be respected and acted upon because it has direct significance to the real world in which the individual or group performs the behaviour or holds the belief. Extrapolating data and information from research samples is important for the planning of targeted interventions or population campaigns (Porter Novelli 1991). Epidemiology is also crucial to understanding risk and particularly personal risk. Interventions should be based on current epidemiology, which is illuminated by needs assessment research for specific target groups. By developing indicators based on such knowledge, planners can more readily develop messages which have relevance for the target population. Such a research framework underpinning the planning of the programme means that specific, measurable outcome objectives can be set and evaluated (Kok and De Vries 1989).

SETTINGS AND TARGET GROUPS FOR HEALTH PROMOTION ON SUN AND SKIN CARE

Interventions can be targeted to specific groups in a community using a range of dissemination points, or to whole populations with the intention of changing the currently accepted norms. Disseminating information means working in a community with as many interfaces as possible at once and over a period of time. Health promotion involves working in specific settings and with specific target groups.

Settings include the community, primary care, schools, the leisure and health industry, the travel industry and retail outlets selling leisure wear. It is important that all those working in each setting are clear about the information they need to know, what message they are promoting and to whom. Healthy alliances need to be created and time invested in planning and developing the initiative and the team. The Health Education Authority's campaign 'Sun Know How' (1994) and the Cancer Research Campaign's 'Play Safe in the Sun' (1994), are examples of such an approach.

The needs of specific target groups have to be understood and addressed so as to maximise the effectiveness of the campaign or the message. This can be done either by social class segmentation or by leisure patterns, or in terms of such factors as foreign travel, age groups and degree of outdoor work. The information needs of different groups vary, so messages should be targeted directly to their needs.

Socio-economic groups

It is significant, however, that the increase in basal cell carcinoma and melanoma in recent years has been greatest in social classes one and two. It is suggested that this is associated with short intermittent bursts of sunbathing and sun exposure and the greater incidence of foreign holidays in this social group is implicated. Travel-related campaigns on skin care need to take this into account.

However, increasingly, numbers of people from other social class groups may take a holiday abroad at least once per year. Others, owing to lack of money or personal choice, will probably remain in the UK. With the likely decrease in the protective ozone layer over the next century, even short periods in the sun may have the effect of increasing the risk of skin cancers and therefore loss of healthy years of life or increased morbidity.

Age groups: children and older people

It is important that the process of education begins in the primary school and then follows the principle of the spiral approach to knowledge throughout secondary and tertiary education. This will enable children to develop positive sun protection habits which will be part of their behaviour from an early age (Foot *et al.* 1993). Changing the sun protection behaviour of children is crucial, and this should include behaviour in their native country and on holiday. A study by Foot *et al.* (1993) shows that children do respond to messages and that the best time for effective sun protection messages is between 9–11 years old. They will then begin their leisure career positively. Understanding how children perceive risk, health, sun, sunbathing, sunburn, protection in the sun and cancer is a prerequisite of effective educational programmes. For too long educators have taken a paternalistic approach to educating children about health; educators encourage parents to take action or do the thinking for them, or educators fall back on the normative approach, 'the professionals know what is best for you, the child.' As the work of Wetton and Collins (1994) shows, children have far more knowledge than professionals usually credit them with, and this can be a powerful educational tool in influencing their parents, friends and families to change behaviour (Wetton and Collins 1994).

Older people, who may over a number of years have had considerable exposure to sun with little or no protection, need to be considered for specific messages. They may have had previous episodes of severe sunburn long before the current information was known, so they may not perceive that they could be at risk. This will dictate their response to a change in their skin or in a mole. It is crucial they understand what such changes are and that with early advice the prognosis is good. This group increasingly present with basal cell carcinoma. What advice and intervention do educators offer them? Increasingly, this group are spending the winter abroad and as a result spend considerable time in the sun. This has become possible through the market for holidays for the over-55s, such as Golden Years Clubs and Saga. These have opened up travel opportunities hitherto not thought about (Newton 1994).

Gender

Traditionally, men have been less concerned with health matters than women. The reasons for this are complex, but generally they are linked to gender specific roles and tasks, cultural beliefs and mores. Men of all ages need special attention in sun protection interventions as they do not readily spot changes in their health, and in this case, skin or moles. Foot *et al.* also found they were less likely to seek advice if they did discover signs of melanoma or skin cancer. (Foot *et al.* 1993). Furthermore, they do not present early for advice or diagnosis with the consequent result that their prognosis is less positive than women even though their incidence rate is less (Newton 1994). Men travelling abroad to work need special advice as the conditions applying to migrant populations may well apply to them particularly in high temperature climes (Armstrong 1989).

HEALTH PROMOTION INTERVENTIONS

There are two major approaches to interventions. These are 'primary prevention' with the emphasis on promoting positive health, reducing risk and preventing illness, and 'secondary prevention' with its emphasis on recognising change and seeking early advice or diagnosis.

Primary prevention

The role of primary prevention is to stop disease starting. So practitioners work with healthy people to encourage them to protect their health. In recent years primary prevention has used positive health promotion strategies, often referred to as lifestyle education. This is based on the premise that the lifestyle an individual has chosen, or fallen into the habit of, can enhance health or reduce risk, or increase risk and jeopardise health. Lifestyle can change when individuals make a voluntary choice based on all the information at their disposal. Primary prevention seeks to help individuals or populations to reduce their risk of ill-health. Reducing risk means changing to a lifestyle that promotes health (Ewles and Simnett 1989; Newton 1994). Protection in the sun is a lifestyle issue and the behaviour of suntanning and over-exposure to the sun can be changed by choice and personal action. This should not be confused with environmental aspects, such as the thinning of the ozone layer, or predisposing factors for which an individual cannot be responsible or indeed change, e.g. their genetic inheritance or skin colour (Dickinson 1994).

The primary prevention messages which interventions should promote are:

- Always wear a close-weave cotton shirt with long sleeves when in the sun.
- Always wear a hat with a peak if possible, especially if you cannot afford sunglasses that are protective.
- Wear sunglasses that are protective (these are expensive and so thought needs to be given to the promotion of this message).
- Stay out of the sun between 11.00 and 15.00 – sit in the shade or go indoors.
- Always wear shirts, hats and sunglasses when sightseeing as concrete reflects sunlight.
- Always protect the body with suntan lotion with a factor 8+ for adults and 15+ for children if swimming.
- Sunblocks for the face are essential for outdoor sports persons, children, walkers, cyclists and when playing on the beach.
- Read the instructions carefully on sun protection lotions and creams. These should be matched with skin type. Application of sun lotion means that you can extend the time you sit in the sun. It does not mean you are protected from sunburn

(e.g. if you have a fair to moderate skin, exposed for 10 minutes without a sun lotion, it will redden. Applying a sun factor 6 means you could extend the time before reddening to 60 minutes. If you swim during that time, you decrease the time it takes to redden. For darker skins, a higher factor will increase the delaying of reddening. It does not prevent sunburn if you continue to overexpose (Dickinson 1994).

- The promotion of suntan lotions is not necessary as part of an intervention although giving correct information about SPF numbers may be. Changing behaviour is the main aim.

Secondary prevention

Secondary prevention as part of positive health promotion is aimed at halting the progress of the disease, increasing the chance of a positive prognosis, reducing the risk of morbidity and early mortality. In the promotion of messages about reducing the risk of skin cancers, there are key messages which are very important. These fall into two categories:

- messages that will encourage members of the public to seek advice early if they notice a change in their skin which does not heal as normal or a change in a mole;
- messages that should be part of a professional basic and post-basic training in primary care and dermatology departments, these are the seven-point change scale for assessing moles and the Breslow thickness test. Although this may not be a significant aspect of a campaign, it is an important message to all target groups so that they seek early advice and therefore have the possibility of a positive prognosis.

THE PRECEDE PROCEDE MODEL

The Precede Procede Model (Green and Kreuter 1991) sets out a framework from which community and population interventions can be designed. It is useful for developing specifically targeted messages in a range of settings, including campaigns, using a collaborative approach. Yet it recognises the impact of both internal and external factors which may operate in any given point in time, these being the political, economic and environmental conditions. The model acknowledges the powerful effects of such factors but encourages practitioners to make an objective assessment of them. This helps ensure that interventions succeed in empowering individuals or whole communities within the context of their social reality.

The model uses a research framework to develop understanding of all the aspects of a health issue before designing the intervention. It therefore combines the epidemiological evidence on which policy is based with appropriate research to illuminate how and why individuals think as they do, behave as they do, and how they value health and behaviour change. It also seeks to be realistic, separating throughout the research phase those factors that are changeable, and therefore worth attention, and those that are not. Resources are then devoted to elements of the programme most likely to be successful (Green and Kreuter 1991; Porter Novelli 1991). There are several steps identified in the precede or planning phase of the model. In the remainder of this chapter these will be discussed in relation to campaigns aimed at encouraging sun protection.

Epidemiology and health policy

The analysis of the resources within an organisation to support the safe-sun message as a priority target should be the aim of this phase. A key target of the *Health of the Nation* white paper is to reduce or halt the year-on-year rise in skin cancer and melanoma in England by the year 2005. This national policy decision, like those of European and international policy, is based on epidemiological data which show that incidence and mortality of skin cancer and melanoma are rising among white-skinned populations. The incidence of malignant melanoma varies one hundred fold around the world from a low of 0 to 0.2 per 100,000 population in parts of Japan to nearly 40 per 100,00 population in Queensland, Australia. Thus, as a cause of illness and death, its importance varies considerably. It is important for all those involved in planning to understand the epidemiological basis on which policy and priorities are decided. Discussing malignant melanoma, Dickinson (1994) cites Armstrong (1989: 835–48).

> It is an important cause of death in Australia even though the survival rate (5 year) is in the order of 85%. Its importance as a cause of premature death arises because of the young age at

which it occurs. In the age range 25–44 it was the most common cancer and the third most common cause of death in 1982.

It is important to see the problem in real terms, and although Australia is an extreme example, all white populations face the same problem over the coming years, exacerbated by international travel and therefore the possibility of more time in the sun. Difficulties with recording of statistics in some countries mean that an accurate picture is difficult to obtain, but we have sufficient information to estimate fairly reliably that, in the world, three-quarters of a million people die from cancer each year. Cancer is the second most common cause of death. A further million people develop cancer each year. Of these, 5,000 deaths result from melanoma and around 17,000 individuals develop the disease. The predicted increase in these numbers is between 3–7 per cent per annum. Much of the problem is in Northern Europe. European statistics show an increased incidence in the last ten years. Mortality has also increased but has not grown at a similar rate.

In the UK skin cancer is the second most common form of cancer and has the fastest-growing increase in incidence of all cancers. Most of these skin cancers are preventable and the majority of deaths avoidable with a change in lifestyle and behaviour (primary prevention), and early detection of diagnosis (secondary prevention). Figures issued in February 1993 show 34,000 new cases of skin cancer, with males having a slightly higher increase than females. Of this total number there were 3,600 new cases of malignant melanoma representing an increase of 108 per cent between 1974 and 1987. Deaths from malignant melanoma rose from 743 in 1974 to 1,288 in 1991: an increase of 73 per cent.

Overall survival rates (five-year) for all skin cancers is 97 per cent whereas the overall survival rate for melanoma (five-year) is only 65 per cent. Male survival rate was 52 per cent compared to a female survival rate of 75 per cent. This difference may be due to the fact that females present for diagnosis earlier than males. Of the total male cases of skin cancer, melanoma was 8 per cent but it continues to be twice as common in women, representing 14 per cent of the total number of female skin cancers. (Figures show similar trends in Denmark, The Netherlands, Canada, Australia and Scotland.)

It is essential that all those involved in a slow protection programme know and understand the basis on which policy decisions are based and the implications this has for inclusion in local planning and for resources. Knowing and understanding epidemiology gives the programme authority. Interpreting these facts for the consumer remains the task of the collaborative partners involved in planning and implementing the programme (Vågerö et al. 1990; Cancer Research Campaign 1992).

Environmental considerations

This phase of the planning cycle seeks to understand the external factors that influence risk and to be clear what can and cannot be changed. The incorporation of these factors in the safe-sun message is important. To increase understanding of the synergistic aspect of these factors to an individual's lifestyle risk is a key task for health promoters. Making science understandable is part of that task. Fatalism is a reason both professionals and the lay public give for not implementing health messages. It is essential that the intervention is not doomed to failure by its own failure to interpret the important message about the environmental and genetic factors which may increase risk. Planners cannot leave the perfect loophole for people to avoid taking action because they believe that are doomed anyway by factors outside their control. The perfect foil! Sunshine is solar energy in the form of electromagnetic radiation. The shorter the wavelength, the greater the energy; thus the midsummer sun rays are the most severe. Sunlight has both UVB and UVA rays, that is ultraviolet light. The effect on the skin of ultra violet light is to produce melanin and to stimulate pre-formed melanin which gives the suntan. This sequence of events differs from person to person depending on other factors such as skin colour and length of exposure, and protection factors such as clothes, hats, glasses, sun lotions and geographical place (Armstrong 1989). If people change their environment, migrate or temporarily migrate, as on holiday, then risk may increase (Armstrong 1989). Reflection intensifies the reaction. The maximum protection from melanin develops within fourteen to twenty-one days. Burning is caused by the UVB more than UVA but long-term skin damage and skin cancers could be due to both. The ozone layer has acted as a filter for these harmful rays. With the decreasing depletion of the ozone layer, the amount of UVB rays reaching the earth is increasing all over the world and not just in the UK or Europe. Other harmful effects of UVB can damage the genetic material DNA. It can suppress the immune system, damage the eyes, and damage plant life and crops. Some evidence shows that marine and fresh-water life can also suffer. The effect of ultra violet light is the same if produced artificially, so tanning by using sunbeds and lamps should be discouraged.

The Anti-Cancer Foundation of Western Australia (1990) estimates that the depletion in the ozone layer will increase our skin cancer risk by 3–6 per cent for each 1 per cent decrease in the ozone layer. Understanding the sun, sunshine and the effects of the ultra violet light and the problems of the ozone layer may well help individuals and populations to understand that it is not just the effects of their own personal behaviour that increases their risk. It is a combination of both, yet the most significant thing they can do to reduce risk is to change their behaviour. These external factors are unlikely to be changeable. The time of the day, the nearer you are to the equator, and the season all increase the risk. So the most important and lethal combination is midday, in the height of summer, in countries near the equator. Changing only this one factor and the behaviour of sitting in the sun at this time will be a first step in risk reduction. If people can be encouraged to take one step and be successful, they will usually try the next. This could be staying covered using a shirt of close-woven material and a hat combined with sunglasses: three factors for reducing risk which are also cheap, practical, effective and reliable. Understanding the effects of being in a place where the sun's rays are likely to be scattered and the subsequent increased risk is also important. Sunburn happens even on cloudy days, as the clouds block out the heat-producing infrared rays, making it feel cool. People associate suntanning with feeling warm and so fail to protect themselves if they feel cool.

Lay and professional beliefs about the sun and skin

It is important to understand the perceptions and knowledge of people in the community about protection in the sun, sunbathing, risk, sunburn and their attitudes and behaviour in the sun especially on holiday. It is important to find out what and how much they know, what information has made an impact and why.

It is also necessary to use this information as baseline data against which to measure any change the intervention might make. Planners and implementers cannot possibly say what effect an intervention has had if they have no baseline data against which to measure. In the epidemiological analysis it is essential to study professional and public attitudes, assess knowledge, and seek understanding of behaviour so specific outcome objectives can be set and subsequently measured.

Research has shown that professionals involved in cancer prevention programmes (as part of positive health promotion and protection) have a poor understanding of the epidemiology of the issue. As well as this, they are confused about cancer prevention and the associated risk factors other than smoking, and have scant belief that cancer can be prevented. Research also shows that their personal experience of cancer over the lifecycle also affects their belief in prevention. For those in tertiary care, the impact of experience that is negative reduces the belief in prevention. This mirrors the beliefs and attitudes of the lay public. Because there is generally a confusion in both groups about the difference between risk and probability, facts about incidence, morbidity, mortality and survival have little real meaning. Personal experience has far more impact: someone always knows someone who has died painfully and horribly from cancer. These stories become the basis of community myths and misconceptions (Weston 1994).

The key tasks of professionals involved in the promotion of safe-sun messages is to know and understand these facts themselves. They also need to have the opportunity to explore their own beliefs and attitudes about cancer and cancer prevention and its role in health promotion. Through this process they will be able to interpret the picture more realistically for the public and target groups within it. More importantly, the nature and tenor of the messages they promote will be more positive. In turn they will be able to talk with the public about cancer, openly and supportively. To promote positive protection in the sun means that individuals' fears and anxieties about cancer cannot be denied. Denial, fear and anxiety block the communication process with the result that messages are ignored or treated cynically. The epidemiological evidence needs to be understood in the local setting too. Breaking the picture down so that it has meaning in one's own community or group is important. It can be easier to ignore global data as it is outside the realm of personal experience, but not so easy when it comes closer to home. Researchers need to develop ways of colourfully depicting the local situation. This all helps the individual to have a whole picture. Educators know from learning theory that learning is more effective when individuals have the whole picture: all the parts must come together for it to be remembered and acted upon (Weston 1994).

Socio-cultural determinants of sun behaviour

Research is required in this phase to understand the culturally and socially specific attitudes and behaviours that lead individuals to put themselves at risk. Populations have not always sunbathed with such abandon as is the norm currently. Understanding the complex combination of factors which have combined together historically and culturally to attract individuals to sunbathe is necessary if planners are to understand the values placed on such rituals and the value individuals will place on change (Porter Novelli 1991).

The social context in which individuals have lived and currently live has a bearing on their beliefs, attitudes and behaviour, in other words on their lifestyle. The social and peer group in which they move and spend their working and leisure lives is important in influencing their lifestyle and choices. The impact of the media, social and community activities also influences choices.

The historical picture is also important in understanding how patterns of behaviour and lifestyle develop and are maintained. With sunbathing, socio-economic factors are also indicators of possible other social factors that are important. Aspiring to a suntan was once a popular hobby. Young people in the 1970s and 1980s pursued suntans as a measure of beauty, sexuality and fashion. Even during the winter health clubs, beauty parlours and health farms encouraged individuals to spend time on sunbeds or in solariums. The media in its promotion of fashion encouraged (first stimulated by Coco Chanel) brown bodies as fashionable and worth aspiring to in order to be attractive.

Individuals used various methods to help their suntan along, such as olive oil, cooking oil, and tin foil to reflect the heat (there were even deaths from the use of tin foil). The suntan industry was assured of a successful market when it developed suntan lotions. With the promotion of such lotions there was the false sense of security: individuals could sunbathe safely. Only relatively recently did it become known that this might be at the price of health and life. Common sense was abandoned as deep and dark tans were pursued. In the 1950s there was common sense about the sun, with mothers protecting their children with cotton vests, hats and shirts when in the sun and the use of calomile lotion if children did get burned. Children played outdoors much more all through the year and so had the benefit of the less fierce spring sun and of tanning slowly and naturally. New Zealand experts still hold this view, that just as outdoor workers may be protected from melanoma by their slow exposure to ultra violet light, so might we all. However, this may indeed increase the risk of basal cell carcinoma. There is still argument about just what constitutes a safe message (Newton 1994).

History can give clues to the way sunbathing patterns develop and become maintained. In continental Europe the historical patterns differ, but all the indigenous populations remain out of the midday sun, and the midday siesta has encouraged and formulated cultural patterns that protect from the sun and benefit health too. Even in springtime the indigenous populations cover their heads and necks as protection. It is an interesting feature of the British on holiday that they continue culture-specific behaviour in another country rather than follow the role model of the indigenous population.

The film and arts industry also played its part with the golden brown bodies of the Californian beauty, sunbathing all the year. Just as in promoting the image of a smoker as successful, cool and in control, so they promoted the golden body in the same way. Is it any wonder that individuals wanted to emulate this image in their own bid to choose lifestyles that appeared wealthy, successful and attractive? To understand how the behaviour developed is also to understand how it can be encouraged to change. It is not as simple as seeking to reverse the pattern. Unravelling all these entangled beliefs and attitudes can give the clues for catalysts to change.

Promoting the image of the successful attractive person without the suntan can encourage safe-sun behaviour. One need only look how promoting *not* smoking as the norm has changed what is acceptable in society and what is not, with the added bonus of reducing deaths from lung cancer. History also shows that in the

1920s when the wealthy did go abroad they remained covered and sheltered from the sun as they valued their delicate white skin; during British colonial history this also remained the case. This was reinforced by the army, navy and airforce who always insisted on protection against the sun for servicemen.

So behaviours have been positive in the past with great respect for the power of ultraviolet light and for the damage it can do both in terms of ageing and sunburn. Why was this cultural pattern reversed and how can it be reinstated? Grappling with these issues is the task for researchers and planners (Dickinson 1994; Newton 1994; Weston 1994).

Individual assessments of risk

Research can include, in the behavioural and social diagnosis, different ways of understanding all the factors individuals believe lead them to want to sunbathe, to have tans and to take risks. Understanding the concept of risk is essential in this part of the needs assessment. As well as this, educators need to know how much knowledge individuals have about their own predisposing factors for at-risk behaviour. This includes the knowledge they have about all the environmental factors described above, as well as their personal predisposing factors (McWhirter and Weston 1994; Wetton and Collins 1994). As planners and educators it is important to know how people estimate:

- skin type and colour;
- age and risk;
- fair or red hair and green or blue eyes;
- tendency to freckle;
- moles on the body (40+ is a risk factor);
- previous episodes of sunburn especially in childhood;
- family history of melanoma (and the effects on people if this is raised as a risk factor).

And they need to know how they estimate their external risk factors such as:

- intensity of sunlight;
- geographical location;
- altitude (which applies to skiers and mountaineers);
- wind force (sailors and also watersportsmen of all types);

- atmospheric conditions;
- exposure and time of day.

The influence of peer group and social indicators of success and wealth cannot be ignored in the choice of lifestyle and therefore risk behaviour as predisposing factors. These can act as powerful reinforcing factors, continually maintaining risk – affecting behaviour even when individuals accept the safe-sun message. This is where population messages through campaigns which aim to change the ethos and norms of a population and culture can be useful. Change the accepted culture and, in turn, behaviour will be affected: no smoking is the norm now, for example, and educators need to reach a stage where safe-sun behaviour is the norm. The power of population campaigns cannot be ignored when planning interventions (Sanson-Fisher 1990; Wetton and Collins 1994).

Enabling people to change their behaviour

As the social diagnosis aims to understand complex cultural and social patterns, the behavioural diagnosis seeks to explore the factors that combine to form behavioural repertoires. These may be individual or community based. To understand behaviour it is necessary to understand the historical context, culture and atmosphere in which it has been shaped and maintained. Beliefs and attitudes, social mores and values give added meaning to these patterns. The pathway of triadic influence shows clearly just how many strands there are to unravel in understanding why people behave as they do, even though they know and sometimes believe that it is detrimental to their health (Prochaska 1992; Hill and Sanson-Fisher 1993). Research with appropriate methodology is needed to understand these factors, with sampling that is valid and from which sound extrapolations can be made for each target population. In considering population approaches for safe-sun messages it is still necessary to understand the basis of behaviour.

With specific populations it is also important to understand the stage an individual is at in terms of wanting to change: in other words, the behaviours they are prepared to exchange for new ones to benefit their health. Lifestyle behaviour change is about the exchange of values, it has to be a valued exchange. Following the work of Prochaska, educators can understand the optimum points of influence in the behaviour change cycle and also appreciate how difficult change can be, with individuals making as many as five attempts over seven years to change behaviour (Prochaska 1992). Measuring behaviour change therefore needs an intervention which is planned over a number of years to monitor such change accurately (see the Australian model). Even in population programmes where there is a campaign message rather than a message to specifically targeted populations, it is possible to measure behaviour change (Kok and De Vries 1992). Consideration of the specific outcome objectives for a programme, whether it is for specific target groups or population based, needs to be founded on research that uses appropriate methodology for understanding behaviour, behaviour change and behavioural indicators for measuring change, if it is to be successful. If individuals value their current behaviour with its inherent risk more than they would value what is on offer from the interventions, then educators are unlikely to be successful. Planners need to know that the message they design will be valued by the client group because they have researched thoroughly what the clients do indeed value. If sunbathing is to be only a small part of the holiday, do they run the risk of feeling they have not had a holiday? What would they value in place of sunbathing? To know is to be successful in communicating the right message (Porter Novelli 1991; Green and Kreuter 1991).

A creative approach is needed to integrate all the research in the planning phase in the design of the intervention. This should encourage populations and individuals to make changes in their behaviour and to maintain them in the long term. In other words, the new behaviour becomes part of their construct system. The research should be used to extrapolate these factors for populations and specific target groups and as the basis for a campaign or more specifically targeted messages. Coupled with the epidemiological profile of populations or target groups, this is a powerful tool. Children can tell us what they know, how they perceive risk, how they perceive sun and sunbathing, and what precautions they should take when in the sun. When compared to Australian children who have been the target of ongoing safe-sun messages, research shows that British children do not have as much knowledge about keeping themselves safe in the sun. By this comparison it is easy to see where gaps in knowledge lie and how they might be solved (Wetton and Collins 1994). The profile of personal behaviour factors including internal motivation and knowledge of the external factors that influence behaviour and risk should give clear leads for planners (Tones 1992). All partners can have a role in such interventions. This is where resources and skills can be pooled. Each collaborative partner will have a role in deciding the most appropriate task for them both in design and implementation of the message.

Empowerment is a word much used and even less understood by those who use it. Making choices in lifestyle or life depends on the many internal and external factors operating for a person at a given point in time. However, this is not a static process and many catalysts can be used to influence an individual to change his or her behaviour. Increasing a person's ability to make choices and control one aspect of their life is a start, it gives them the first taste of taking responsibility for themselves and taking some control for their lives. It is like whetting the appetite, one small taste can have a powerful effect. Success means they will try again. The work of Rowe (1988) with severely depressed patients shows that this is possible when one seeks to understand the roots of behaviour, attitudes and beliefs. If, as educators or positive health promoters, one then maintains the awareness or support, this increases the success rate of change which is maintained. The heady power of this feeling in control acts as an aphrodisiac which encourages more. For safe-sun behaviour one needs to ensure that people can go on enjoying the outdoors and the sun safely. Empowerment means that they can control how and when they make a change based on the facts, and then when they choose to make the next one. This way they take control of their own risk reduction and positive health (Rowe 1988; Tones 1992; Prochaska 1992; Weston 1994).

Planning, implementation and evaluation

Having understood the task before them, planners need to assess the resources, both financial and human, and the extent of skills and experience they have at their disposal to implement such a programme. Managerial support for such a programme is essential. With priorities being determined by epidemiology, it is essential to ensure that the sun protection programme is a priority and that the management will support it from beginning to end. Public health programmes which will be monitored for efficacy and effectiveness need to be developed within a framework that supports each element of the programme. It is essential, therefore, to carry out an audit of, first, the resources available internally within the organisation responsible for overall intervention and, second, the resources available externally in the community to support such a programme. Too often in the past, programmes have been based on the good idea of one or more individuals, who then have to struggle without the appropriate resources to make the programme work.

As reduction in skin cancer is the target of the *Health of the Nation* in England and such targets have been set in Scotland and Wales along with other states in Europe and beyond, this should not be a problem in theory. In reality, however, it can be – as policy is often resource–neutral, and the expectation is for current resources to be used, or for organisations to combine in a collaborative way to share resources to implement programmes. This takes time and an essential task for managers is to ensure that time is invested in developing healthy alliances, team development, and in an audit of what is currently being done about sun protection in their local area as well as nationally. Reinventing the wheel should be avoided. The Australian sun protection programme based on behavioural science principles is an excellent model to use as a guide (The Anti-Cancer Foundation of Western Australia 1990). Understanding what has worked and been successful, and with whom, is a good way to start. The Australian campaigns have been evaluated and this provides useful information about strategies adopted in population or specifically targeted programmes, e.g. the educational process and language employed and the role of the media, schools, community and beach work (Green and Kreuter 1991; Kok and De Vries 1992).

Implementation: the questions to ask

To summarise, successful sun protection programmes are a combination of the following:
- quantitative evidence, i.e. epidemiology of global, national and local levels of incidence, morbidity and mortality as well as cure rates forming the basis of the programme and being explained adequately to the consumer;

- qualitative data that illuminates the quantitative information and gives some understanding about how populations and individuals perceive the issue of safe-sun behaviour;
- planning that is based on the combination of both of the above and which sets measurable outcome objectives;
- implementation of either population-based campaigns, intended to raise awareness, change the culture and change behaviour or specifically targeted programmes which include individual behaviour change objectives. These are not mutually exclusive but can be integrated to enhance impact. This has a pilot phase;
- formative evaluation following a pilot programme and then full implementation.
- summative evaluation which seeks to measure outcome objectives and effectiveness including behaviour change;
- healthy alliances and collaborative actions which seek to find creative ways to promote the safe-sun message;
- a combination of primary prevention, promoting positive health and protection in the sun, and secondary prevention to raise awareness of signs of change and the importance of seeking early advice.

The interventionist approach gives an opportunity to develop programmes in a single context. Safe-sun messages can be strategically and systematically planned. In the planning phase an attempt is made to answer five questions:

- How serious is the problem?
- Which behaviours are involved?
- What are the determinants of that behaviour?
- What options are there for change?
- How can these options be implemented? (Kok and de Vries 1992)

Planning takes into account many variables including:

- attitudes to cancer, public and professional;
- social and environmental issues;
- re-inforcing factors for such behaviour;
- enabling factors which may promote change and then reinforce change.

This framework for cancer prevention, of which safe-sun behaviour is part, is:

- integrated within existing health promotion programmes and budgets;
- intersectoral and involves collaboration between agencies;
- integrated with other chronic disease programmes and training;
- based on the principles of behavioural science.

Interventions, of which safe-sun behaviour is one, should:

- have measurable but realistic and achievable goals;
- be based on research that informs the planners, i.e. starts where the population or the individual is;
- provide opportunities for interaction with the client;
- offer support and maintenance programmes to sustain behaviour change;
- congratulate successful achievers;
- systematically build on that success.

Outcome evaluation asks the questions in reverse and measures changes in awareness, knowledge, attitudes and behaviour against the baseline data collected in the planning phase. Effectiveness studies have been shown to affect positively the quality of the planning (Kok and De Vries 1992; Green and Kreuter 1991; Porter Novelli 1991).

CONCLUSION

For those travelling either for work or leisure, the health promotion message should be consistent, promoted across a range of relevant settings, and be specific to different target groups. Travellers and holidaymakers should have the relevant information about the risk of sunbathing and their personal risk profile, the climatic conditions in the country they are visiting or during the summer at home, relevant information about sun-protection lotions, and information about the benefits of changing their behaviour.

Professionals need to know and understand the epidemiology on which the messages are based so that they may promote messages that are credible. They should form healthy alliances with a range of agencies and industry, and have sufficient resources to promote the campaign and to evaluate effectiveness. Promoting safety in the sun messages entails the development of such links with the travel, tourism and leisure industries as these provide the opportunities and promote the context for sun exposure on holiday. The safe-sun message means that everyone can go on enjoying the sun and the outdoors, if they respect the sun and its power. Educators need to take the same kind of common-sense precautions that are necessary in using any tool, driving the car or learning to swim. The message is: 'Enjoy the sun, make the most of warm sunny weather, but take care'. Health educators are not killjoys – too many enjoy the sun themselves!

REFERENCES

Alleyne, G. (1991) 'Health and tourism, the intersectoral linkages' in H. O. Lobel, R. Steffen and P. E. Kozarsky (eds) *Travel Medicine 2*, Proceedings of the Second Conference on International Travel Medicine: ISTM.
Armstrong, B. (1989) 'Epidemiology of malignant melanoma; intermittent on total accumulated exposure to the sun?', *Journal of Dermatology Surgical Oncology* 14, 8: 835–48.
The Anti-Cancer Foundation of Western Australia (1990) *Do You Want to Save Your Child's Skin?*, Melbourne: Anti-Cancer Foundation of Western Australia.
Box, V. and Anderson, Y. (1993) *Professional Attitudes to Cancer Survey, Southampton*: Southampton University.
Cancer Research Campaign (1992) *Be a Mole Watcher*, London: Cancer Research Campaign.
Department of Health (1992) *The Health of the Nation: a Strategy for Health in England*, London: HMSO.
Dickinson, L. (1994) 'Sun exposure; the risks and issues' in L. Dickinson, and D. Pizzala (eds) *Safe in the Sun*, Bexhill-on-Sea: South East Thames Regional Health Authority.
Doherty, V. R. and Mackie, R. M. (1989) 'Experience of a public education programme in early detection of cutaneous malignant melanoma', *British Medical Journal* 297: 388–91.
Ewles, L. and Simnett, I. (1989) *Promoting Health: A Practical Guide to Health Education*, Chichester: Wiley.
Foot, G., Girgis, A., Boyle, C. A. and Sanson-Fisher, R. W. (1993) 'Solar protection behaviours: a study of beachgoers', *Australian Journal of Public Health* 17, 3: 209–14.
Forman, J. (1991) 'Ozone hole set to grow', *Financial Times*, 16 October.
Green, L. W. and Kreuter, M. W. (1991) *Health Promotion Planning: an Environmental and Educational Approach*, Mayfield: Palo Alto.

Hall, A. (1992) 'Lay beliefs about cancer', in T. Heller, L. Bailey, B. Davey and S. Pattison (eds) *Reducing Risks of Cancer*, Oxford: Oxford University Press.
Hill, M. and Sanson-Fisher, R. W. (1993) *Behavioural Science Workshop Proceedings*, Amsterdam: UICC.
Ingrams, R. (1994) *Observer*, 1 May 1994.
Kok, G. and De Vries, H. (1992) 'Primary prevention of cancers: the need for health education and intersectoral health promotion', in *Reducing the Risk of Cancers*, Oxford: Oxford University Press.
Mackie, R. M. (1986) *An Illustrated Guide to the Recognition of Early Malignant Melanoma*, Glasgow: Glasgow University.
Mackie, R. M. and Aitchison, T. (1982) 'Severe sunburn and subsequent risk of primary cutaneous malignant melanoma in Scotland', *British Journal of Cancer* 46, 955–60.
McWhirter, J. and Weston, R. (1994) 'Sharks, cliffs and jagged rocks', in *Children's Concept of Risk*, Health Education No. 2. Manual 1994: MCB University Press.
McWhirter, J., Wetton, N. and King, A. (1994) *The Health Authority: Best of Health Project*, London: Health Education Authority.
National Cancer Institute and American Cancer Society (1991) *Report of the Sixth International Conference on Cancer Communication*, Washington.
Newton, J. (1994) 'Education and action for skin care', in L. Dickinson and D. Pizzala (eds) *Safe in the Sun*, Bexhill-on-Sea: South East Thames Regional Health Authority.
Porter Novelli (1991) *Psychographic Analysis*, 1 & 2: Washington Office of Cancer Communications.
Prochaska, O. J. (1992) 'What causes people to change from unhealthy to health enhancing behaviour?', in T. Heller, L. Bailey, B. Davey and S. Pattison (eds) *Reducing the Risk of Cancers*, Oxford: Oxford University Press.
Rolls, L. (1992) *Team Development: A Manual of Facilitation for Health. Educators and Health Promoters*, London: London Health Education Authority.
Rowe, D. (1988) *Choosing not Losing*, London: Fontana.
Sanson-Fisher, R. W. (1990) 'A critical review of Australian cancer organisations' public education material', *Community Health Studies* XIV, 2: 171–4.
Storm, H. and Manders, T. (1991) *Cancer Incidence in Denmark 1988*, Danish Cancer Society.
Tones, K. (1992) 'Empowerment and the promotion of health', *Journal of the Institute of Health Education*, 30, 4: 133–7.
Vågerö, D., Swerdlow, A. J. and Bera, I. V. (1990) 'Occupation and melanoma: cancer registrations in England and Wales and Sweden', *British Journal of Industrial Medicine*, 47: 317–24.
Weston, R. (1992) 'Cancer prevention programmes in health promotion', *European Journal of Cancer Prevention* 2, Supplement 2: 27–9.

—— (1994) 'Cancer communications: the health promotion challenge', *European Journal of Cancer Care* 3, 3: 102–15.
Wetton, N. and Collins, M. (1994) 'Children's perception of the sun on the skin: the missing link', in L. Dickinson and D. Pizzala (eds) *Safe in the Sun*, Bexhill-on-Sea: South East Thames Regional Health Authority.
Youell, R. (1994) *Leisure and Tourism*, London: Pitman Publishing.

Chapter 13

International tourists
A specific target group for AIDS prevention programmes

Georg Bröring

INTRODUCTION

One of the most striking phenomena of the world today is the ever-increasing mobility of people. The motives for this mobility are numerous. People move in order to flee war zones or to escape from political, economic or ecological crises. Migrant workers are also a significant mobile population, as many national economies depend on the human power of foreigners. Furthermore, the world-wide operation of industrial or commercial companies leads to extensive business travel and this makes a considerable contribution to international mobility. Last but not least, an important reason for movement across national borders is tourism. The tourist sector is vital to the economies of many countries and in many societies travelling has become part of the general lifestyle. In the European context, the relaxation of travel restrictions between Central/Eastern European countries and Western countries has had a significant impact on the mobility between these regions. Tourism has increased, greater labour migration has taken place, and an increasing number of business people travel to and from these countries.

Mobility in itself does not necessarily have medical consequences. However, people in an alien environment – be it for a short time as a traveller or a longer time as a member of an ethnic minority group – are influenced in their attitudes and behaviour by the fact that they lack certain aspects of their usual social and cultural settings. It is the behaviour of mobile people and their ability to cope in unfamiliar surroundings which determine the likelihood that they may run risks to their health.

Growing mobility has clearly had an impact on the epidemiology of HIV and AIDS and efforts to stop the further spread of HIV must, therefore, take the mobility factor into account. People from regions with low HIV-prevalence move to countries with a higher HIV-prevalence and vice versa – in this connection, one might think about the mobility between countries in Central/Eastern Europe and Western Europe. Tourists from epidemic centres travel to places where HIV is still very rare and the other way around – here, one might think about the (sex) tourism to countries in East Africa.

An interesting example for the impact of mobility on the spread of HIV is reported from a small town in the foothills of the Himalayas which is located far away from any HIV epidemiological centre. In this town, HIV was detected in one family (parents and child). The route of transmission could be traced and linked to the husband's profession: as a truck driver he regularly travelled the whole country, he used to stay away from home for longer periods and had sexual encounters during these times.

Through travel, people with different social and cultural backgrounds, as well as different levels of education, come in contact with one another. Concepts about sexuality can vary and the availability of health services can differ considerably. Consequently, HIV/AIDS prevention activities are affected by mobility as well.

In Europe, an important project that is specifically involved in supporting prevention programmes aimed at mobile populations, is the European Project 'AIDS and Mobility'. The first part of this article describes the origins and development of this project and briefly summarises its work with travellers, ethnic minorities and migrant communities. In the second part of this chapter, the needs, possibilities and restrictions of AIDS prevention programmes aimed specifically at international tourists will be reviewed. Examples of campaigns undertaken in Europe to alert tourists to the risks of HIV infection will be provided.

THE EUROPEAN PROJECT 'AIDS AND MOBILITY'

In 1990, the European Project 'AIDS and Mobility' ('A and M') was established at the request of the World Health Organisation. The project is located within the Dutch Centre for Health Promotion and Health Education in Utrecht and is funded by the European Commission, the World Health Organisation and the Ministry of Welfare, Health and Culture of the Netherlands.

The 'A and M' Project is advised by an international and a national steering committee. The participants of these committees are recruited from AIDS service organisations, migrant and tourist organisations, and research institutes. Policy-makers participate in the steering committee as well. The steering committees give an essential input to the development of the 'A and M' Project. They advise on the focus of the planned activities with regard to geographical and target group priorities. Priorities are defined according to the needs of professionals in the field and in relation to the (perceived) risk behaviour of possible target groups.

In the first stage of the project, a central aim was to undertake a broad survey of issues that are connected with the subject of AIDS and mobility. This necessitated the definition of different categories of mobile populations, a review of the most significant risk situations with regard to the transmission of HIV which could arise in the context of travel and international mobility, and an examination of the most appropriate ways of developing preventive interventions in this area (Hendriks 1991). On the basis of this initial survey, the implementation phase of the 'A and M' Project started in 1992. In general, the services and activities of the project can be divided into three fields: a documentation service, an international network of institutions and individuals, and the development of small-scale pilot projects and organisation of international workshops.

The 'AIDS and Mobility' documentation service

In the field of AIDS education and prevention, one can observe an increasing focus on mobile populations. One of the indicators of this phenomenon is the number of research studies and publications on this subject that have been released in recent years (see Table 13.1). Research projects have investigated sexual behaviour of tourists (Wilke and Kleiber 1992; Herold *et al.* 1992; Daniels *et al.* 1992; Ford 1991); reports have discussed AIDS prevention programmes for ethnic minorities (Haour-Knipe 1991); and reports have explored the need and possibility of health education designed for migrant sex workers (Bröring 1993a). The 'A and M' documentation service collects these publications

Table 13.1 Number of publications in the 'AIDS and Mobility' database by year of publication

Year	No. of publications
1983	1
1984	3
1985	4
1986	4
1987	8
1988	12
1989	31
1990	101
1991	93
1992	71
1993	72
1994	59*

Note:* Preliminary figure

and the 'AIDS and Mobility – bibliography of publications about travellers, ethnic minorities, migrant communities and HIV/AIDS' (Arends and Hommes 1994) is updated and disseminated on a regular basis.

In addition to books, articles and reports, the 'A and M' Project also collects educational materials that are developed for migrants, ethnic minorities and travellers. These materials include leaflets, posters, audio and video cassettes, stickers and brochures. A compilation of educational materials available in Europe, *AIDS and Mobility – Materials for HIV/AIDS Education Aimed at Travellers, Ethnic Minorities and Migrant Communities*, is available (Hommes and van der Vleugel 1993). (See Figure 13.1 for examples of HIV prevention campaign materials aimed at travellers/holidaymakers.)

The 'AIDS and Mobility' network

The database of the 'A and M' network currently includes approximately 800 individuals and representatives of organisations (see Table 13.2 for a list of network members). These include researchers in higher education institutions, health professionals working in public health services, governmental and non-governmental AIDS or health agencies, migrant organisations, and representatives from the commercial tourist sector.

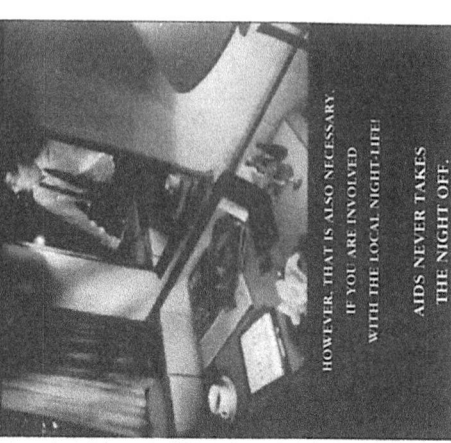

Figure 13.1 Health education materials promoting safer sex in the context of travel from Australia, the United Kingdom and Denmark

AIDS prevention programmes 265

Table 13.2 'AIDS and Mobility' network members

Country	#	Country	#	Country	#
Albania	4	Indonesia	1	San Marino	111
Algeria	2	Irish Republic	7	Serbia	17
Armenia	1	Israel	5	Slovakia	6
Australia	4	Italy	27	Slovenia	12
Austria	6	Japan	2	South Africa	2
Azerbaijan	1	Kazakhstan	1	Spain	46
Belarus	2	Kirghizia	1	Sudan	1
Belgium	34	Kuwait	1	Sweden	22
Benin	1	Latvia	4	Switzerland	8
Botswana	3	Liechtenstein	2	Syria	1
Bulgaria	14	Lithuania	6	Tadjikistan	1
Canada	5	Luxembourg	7	Tanzania	1
Chile	1	Macedonia	1	Thailand	2
Croatia	4	Malta	4	Trinidad	1
Czech Republic	12	Morocco	24	Tunisia	5
Denmark	22	Mexico	1	Turkey	18
Egypt	2	Moldavia	1	Turkmenistan	11
Estonia	6	Monaco	3	Ukraine	1
Finland	5	Nepal	2	United Kingdom	95
France	50	Netherlands	62	United States	8
Georgia	2	Nigeria	2	Zambia	1
Germany	80	Norway	15		
Ghana	2	Philippines	1		
Greece	10	Poland	20		
Hong Kong	1	Portugal	13		
Hungary	12	Qatar	1		
Iceland	4	Romania	5		
India	4	Russia	13	Total	805

One important purpose of the 'A and M' network is to facilitate communication between its members. For example, if a health service or an AIDS service organisation is planning activities in a certain field (e.g. a prevention campaign for tourists in a holiday resort) the 'A and M' staff members can put them in touch with people who have already developed expertise in this field. For example, the experiences that have been acquired in the 'Sea, Sand and Safer Sex' campaign of the Plymouth and Torbay Health Authority (see Chapter 14 this volume) were useful for the development of comparable interventions in Greece; health authorities in Switzerland and in the Netherlands that are planning AIDS prevention activities for sex workers from Central/Eastern Europe were put in touch with experts that were involved in the bilateral project between Poland and Germany organised by 'A and M'; outreach workers in Berlin and Amsterdam who provide Polish and Romanian male prostitutes with AIDS education, were given the possibility to exchange their experiences in an 'A and M' pilot project (Bröring 1994).

Communication between the 'A and M' staff members and the network has two dimensions. On the one hand, the 'A and M' Project informs the members of the network by regular mailings about the project's activities and publications. On the other hand, the members of the network indicate specific problems and the need for action in relation to mobility and risks of HIV infection. Communication with the network is important for defining the priorities of the 'A and M' Project and for the planning of activities.

Pilot projects and the international workshops

Since its inception, the 'A and M' Project has organised a number of activities to stimulate and support the development of prevention initiatives in the field of mobility and AIDS. These have involved the development of educational materials, the organisation of workshops and expert meetings, and the co-ordination of small-scale prevention programmes. An important part of each 'A and M' pilot project is the report of the activity in order to disseminate the experiences towards the members of the 'A and M' network and to stimulate follow-up activities.

Previous 'A and M' pilot projects include:

- a bilateral prevention project between Poland and Germany aimed at female Polish sex workers in Berlin (Bröring 1993a);
- a workshop on AIDS prevention programmes aimed at Turkish migrant populations in Europe (van Duifhuizen and Cinibulak 1992);
- a project to investigate the possibilities of including European airline companies in prevention activities aimed at air travellers;
- the development of educational materials for young men from Central/Eastern Europe who engage in prostitution in Western European cities (Bröring 1994);
- workshops on drug use, mobility and HIV in Europe: Amsterdam, May 1993 and Prague, December 1993 (Bröring and de Jong 1993);

Figure 13.2 HIV/AIDS prevention materials produced in Santorini in association with the AIDS and Mobility project

- an evaluation meeting on educational materials for Turkish migrant populations in Europe;
- a workshop on AIDS prevention campaigns aimed at Maghreb speaking ethnic minorities in Europe (Sahraoui and van Duifhuizen 1993);
- the initiation of AIDS prevention activities aimed at tourists in Greece (Bröring 1993b) (see Figure 13.2 for examples of HIV/AIDS prevention materials produced in Santorini).

The *AIDS and Mobility Manual for the Implementation of HIV/AIDS Prevention Activities Aimed at Travellers and Migrants* (van Duifhuizen and Bröring 1993) gives an overview of a diversity of prevention projects carried out by the 'A and M' Project and other health/AIDS organisations in Europe.

Current activities

The 'A and M' Project strives to put the 'AIDS and Mobility' issue on the agendas of governmental and non-governmental organisations and institutions. This happens partly by the direct involvement of representatives from national ministries into 'A and M' workshops, and partly through the participation in international meetings (e.g. organised by the World Health Organisation) that are attended by representatives from national governments. Presentations are given at AIDS-specific as well as mobility-specific conferences, for example International AIDS Conferences (van Duifhuizen and Hendriks 1992; Bröring and van Duifhuizen 1993) as well as conferences on Migration and Health and on Tourism and Health (Bröring 1992; Bröring 1993c). Furthermore, contributions have been made to various publications. Reports about pilot activities that are relevant for the development of appropriate policies (e.g. the report of the workshop on drug use and mobility, Bröring and de Jong 1993) have been brought to the attention of national and European policymakers.

The 'A and M' staff members are increasingly asked to contribute to other projects aimed at mobile populations; they participate in consultative committees, give advice on research studies and project designs, and comment on educational materials that are developed for travellers, migrants and ethnic minorities. Currently, the 'A and M' Project participates in steering committees of the 'Migration, Health and AIDS' Project (implemented by HIV Denmark), the 'European Symposium on Health and the Sex Industry' (organised by the Network of Sexwork Projects in Edinburgh/UK) and the 'Migrants, AIDS and Human Rights Conference' in Leuven/Belgium. Contributions were also made to the 'Travel, Lifestyles and Health' Project in Canterbury/UK, the 'Projet Migration Santé' in Strasbourg/France and a project aimed at Turkish and Kurdish ethnic minorities implemented by health authorities in Hackney/London.

The focus of present activities lies on the mobility of sex workers who travel from Central/Eastern Europe to Western and Southern European countries. Although quantitative data about prostitution and East–West migration are lacking, health workers in Western cities frequently report this phenomenon. In the metropolitan areas of Berlin and Amsterdam, for example, an increasing number of male prostitutes from Poland, Romania and the Czech Republic can be observed, since travel restrictions in former socialist countries have been relaxed (Marijnissen 1994; Kouters 1994; Bröring 1994). Mobility of female sex workers is also frequent between countries of the former Soviet Union and Turkey (Briggs 1993). An 'A and M' pilot project on female prostitution, mobility and HIV prevention in the Black Sea Region (Turkey and Georgia) was implemented in 1994.

Another focus is on asylum-seekers in Western Europe and their specific needs for AIDS education. Furthermore, the 'A and M' Project is involved in activities aimed at various migrant communities and the development of an AIDS prevention project aimed at mobile drug-users in EU member states. The 'A and M' working plan for 1994 gives a summary about the various activities in this field (van Duifhuizen 1994).

THE 'AIDS AND MOBILITY' PROJECT AND TOURISM

Within the scope of the 'A and M' Project, tourists are one target group among others. The 'A and M' Project has contributed to HIV/AIDS prevention programmes aimed at tourists in a number of ways: by participating in advisory committees; by networking between institutions that are involved in activities directed towards tourists; and by organising a small-scale pilot project in Greece

(Bröring 1993b). Furthermore, the 'A and M' Project strives to create or maintain the awareness of the tourism industry with respect to tourism and AIDS, for example by making presentations at international conferences on tourist health.

Rationale for specific prevention activities aimed at tourists

A number of recent publications have stressed the impact of international travel on health hazards in general (Cossar and Reid 1989) and on the spread of sexually transmitted diseases (STDs) and HIV in particular (De Schrijver and Meheus 1989; Hawkes 1992; von Reyn et al. 1990; Daniels et al. 1992; Mulhall 1993). Although it is hard to measure how many people actually acquire HIV infection abroad, there are numerous indications for the need of specific HIV/AIDS prevention efforts aimed at tourists. Psychological factors influence human behaviour while on holiday (Pearce 1982). Tourists want to relax and do not want to worry about any inconveniences or health hazards. With greater time and opportunity it is easier to meet people, and tourists are more receptive to new contacts. A number of research studies have been carried out to investigate the sexual behaviour of tourists (Ford 1991; Conway et al. 1990; Kleiber 1991; Wilke and Kleiber 1992). These studies demonstrate the following point:

- Sexual activity of unaccompanied travellers with fellow tourists and the local population is particularly frequent on holiday (Conway et al. 1990: 69–70).
- Condom use in sexual contacts with fellow tourists and the local population is far from consistent (Ford 1991: 106–9).
- Many young people make new friends on holiday and build up relationships that include sexual contacts, which are to a considerable degree unsafe (Ford 1991: 106).
- Alcohol consumption has an important impact on the sexual behaviour of tourists (Conway et al. 1990; Ford 1991).

It can be concluded from these studies that factors like age, holiday setting (travelling alone or with a partner) and co-determinants of sexual behaviour like alcohol consumption have to be taken into consideration when planning and implementing HIV/AIDS prevention programmes for tourists. An interesting aspect is the fact that 'short-tem relationships' on holiday are often associated with intimacy and love (Kleiber 1991: 24) and that they are not seen as 'casual contacts'. Under these circumstances, the necessity of safer sex is frequently neglected. Certainly, tourists should not be considered a specific risk group. Tourism should rather be seen as a specific situation – like going out to a disco – that can lead to risky sexual behaviour and that requires specific AIDS prevention approaches. Finally, if prevention campaigns in a tourism setting are implemented successfully, holidays could be an important 'practice ground' for health educators on the principle that 'If they can do it there, they can do it everywhere'.

Principles underpinning AIDS prevention activities with tourists

Hendriks (1991) lists a variety of preconditions for successful AIDS prevention activities geared towards tourists, some of which will be reviewed below. There are a number of basic principles for AIDS prevention campaigns in a holiday setting.

- Campaigns should avoid any suggestion of blaming tourists for the spread of HIV; the stigmatisation of the tourist sector would have counter-productive effects.
- Prevention campaigns should not interfere with the main objectives of holidays, namely relaxation and entertainment, and it should be emphasised that holidays can be enjoyed as long as sensible precautions are taken.
- Prevention campaigns for tourists should fit in with other prevention activities in the home country and the country of destination in order to prevent confusion.
- Prevention messages need to be culturally acceptable for the tourist population and the host society alike. This is particularly important as issues like sexuality, homosexuality and drug use have to be addressed. In this connection it should be mentioned, however, that many issues can be addressed more readily than health workers and health authorities often expect. Safer sex can be discussed on the Greek Islands as well as in British holiday resorts, and air travellers are not shocked if they find a condom in their overnight kit on the plane. There is thus no need for excessive shyness.
- AIDS prevention activities for tourists should be based on a broad range of co-operative partnerships. Support should be

sought from health services, the tourist business, AIDS service organisations and political bodies. Furthermore transport agencies (air carriers, railway and bus companies) and tour operators should be asked for collaboration. An important group that should be involved in AIDS prevention activities is seasonal workers (see Ford 1991; also Ford and Eiser, Chapter 8 in this volume). In general, they have good access to the target group, they know the best ways to address tourists and are therefore very feasible intermediaries.

- If possible, prevention campaigns should provide practical information, e.g. where to obtain condoms, the phone number of the AIDS hotline, or how to contact local health services.

Problems encountered in AIDS prevention work with tourists

A major obstacle with which AIDS prevention programmes for tourists have to contend is the diversity of the target group. Holidaymakers can be distinguished according to their mode of travelling (alone; with a partner/family; in a group) and in relation to the primary motivation served by their holiday (relaxation; culture; adventure). These factors contribute to the degree tourists might be at risk of HIV infection and the need for preventive activities. Therefore, it is essential that it is made clear beforehand who exactly should be reached with a campaign and what the appropriate messages and means of communication should be.

The specific situation on holiday can be another obstacle. Tourists want to enjoy themselves on vacation and do not want to be faced with problematic issues. Good intentions are sometimes set aside for a carefree time and the threat of health hazards is not taken seriously.

The co-operation with the tourist business can also be a problem. Providing information on health issues and diseases is not a high priority on the agenda of the travel industry as it strives to provide its clientele with a trouble-free product. AIDS prevention campaigns can remind customers of potentially unpleasant consequences and this does not sit easily within a time and pattern of activities which are expected to be enjoyable. However, many of these obstacles can be overcome if the right messages are formulated, if appropriate activities are implemented, and if key persons are involved.

Furthermore, AIDS prevention campaigns geared towards tourists are restricted by the AIDS awareness in the general population. Too often, AIDS is still seen as a disease that affects mainly specific subgroups of society (Conway, Gillies and Slack 1990). In this context, prevention campaigns should emphasise the fact that it is not the attachment to a certain group which puts people at risk but their sexual behaviour.

Finally, there is a lack of research with regard to tourism and AIDS. There is little knowledge about the actual number of HIV infections acquired on holiday and evaluation studies of AIDS prevention campaigns for tourists are insufficient. There are studies about the acceptance and the recall rates of prevention activities (e.g. Alexander 1992; Gruer et al., 1993), but the knowledge about the effects of campaigns on the sexual behaviour of the addressed population is rather scarce. In this field, additional efforts are necessary.

EXAMPLES OF EUROPEAN CAMPAIGNS AIMED AT TOURISTS

Over the last decade, a variety of AIDS prevention programmes aimed at tourists have been implemented. It is virtually impossible to give a complete review of these activities as many of them have been organised on a local level and have not been well documented (see Chapter 11 in this volume for discussion of campaigns in the United Kingdom).

The examples described below represent campaigns on a national, regional and local level. (Further details and illustrations of the materials used can be found in Hommes and van der Vleugel 1993.) In 1992, the Danish National Board of Health developed a series of advertisements to address travellers in different settings: business travellers, backpackers, unattached travellers to the Mediterranean, sex tourists and others. The advertisements were published in inflight magazines, lifestyle magazines and other publications.

In Australia, the Commonwealth Department of Health, Housing and Community Services in co-operation with the National Council on AIDS launched a nationwide 'Travel Safe' campaign in 1989. Posters were displayed at international airports and leaflets and give-aways were distributed by travel agencies and tour operators. This campaign was accompanied by an extensive evaluation study which reported a high level of acceptance by the target group. The overall recall rate of the campaign was 46 per cent (n = 430); those posters that were displayed in the airport toilets were recalled by 87 per cent of the travellers that had used the toilets. Seventy-eight per cent of the respondents agreed strongly or very strongly that the campaign 'reminded me about HIV/AIDS infection'; 86 per cent felt that the campaign was 'not embarrassing'; 84 per cent felt strongly or very strongly that the campaign was 'not a waste of time and money'; and 80 per cent agreed strongly or very strongly that it 'should be given to all travellers' (Alexander 1992).

The Health Education Authority (HEA) in the United Kingdom has undertaken a number of travel and holiday-related campaigns involving collaborative work with radio channels, advertising in the youth press, and production of posters. Advertisements for condoms were displayed at international airports under the motto 'Don't go too far without it!' In 1993, the HEA funded an insert in MIZZ magazine on 'Summer Love'. In addition, the Department of Health has undertaken a major national campaign ('Travel Safe') through newspaper advertising and the production of leaflets and posters to alert travellers of the risks of HIV infection. This has been evaluated and the campaign was re-run in the summer months of 1994 (see Stears, Chapter 11, this volume, for details).

The STD foundation in the Netherlands has developed leaflets and posters about AIDS and STDs in various languages which are specifically designed for young tourists. These materials are available at railway stations, travel agencies and in youth hostels.

In Germany, in 1991 the Federal Health Education Authority produced television advertisements to promote condom use in unattached travellers. These were broadcast regularly during the summer months of 1992 and 1993.

At a regional level, the 'Sea, Sand and Safer Sex' project undertaken by the Plymouth and Torbay Health Authority in the United Kingdom should be mentioned. During the summer months of 1992-4, specially trained young peer educators organised party nights in numerous tourist venues. They involve customers in quizzes and distribute prizes, condoms and AIDS education materials. These activities involve a high degree of co-operation with the local holiday industry (see Ford, Inman and Mathie, Chapter 14, this volume).

On a local level, health authorities tend to address travellers at airports and railway stations. Such activities have been organised at the airport in Glasgow (Scotland) and the railway station in Düsseldorf (Germany). In major cities of the Netherlands, 'Gay Tourist Info' is available. This brochure gives information about tourist attractions, safer-sex guidelines and health services for gay men visiting the Netherlands. Experiences with regard to the co-operation with the tourism industry vary considerably. In the preparatory stage of a pilot project aimed at tourists in Greece implemented by the 'A and M' Project, the local businesses catering to tourists proved to be very willing to collaborate. The Plymouth and Torbay Health Authority had the same positive experience during their 'Sea, Sand and Safer Sex' campaign. On the other hand, attempts made by the 'A and M' Project to motivate airline companies to get involved in AIDS prevention campaigns were received very reluctantly. Although the need for action was widely acknowledged, the companies were anxious about being linked with the spread of a disease and collaboration was virtually impossible. An interesting exception is the Austrian airline company 'Lauda Air'. They have provided their long-distance travellers with condoms that are distributed through the overnight kits. This initiative was widely appreciated by the customers. Once the word has spread that the responsibility of the tourist business for their clients can create a positive image, more of these initiatives might be realised.

Future developments

In the future, the possibility for European-wide AIDS prevention programmes for tourists should be investigated. In this context, one might think about a concerted action in which all international airports in Europe display multilingual prevention materials. Travellers would be addressed in the country of origin with the same messages as in the country of destination. The message that AIDS does not recognise borders could be more widely broadcast. The Conference of European Community Parliamentarians on HIV/AIDS that was held in April 1993 in London stressed both the relevance of mobility-related issues and the importance of international collaboration in the fight against AIDS (British All-Party Parliamentary Group on AIDS 1993). European-wide

AIDS prevention efforts aimed at international travellers – and the funding of activities – could prove that the statements in the Conference's report are more than mere good intentions. Another issue that should be addressed in the future is the travelling of ethnic minorities to their country of origin. On the one hand, it seems that sexual behaviours are different in the country of origin to those in the host country; in that sense that safer sex is less consistent in the country of origin. On the other hand, travelling ethnic minorities might be suitable intermediaries to spread information on AIDS and safer sex in their country of origin. In this connection, one might think about travellers between European countries and their former colonies, e.g. between the United Kingdom and India; between France and West Africa; between the Netherlands and the Antilles; and so on. Travel agencies that are specialised in providing services to specific ethnic minority groups could be involved in AIDS prevention activities for these target groups.

International mobility – be it migration, tourism or business travel – is a prominent feature of virtually all societies now and will continue to be into the future. In the field of health education in general and AIDS prevention in particular, policies and activities have to be developed to respond in an appropriate way to this phenomenon and to provide optimal health protection and advice.

REFERENCES

Alexander, J. (1992) *Evaluation of the Information for Travellers' Campaign 'Travel Safe'* (preliminary executive summary), Sydney: AGB.
Arends, R. and Hommes, M. (1994) *AIDS and Mobility: Bibliography of Publications about Travellers, Ethnic Minorities, Migrant Communities and HIV/AIDS*, Amsterdam: European Project 'AIDS and Mobility'.
Briggs, M. (1993) 'Russische prostituées vinden Turkse goudkust', *Het Parool*, 18 September 1993.
British All-Party Parliamentary Group on AIDS (1993) *Report of the 1993 Conference of European Parliamentarians on HIV/AIDS*, London.
Bröring, G. (1992) *AIDS Prevention for Tourists: Needs, Possibilities, Restrictions*, presentation at the Fourth International Conference on Tourist Health in Antalya/Turkey.
—— (1993a) *Bilateral Project Poland – Germany: AIDS Prevention for Polish Sex Workers in Berlin – Final Report*, Amsterdam: European Project 'AIDS and Mobility'.

—— (1993b) *AIDS Prevention Activities for Young Tourists in Greece – Report of the Preparatory Visit to Athens, Santorini and Crete*, Amsterdam: European Project 'AIDS and Mobility'.
—— (1993c) *Tourism and AIDS: a Challenge to Health Education*, presentation at the World Congress on Tourist Medicine and Health in Singapore.
—— (1994) *Male Prostitution and Mobility. Report of a Pilot Project Aimed at Young Men from Poland and Rumania Who Engage in Prostitution in Western European Cities*, Amsterdam, European Project 'AIDS and Mobility'.
Bröring, G., and van Duifhuizen, R. (1993) *AIDS and Mobility: International Co-operation in AIDS Prevention Activities for Mobile Populations*, poster presentation at the Ninth International Conference on AIDS, Berlin.
Bröring, G. and de Jong, W. (1993) *Drug Use, Mobility and the Spread of HIV – Report of the Workshop Held in Amsterdam*, Amsterdam: European Project 'AIDS and Mobility'.
Conway, S., Gillies, P. and Slack, R. (1990) *The Health of Travellers*, Nottingham: Department of Public Health Medicine and Epidemiology.
Cossar, J. and Reid, D. (1989) 'Health hazards of international travel', *World Health Statistics Quarterly* 42: 61–9.
Daniels, D., Kell, P. and Nelson, M. (1992) 'Sexual behaviour amongst travellers: a study of genitourinary medicine clinic attenders', *International Journal of STD and AIDS* 3: 437–8.
Duifhuizen, R. van (1994) *AIDS and Mobility Annual Report for 1993 and Working Plan for 1994*, Amsterdam: European Project 'AIDS and Mobility'.
Duifhuizen, R. van and Bröring, G. (1993) *AIDS and Mobility: A Manual for the Implementation of HIV/AIDS Prevention Activities Aimed at Travellers and Migrants*, Amsterdam: European Project 'AIDS and Mobility'.
Duifhuizen, R. van and Cinibulak, K. (1992) *Workshop Report: Workshop on AIDS Prevention Towards the Turkish Population in Europe*, Amsterdam: European Project 'AIDS and Mobility.'
Duifhuizen, R. van and Hendriks, A. (1992) *AIDS and Mobility: the Impact of International Mobility on the Spread of HIV/AIDS*, poster presentation at the Eighth International Conference on AIDS in Amsterdam.
Ford, N. (1990) *A Comparative Analysis of the Socio-Sexual Lifestyles of Workers in the Tourism Industry with Other Young Residents in Devon and Cornwall*, Exeter: Institute of Population Studies University of Exeter.
Ford, N. (1991) *Sex on Holiday: the HIV-Related Sexual Interactions of Young Tourists visiting Torbay*, Occasional Working Paper No. 14, Exeter: Institute of Population Studies, University of Exeter.
Gruer, L., Cowan L., Elliott, L., Farrow, K., Henderson, A. and Sloan, D. (1993) *A Safer Sex Campaign at an International Airport*, poster presentation at the Ninth International Conference on AIDS, Berlin.

Haour-Knipe, M. (1991) *Migrants and Travellers Group. Final Report*, (Assessing Aids prevention. EC concerted action on assessment of AIDS/HIV preventive strategies), Lausanne: Institut Universitaire de Médecine Sociale et Préventive.
Hawkes, S. (1992) 'Travel and HIV/AIDS', *AIDS Care* 4, 4: 446–9.
Hendriks, A. (1991) *AIDS and Mobility – The Impact of International Mobility on the Spread of HIV and the Need and Possibility for AIDS/HIV Prevention Programmes*, Copenhagen: World Health Organisation.
Herold, E., Corbesi, B., Garcia, R. and DeMoya, T. (1992) *Canadian Tourists and Sexual Relationships*, poster presentation at the Eighth International Conference on AIDS in Amsterdam.
Hommes, M. and Vleugel, H. van der (1993) *AIDS and Mobility: Materials for HIV/AIDS Education Aimed at Travellers, Ethnic Minorities and Migrant Communities*, Amsterdam: European Project 'AIDS and Mobility'.
Kleiber, D. (1991) 'AIDS und (Sex-) Tourismus', *Edition AIDS* 11: 1–28, Hanover: Nieders[um]achsisches Sozialministerium.
Kouters, S. (1994) 'Tsjechische jongens werken harder in bed', *Volkskrant*, 7 March.
Mangla, B. (1994) 'Hitching a ride', *WorldAIDS* 31: 11.
Marijnissen, H. (1994) 'Oosteuropese hoerenjongens zijn populair', *Trouw*, 14 February.
Mulhall, B. (1993) 'Sexually transmissible diseases and travel', *British Medical Bulletin* 49, 2: 394–411.
Pearce, P. L. (1982) *The Social Psychology of Tourism*, Oxford: Pergamon.
Reyn, C. von, Mann, J. and Chin, J. (1990) 'International travel and HIV infection', *WHO Bulletin* 68, 251–9.
Sahraoui, D. and Duifhuizen, R. van (1993) *Rapport Final – Premier séminaire sur la prévention du VIH auprès des Maghrébins vivant en Europe: rencontre Euro-Maghrébine*, Amsterdam: European Project 'AIDS and Mobility'.
Schrijver, A. de and Meheus, A. (1989) 'International travel and sexually transmitted diseases', *World Health Statistics Quarterly* 42: 90–9.
Wilke, M. and Kleiber, D. (1992) *Sexual Behaviour of Gay German (sex) Tourists in Thailand*, poster presentation at the Eighth International Conference on AIDS, Amsterdam.

Chapter 14

Interaction to enhance mindfulness
Positive strategies to increase tourists' awareness of HIV and sexual health risks on holiday*

Nicholas Ford, Marlene Inman and Elspeth Mathie

INTRODUCTION

Whilst national mass-media approaches have been widely employed to alert potential tourists to sexual health and, more specifically, HIV/AIDS risks related to travel, relatively little work has been undertaken to bring such issues to the notice of tourists when they are in resort areas. This possible reticence to highlight HIV risk in tourist resorts may well derive from two underlying concerns; first, the obvious commercially based wish not to discourage tourists from visiting particular resorts, and second, an uncertainty relating to whether locality-based, tourism-oriented HIV prevention strategies are feasible, and if so, what form they could take. However, as discussed in Chapter 8, for a subset of tourists at least, the resort environment has a liminal quality which can override the health promotion messages disseminated in their home areas. This chapter discusses one specific HIV prevention/sexual health promotion project which has been designed to have a direct impact upon tourists' sexual practices within a tourist resort environment.

The project has emerged from Torbay Health Authority's long-running concern with developing its work in health promotion, and in particular, HIV prevention, in close relation to the distinctive characteristics of its local environment. A series of AIDS-awareness and sexual lifestyle surveys undertaken by the Institute of Population Studies revealed the high levels of sexual interaction between tourists and locals (Ford 1990a) and seasonal tourism workers (Ford 1990b). Subsequent collaborative projects focused upon tourists' socio-sexual interaction (Ford 1991) and the detailed evaluation of the tourism-oriented intervention project (Mathie and Ford 1993), which is the focus of this chapter. Following a discussion of the problems involved in addressing the sexual health of tourists within resorts, the chapter discusses some potential approaches to promoting 'safer sex' among tourists, and then outlines the design, implementation and partial evaluation of the 'Sea, Sand and Safer Sex' (it was felt that 'sun' could not be guaranteed in the English summer!) Project being conducted in Torbay, England.

PROMOTING THE SEXUAL HEALTH OF TOURISTS IN RESORTS – SOME ISSUES

As noted in Chapter 8, survey findings indicated that although only a minority of young visitors to Torbay engage in sexual intercourse with a new partner on holiday, most of those who do engage in 'unsafe' practices. Evidence for substantial levels of unsafe sexual behaviour associated with the tourist season in the South-West of England was also provided by an audit of the seasonal demand for terminations of pregnancy (TOP) in a Cornish resort (Ford 1990b). This audit revealed clear peaks in the numbers of TOP requests occurring in the months of June and September at the beginning and end of the tourist season. It was felt that the June increase in TOP requests may reflect the arrival of large numbers of tourism industry staff in April and May, and that September reflected levels of sexual activity during July and August, the peak of the tourist season. It must be noted, however, that it is difficult to identify the full scale of sexual health-related problems associated with the tourist season, given that most such visitors will be unaware of any problem until after their return to their home area.

It is the very transience of tourists which makes them a difficult group to target with sexual health promotion. The short, temporary nature of the tourist visit clearly negates the possibility of comprehensive strategies which seek to have a sustained impact upon sexual lifestyles. Such strategies can, of course, be addressed to the resident populations of tourist resorts. However, for tourists in resorts, the most that could be addressed, perhaps, is to ensure easy access to protection (for instance in condom distribution) and to enhance their mindfulness of risk to encourage safety in sexual interactions taking place during the holiday.

It is important to stress that it is probably only a minority of visitors who are likely to be involved in sexual risk-taking on holiday. Given that health promotion resources are necessarily limited, it is useful to consider ways to ensure that efforts are directed to those most at risk rather than spreading information more superficially to the whole population of tourists.

In any given tourism setting the particular groups likely to engage in risky sexual behaviour will depend upon the nature and interaction of the host and source sexual cultures. In different tourist settings variations in tourist/host community sexual interactions will reflect such factors as: sexual orientation, age distribution, gender mix and the incidence of commercial sex work. In the Torbay setting the majority of tourists originate from other parts of the UK, there is relatively little commercial sexual activity, with the highest levels of sexual interaction with new partners on holiday taking place among young people in their late teens and twenties (Ford 1991).

Survey findings highlighted the need to address HIV prevention efforts to that minority of young people who multiply their sexual health risks through both their numbers of sexual partners and non-use of condoms on holiday. However, beyond the broad parameters noted above, it is very difficult to identify this subset of young people in terms of socio-demographic characteristics, except in terms of their patterns of leisure activities. A high level of sexual interaction on holiday was found to be associated with leisure behaviours involving regular frequenting of pubs and nightclubs and associated high levels of alcohol consumption. Thus, the nightlife venues provide a useful focus for the direction of sexual health promotion activities.

THE 'SEA, SAND AND SAFER SEX' PROJECT

In formulating and designing the 'Sea, Sand and Safer Sex' three-year project in Torbay an attempt was made to draw upon and operationalise some major lines of health promotion theory. At a macro level there is a need for the widespread acceptance of 'safer sex' as the social norm. Romer and Hornik (1992) have articulated this in terms of the basic prerequisite of a strong social consensus in favour of 'safer sex', including condom use, such that consistent protective practices are supported by the social environment. Such a macro-level approach supports the need for mass-media-based strategies to promote safer behaviours. However, impersonally disseminated information alone is unlikely to make much impact upon behaviour. Thus there is a need to develop strategies that interact personally with visitors. Furthermore, there is a need to present the information that engages the attention of visitors in ways that blend harmoniously and positively with the holiday experience. There is evidence to show that condom use promotion has greater success when messages are positively expressed (DiClemente *et al.* 1992). Recognition of these factors helped shape the content and format of the nightlife events outlined below.

In order to influence the broad social climate and to engage tourists within the resort personally, a varied programme was implemented using a community-based strategy. Such a strategy involved drawing upon the advice of a wide range of groups and organisations, mobilising social inputs to facilitate tourist contact with the programme, and most importantly, *enabling* the key group – young people – to become actively involved in its development and implementation.

At the core of the 'Sea, Sand and Safer Sex' Project was a commitment to develop and evaluate a peer education strategy. Peer education involves the sharing of information, attitudes or behaviours by people who are not professionally trained educators, but whose goal is none the less to educate (Finn 1981). The terms peer 'educator', 'facilitator' and 'tutor' are often used interchangeably, to refer to someone who is of the same status (in terms of age, occupation or interest) to the audience to be addressed. In this project the peer educators were drawn from the same age ranges as the young tourists frequenting the town's pubs and nightclubs. Peer-based strategies have been used for various health-related programmes, including smoking and drug misuse (Perry *et al.* 1986), alcohol (McKnight and McPherson 1986; Perry *et al.* 1986) and more recently, HIV/AIDS awareness (Rickert *et al.* 1991). A number of sexual health programmes have also worked with peer educators to inform young people but very few of these programmes have been evaluated.

There are a number of rationales for peer education but the main one underpinning this programme concerns the value of peers 'speaking the same language' and being able to relate easily to the youth in the nightclubs. Peer educators can comprise a:

readily accessible forum... for young people to connect easily with persons who will discuss with them, in an open, non-judgmental and supportive fashion the kinds of problems and concerns which are common to both parties of the transaction.

(Carrera 1976: 64)

A peer educator may well have more credibility to challenge or reinforce peer attitudes than, for instance, a 'health education expert', whose life may be perceived as being too far removed from that of youth, to be considered as a useful source of information. A second major reason for following a peer-based strategy is that sexual health promotion workers in the resort have noted the interest in sexual health and HIV-prevention matters shown by many young people, who wish to link up with, and help shape the work being initiated by the health authority. An underlying goal of the peer education training and experience is to assist the empowerment and social skills development of those involved.

Project aims and organisation

The aims of the programme were four-fold:

- to raise public awareness of the dangers of unprotected sexual intercourse in a resort in which, during the holiday season, there is a highly mobile population;
- to promote correct, consistent use of condoms to reduce sexually transmitted infections including HIV, and to reduce the number of unplanned pregnancies and the need for abortion;
- to minimise the harm from intravenous drug use and alcohol misuse;
- to reduce prejudice and stigma around HIV issues and to promote a caring and helpful attitude to those whose lives are affected by HIV/AIDS.

Owing to both the extensive ramifications of HIV/AIDS and the need for a community-based strategy to implement the project, considerable efforts were made to liaise with a wide range of groups and organisations in planning and developing the programme. A general draft of the project was discussed with relevant policy-makers and heads of services one year before the funding was approved. The first step was to identify appropriate people to represent the participating/supporting organisations and agencies, which included:

- Torbay and Plymouth Health Authority
- South Devon Healthcare Trust
- Community Health Council
- Local Education Authority
- Community Education
- college and 'special needs' departments
- language schools
- Local Authority Council, 'Arts and Recreation' and 'Health' Committees
- holiday industry
- Torbay AIDS Support Group
- Body Positive
- Devon AIDS Association
- Institute of Population Studies, University of Exeter
- television, radio and the press.

The overall management team for the 'Sea, Sand and Safer Sex' Project comprised a full-time Project Co-ordinator (appointed with a background in youth work), a part-time Project Manager (HIV/health promotion co-ordinator) linked to the health authority administration, and the steering committee consisting of the range of groups and organisations involved in the project.

The steering committee meets monthly to receive an update on the progress of the project and to give advice and guidance for its development. This has facilitated the smooth implementation of what could be considered by some to be a controversial project. Informing a wide range of organisations about the rationale for an HIV/AIDS project in a resort is vital in allaying fears that such a campaign may have an adverse effect on the resort's image and its promotion by the tourism industry as a safe and desirable destination to visit. The point was stressed that the project should be presented as evidence that project organisers cared about the health of both tourists and local populations.

In the first year of the project the main focus of activities was upon identifying, training and establishing the team of peer educators, developing a core of sexual health/HIV prevention information and materials, and staging a programme of nightlife-oriented health promotion and other awareness-raising events.

A broad overview of these activities is outlined followed by the key findings from the detailed evaluation of the peer-based component. Twenty-four peer educators attended the training residential weekend and an additional nine environmental health students also joined the team of peer educators. Twenty-six of these trained peer educators actually carried out some peer education. Reasons for drop-out included additional work commitments, moving out of the area, and the insuitability of three peer educators (a conclusion reached after the residential weekend).

Following training of youth tutors and the peer educators, the project was launched by the Mayor on 12 June 1993 and events comprised a 'karaoke talent competition' organised in public houses, bars and drinking establishments. Six competitions were held and 'the grand final' was held as part of the 'National Music Weekend' entertainments. The peer educators wore project promotional clothing of a jockey cap, tee-shirt or sweatshirt, all showing the project logo. The karaoke events provided an introduction to the project for both the peer educators and nightlife venues. The peer educators distributed promotional materials and information as well as making condoms freely available. Specific local information was disseminated concerning the whereabouts and times of opening of services for family planning, genito-urinary medicine, addictions, 'clean needle' exchange, HIV/AIDS counselling, and Torbay AIDS Support Group, as well as telephone numbers of local and national helplines.

Throughout the months of June, July and August the peer educators undertook 'safer sex' promotion in nightclubs and bars. In total, twenty-nine 'party-nights' were held. The majority of the nightclubs had four events spread over the three months. The venue disc jockey ran competitions during the early part of the evening before the nightclubs became too noisy. Peer educators circulated amongst the patrons of the venues and engaged them in conversation about the project and also encouraged participation in the competitions. The events were staged in a 'fun/party' atmosphere with balloons and stickers (featuring the 'Sea, Sand and Safer Sex' logo). The competitions in the venues included a 'safer sex' crossword, a word search, poster design and search for an appropriate slogan for the promotion of safer sex. These competitions aimed to raise awareness and improve knowledge of sexual health. Prizes were awarded which had been donated from various local organisations. Leaflets, free condoms and information about sensible alcohol intake and about drug use were available and distributed.

In addition to the events in the nightclubs and bars, ten other events were held. These events included having a trailer van or display at National Environmental Week, Community Care Week, National Music Day activities, Teignmouth Youth Day, Paignton Youth Day, the karaoke rock concert, a music event held at the Place Avenue Theatre, Hollywood Bowl (bowling alley) and two 'Radio One' road shows.

Media attention was achieved through the Project Co-ordinator and the peer educators talking about the project on air at the two road shows. A documentary was filmed for a local television programme. The documentary included interviews with the Mayor, the disc jockeys in the venues, the peer educators, venue owners and other people from the steering committee about their feelings towards and experience of the project. In addition, all the events were publicised in the local newspapers and numerous features and articles were printed. Radio interviews relating to sexual health and holidays were undertaken on local, regional and national stations throughout June, July and August 1993.

Project evaluation

Evaluation of the first year of this project placed emphasis on the experience of the peer educators and other disseminators. Questionnaires were completed by the peer educators at the beginning and end of the project (pre-test and post-test). These questionnaires aimed to identify the peer educators' levels of sexual health knowledge, attitudes and behaviours before and after the project, in order to measure any change. In addition, the peer educators filled in an evaluation questionnaire after the weekend training and also after each event in the nightclub or pub. These feedback questionnaires were useful for gathering information about the practicalities and success of events at each venue and numbers of people spoken to and topics discussed. The venue owners, disc jockeys, bar staff and security staff in each venue also completed a questionnaire at the end of the project to give their views on the project. A short questionnaire was also left out in the venues for the young people in the nightclubs to give their comments.

One of the aims of this health promotion campaign was to raise public awareness of the dangers of unprotected sexual intercourse in Torbay. As outlined above, media interest was attracted to this project, bringing the campaign at least fleetingly to the attention of millions. The project was also advertised in tourist brochures in numerous outlets. From the questionnaires which were filled in by the peer educators (at 80 per cent of the events), it can be calculated that the peer educators spoke to an average of 37.9 people at each event; which makes the estimated total number of people spoken to at least 1,440 young people. This clearly comprises a substantial level of contact/outreach. In addition, the disc jockey in each nightclub publicised the event to the whole audience. The questionnaires also showed that on average the peer educators spent about three and a quarter hours at each event and the average number of peer educators per event was 3.6. Some preferred to make contact in pairs with members of the audience. The estimated total time that the peer educators were available for peer education (as recorded on the questionnaires) was 437 hours.

The peer educators spoke only briefly to some, and in more depth to others, of the young people. The issues that were discussed included the project itself, sexually transmitted diseases, HIV/AIDS, names and addresses of agencies where free condoms and advice could be obtained, and the competitions that were taking place in the venues. The evaluation questionnaire showed that the 77 per cent of the peer educators did not find it difficult to approach people and 89 per cent were not embarrassed to approach people on these matters. Through opportunistic conversations, competitions and quizzes the peer educators passed on information that was of direct relevance to people of their own age group.

The vast majority of the young people (68) (target audience) who completed the evaluation questionnaires gave positive comments about the project. Over two-thirds (64 per cent) of these respondents felt this type of AIDS education to be very useful, one-third (33 per cent) fairly useful, and only two people found it not useful. The young people liked the relaxed manner in which the information was conveyed and also felt it important that the messages were being given in a nightclub/bar and in a tourist setting. It appears that this age group (18 to 30) is still receptive to AIDS education messages. The free condoms were appreciated and all of them were taken on every occasion; one peer educator said he was 'asked for four times the amount we had'. There was also evidence from both the peer educators and the venue staff that the leaflets were being read.

It is important when evaluating the project to consider how far the original objectives were met. The peer educators and the venue staff were asked 'Do you think the "Sea, Sand and Safer Sex" campaign was effective in achieving its aims; raising awareness of HIV/AIDS and sexually transmitted diseases and safer sex?' Forty per cent of the peer educators and 53 per cent of the venue staff felt the project had been very effective, while 60 per cent of the peer educators and 47 per cent of venue staff felt it had been fairly effective. None of the respondents thought it had not been effective.

The peer educators recorded their perceptions of the audience's reactions. They felt the majority (77 per cent) of the young people were fairly (51 per cent) or very (26 per cent) interested in the project and they received a positive response from 79 per cent of the young people. Overall, the events were rated a success by both the peer educators (84 per cent) and the venue staff (94 per cent). The peer educators felt that a number of factors contributed to the success of the events. A successful evening included being able to talk to lots of people, that people were reading the leaflets, and that generally the young people were being responsive. The disc jockey was also a key to the success of the evening in the promotion of the event and competitions, and this varied from venue to venue. It must also be noted that the Project Co-ordinator (who attended all the events) played a vital role in the organisation of the project and in the motivation and support for the peer educators. The events that were less successful were felt to be so largely owing to the audience's lack of interest. This lack of interest was found for instance in one venue in particular, where the clientele were mostly over 30 years old and who felt that the messages were not appropriate to them. Other reasons included not enough publicity about the event before and during the event and also if the music was too loud. In addition, some of the events took place on the same nights as other entertainments, which distracted from the peer education. Sometimes too there were too few people; such as at the leisure centre and the bowling alley. Lastly, the venue staff and peer educators commented that the events should not take place in the venues too often as the same people were being targeted repeatedly.

The pre-test and post-test questionnaires revealed that the peer educators themselves increased their knowledge of sexually transmitted diseases primarily through the training but also through participating in the project. They also became more confident in carrying out peer education and approaching people to discuss HIV/AIDS. The evaluation also showed that by the end of the project the peer educators had themselves developed a more positive attitude to condom use and a stronger commitment to 'safer-sex' practices. Furthermore, they had developed a greater sense of self-efficacy in being able to put protective intentions into practice, such as through being able 'to say no' or insist on condom use in the event of engaging in intercourse. As the project progressed it became evident that some of the peer educators were not as committed to the project as others. This meant that at some of the events there was an under-representation of peer educators. In the second year of the project it has been decided that the peer educators need only commit themselves for one month at a time rather than for the full three months. Young people often have other commitments over the summer months, including summer jobs and holidays.

The evaluation revealed that the peer educators were successful in spreading the safer-sex message to people of their own age and the education was reaching the young people at a time when perhaps they most needed it. The levels of informal discussion about HIV/AIDS issues between the peer educators and friends and parents also increased during the project period, which illustrated the benefits of this type of project for the diffusion of ideas and information to people beyond the immediate target audience.

The detailed monitoring and evaluation of this project is now being used in the refinement of its second year. The peer education will concentrate on those venues that were most successful and where the disc jockeys were most co-operative. The number of events and the day of the event will also be reconsidered in next year's planning as well as efforts to increase publicity (both before and during the event). Next year's training hopes to use the assistance of this year's experienced peer educators and also offer more than one training session, so that more peer educators can attend.

CONCLUSION

This chapter started by emphasising the need for multi-faceted, interactive HIV prevention/sexual health promotion strategies to address tourists when they are actually in the resort environments. It was also noted that limited resources need to be focused upon subsets of the tourist population who are most likely to face potential risks to their sexual health. Conceptually, the health promotion task is essentially one of overcoming the 'liminal' qualities of the holiday experience and resort environment to enhance tourists' mindfulness and ensure consistent protective practices.

The 'Sea, Sand and Safer Sex' Project being implemented in Torbay was described in terms of its development, implementation and evaluation, as a specific type of tourism-focused project. Key elements within the first year of this multi-faceted project included intersectoral collaboration and peer-based interactive strategies. These were seen to revolve around a consistent 'safer sex' promoting message expressed in a positive and fun style. The overall evaluation of the first year of the project indicates that the peer educators were successful in engaging the attention of young people without embarrassment and were well received. This provides a strong vindication of the approach adopted in this innovative project. The young people attending the events appeared to be interested in, and positive towards, the project; and the peer educators managed to talk to a large number of people. Information, advice, leaflets and free condoms were well received by the young people in the pubs and nightclubs. Such nightlife venues do not usually receive health education inputs and yet may comprise particularly appropriate settings for mindfulness-enhancing promotional activities and cues.

Throughout the project, sexual health promotion was presented in a fun, relaxed format. Although small scale, the evaluation of the response of young people in the pubs and nightclubs to the events was very positive. The peer educators themselves and venue staff also overwhelmingly rated the events successful. The process evaluation of the events has produced much valuable information, providing practical guidance for the refinement of the project for the second year of its implementation. Practical lessons have been learned, for instance, concerning such 'nuts and bolts' issues as the precise contents of the peer education training, the requisite number of peer educators, means of sustaining commitment, the optimal frequency of events per venue, costings and logistics, the timing and integration of advance publicity for events, and the crucial motivational role of the project co-ordinator. The peer educators themselves felt that they had been better able to inform themselves and their friends concerning important sexual health matters. Furthermore, as has been observed in other peer-based projects, they also felt that as a result of their experience of the project they had become more confident, assertive and positive in their general attitudes and communication skills. Also they were able to disseminate the ideas concerning 'safer sexual' practices to their friends and relatives after and outside the discrete project events. One of the key benefits of peer educational strategies is that the education continues informally outside the project itself and the ideas are diffused to a wide population beyond the specifically addressed audience. Once again it is important to stress that to seek to influence behaviours, health authorities need to play a facilitating role which unlocks the creativity of sections of the population being addressed to become part of, and carry forward, health promotion activities. A major emphasis in Torbay HIV prevention work has become one of creating a sustained shift in the direction of effort out of the (health authority) offices and into the community.

Based upon the positive evaluation of the first year's peer-based strategy, a similar programme of activities is to be undertaken in the second year. The evaluation of the first year of the project focused primarily upon the training and experience of the peer educators and process feedback in implementation. In the second year of the evaluation, emphasis is to be focused more broadly upon young tourists visiting the resort, to seek to understand more about *their* awareness and perception of the 'Sea, Sand and Safer Sex' Project and to assess whether attendance of events has an identifiable impact upon any sexual practices that may take place.

Whilst the nightlife-oriented events will continue to comprise a major part of the project, some further components are being added for the second year. First, additional efforts are being made to address key subgroups who *may* be of particular vulnerability to HIV infection. Thus two outreach workers have joined the project to work with gay and bisexual men and injecting drug-users. Second, close links have been established with the foreign language schools in the resort to explore ways of making 'safer sex' promotion available to their very substantial numbers (estimated at 125,000 annually) of students. Contact is also expanding with 'special needs' in the community. This outlining of the further development of the 'Sea, Sand and Safer Sex' Project clearly highlights the overlap between tourist-oriented and more locally focused initiatives. Two important attributes of the project described here are: first, that it is managing to address in practical terms the issues of tourism and sexuality without in any way engendering any sense of negativity or stigmatisation; and second, a dynamic, multisectoral, tourism-oriented project has become the vanguard of sexual health promotion in one of the UK's largest resorts.

ACKNOWLEDGEMENTS

The authors would like to acknowledge with gratitude the work of Meryl Basham, the Project Co-ordinator, and the funding assistance from Plymouth and Torbay Health Authority.

NOTE

* This project was awarded first prize in the 'Healthy Alliance' Health of the Nation competition for innovative work in the sexual health and HIV/AIDS category, 1995.

REFERENCES

Carrera, M. (1976) 'Peer group sex information and education', *Journal of Research and Development in Education* 10, 1: 50–5.

DiClemente, R. J., Durbin, M., Siegal, D., Krasnovsky, F., Lazarus, N. and Comacho, T. (1992) 'Determinants of condom use among junior high school students in a minority, inner-city school district', *Paediatrics* 89: 197–202.

Finn, P. (1981) 'Teaching students to be lifelong peer educators', *Health Education* 12: 13–16.

Ford, N. J. (1990a) *AIDS Awareness and Socio-Sexual Lifestyles of Young People in Torbay and District*, Exeter: Institute of Population Studies, University of Exeter.

—— (1990b) *A Comparative Analysis of the Socio-Sexual Lifestyles of Workers in the Tourism Industry with Other Young Residents in Devon and Cornwall*, Exeter: Institute of Population Studies, University of Exeter.

—— (1991) *Sex on Holiday: The HIV-Related Sexual Interaction of Young Tourists Visiting Torbay*, Exeter: Institute of Population Studies, University of Exeter.

Mathie, E. and Ford, N. J. (1993) *Evaluation of the Peer Education Component of the Sea, Sand and Safer Sex Project – Year One*, Exeter: Institute of Population Studies, University of Exeter.

McKnight, A. J. and McPherson, K. (1986) 'Evaluation of peer intervention training and high-school alcohol safety', *Accident Analysis and Prevention* 18, 4: 339–47.

Perry, C. L., Klepp, K. I., Halper, A., Hawkins, K. G. and Murray, D. M. (1986) 'A process evaluation study of peer leaders in health education', *Journal of School Health* 56, 2: 62–7.

Rickert, V. I., Jay, M. S. and Gottlieb, A. (1991) 'Effects of a peer-counselled AIDS education programme on knowledge, attitudes and satisfaction of adolescents', *Journal of Adolescent Health* 12, 1: 38–43.

Romer, D. and Hornik, R. (1992) 'Education for youth: the importance of social consensus in behaviour change', *AIDS Care* 4, 3: 285–303.

General index

accidents 80, 136, 142, 230; and age 38; and alcohol 38
accommodation 60
advertising 202
advice 80–3
Aedes aegypti 97
Aeromonas hydraphila 49
AIDS 12–13, 26, 67–84, 152–75, 179, 183, 184–5, 187; age of sufferers 184; and travel 73–80; control of 192–3; development of 70; distribution of 67, 71–3; education programme 274; impact on tourist destinations 186; number of cases 70; target group 272; testing programme 185; tourist attitudes to 75–6; tourist awareness of 273; tourist risk groups 152; tourist prevention programme for 271
airlines 4
alcohol 16, 74, 80; and sex 169
altitude, effects of 25
anthrax 6

behavioural studies 157
blackwater fever 7
business travellers 78, 210, 231, 273

Campylobacter; and season 49
casual sex, desire for 169
chancroid 70
chemoprophylaxis 3
child sex 190–2
cholera 6, 35, 58, 90, 98

Coccidia 50
collaboration, intersectoral 13, 17, 19, 41
compensatory leisure hypothesis 155
condoms 16, 37, 76–7, 135, 137–8, 146–7, 164, 167, 174, 187, 217, 274, 280, 282–3, 285, 287, 290; and age 122, 167; and gender 75, 77, 78, 79, 80, 84, 147–8; and number of partners 167; frequency of use 189, 270; in hotels 185; non-use 281; use and alcohol 168
consumerism 202
contraception and gender 167
cruises 212
Cryptosporidium 49
cultural tours 92

dehydration 35, 116
dengue fever 90–1, 94, 97–8, 104
decompression sickness 102
diagnosis 7
diarrhoea 13, 28, 35, 44-64 90, 94, 98, 109, 115, 116, 126, 136, 142; and age 31, 51; and prophylaxis 52; and season 51, 53; causative agents 47–50; definition 44; and destination 31–2, 44, 49–51, 53; economic impact of 44; in children 46; nationality 31; prevention of 58–63; symptoms 46;
diptheria 6, 33, 93

diving holidays 91, 92, 96, 100, 102
drug resistance 6, 95, 96, 103
drug use 266, 283
dysentery 6, 24

E. coli 47–9
economic issues 5
ecotourism 92, 96
education 10, 84, 187, 219
Entamoeba histolytica 49
enteroviruses 50
epidemiological studies 26–32
epidemiology 3, 13, 17, 50–2, 57, 69–73, 223, 238, 247,253, 256; and health policy
Escherichia coli 47–8; and destination 48; and season 47
European Community 60, 90, 152, 215, 224
European Project AIDS and Mobility 261–62; and tourism 269–75; current activities 268–69; database 263; documentation service 262; network 263–66; pilot projects 266–68
exercise on holiday 131

female tourists 186
filariasis 7
flying, effects of 34–5
food 35, 58–9, 63
food hygiene 60, 99, 102
food poisoning by ciguatera fish 102

general practitioners 40, 50, 109, 136, 221
Giardia lamblia 49
gonorrhoea 69–70, 134

health advice 8, 34, 41; and travel brochures 224, 225
health and destination areas 92
health behaviour 216
health education 99, 181, 217; evaluation 286; media participation 286; peer educators 282, 285, 287; questionnaire surveys 286
health facilities 100
health information 10
Health of the Nation 218
health promotion 10, 17–18, 129, 235; aims of 236–38; and airlines 266, 273, 275; and chemists 230; at airports 227–28, 275; empowerment 220; equity 220; internationalism 222; interventions 240–42; lifestyle influences 241; national level 230; needs assessment 222; precede procede model 242–43; principles of 219–22; social skills 222; policy 221; primary prevention 240–42; safer sex 228; secondary prevention 240, 242; strategies 290; target groups 237–40; with tour operators 273; with travel agents 230
health protection 33–8
health tourism 199–212; airline concerns 205; and cruises 204–5; as a business 200; data availability 212; in Hawaii 203–4; market development 200; motivation for 200; popular destinations 201
Heathrow 4, 40
hepatitis A 11, 33, 35, 217
hepatitis B 220
HIV 13–14, 18, 37, 40, 67–82, 155, 163, 185, 188–90, 261, 270, 274; effect on resorts 174; impact of mobility 261; perceived vulnerability to 165; prevention of 134–48, 173; prevention coordination 228; role of nightclubs in prevention 174; tourist awareness of 279–92; transmission of 69–71, 261; *see also* AIDS
holiday benefits; and age 129–30; physical 129; spiritual 130
holiday experience questionnaire 114
holiday romance 142; and sex 142

hospital admissions 30; costs of 30–1
hygiene, personal 62, 64

ice 60
illness; and age 27; and destination 28; and lifestyle 29; and season 28;
immunisation 3, 10–12, 32–4, 217
information, sources of 38–41
insurance 5, 34
international tourists, and AIDS 260–76
international travellers 276
intersectoral collaboration 219, 221, 224–25, 227, 290; and primary health care 227; with pharmacists 227; with travel agents 227

laboratory studies 31
Legionnaires disease 27
legislation 58, 60, 90, 180; tourist motivation for 182
leisure time 235
leprosy 101
lifestyle 217, 235

malaria 5–7, 10, 24, 26, 35, 37, 90–1, 93, 94–7, 100–1, 104, 232; preventatives 37, 40
Malta survey 113; and age 113; and gender 113; holiday experiences 113, 127; methodology 113, 115; training of researchers 113
mature traveller market 210
media reports 3, 5–8, 11–12, 90, 95–6
Medical Advisory Service for Travellers Abroad 6
melanoma, deaths from 243, 244; distribution of malignant 243; in New Zealand 249; survival rates 243, 244
missionaries 24
mortality 29
multi-dimensional approach to health education 219

multidisciplinary approach 219
National Health Service 40
Neisseria 69
Norwalk virus 50

paedophiles 190–2; legislation 190–2
pathogens, and destination 31
peer educators 286, 291; activities of 287; responses to 287; success of 288–90
plague, 3–6, 23; economic consequences of 4
Plasmodioum malariae 94
Plasmodium falciparum 5, 7, 26, 94–5, 97, 101
Plasmodium ovale 94
Plasmodium vivax 94
Plesiomonas shigelloides 49
polio 32–3, 35, 50
preventative measures 80
prevention 217
prostitutes 72, 74, 79–80, 145, 181, 183, 189, 262, 266; 269; and health cards 185; and STDs 185; economic effects of 186; female 269; government attitude towards 186; HIV in 185; male 269
protection 217
Providencia alcalifaciens 49
psycho-social studies 157
public health 6, 53, 57–8, 63, 138; monitoring 254

quarantine 24
questionnaires 51–2; postal 226

rabies 96
risk behaviour, and gender 112; and visitors to Thailand 190
risk-taking behaviour 235, 248, 281; influencing 237
Rota virus 50

safe sex 18, 84, 181, 194, 276, 280–81, 285
salmonella 7

General index 297

Salmonella enteritica 48; and season 48
Salmonella typhi 59
sanitation 100–1
schistosomiasis 35
seaside resorts, function of 156; liminal qualities of 279
self-catering 62
serological studies 13, 32–3
sewage 58–60
sex 36–7; and gender 189; sociology of 148
sex industry 17, 79
sex tourism 155, 179–94; and economies 183–4; and government 184–5; definition of 180; financial benefits of 187; in South-East Asia 181–91; media reports 179
sex tourists 79, 135, 188; heterosexual men 188; outbound from Australia 188
sex workers (*see* prostitutes)
sexual activity 110, 112, 138, 156; and condom use 167; and gender 166
sexual attitudes 163
sexual behaviour 73, 77–8, 80, 108, 128, 134, 136, 144, 157, 164, 181, 218, 221–22, 226, 262, 276, 280; behavioural risk factors 145, 146; cultural factors 145
sexual health 230–31; promotion of 280–1
sexual practices 138
sexually active tourists, characteristics of 167
sexually transmitted diseases (STDs) 69, 78–9, 134, 148, 156, 167, 174–5, 182, 184, 186, 190, 217–18, 232, 270, 274, 283, 287; cultural attitudes towards 187; health implications of 187;
Shigella boydii 48
Shigella dysenteriae I 48
Shigella flexneri 48
Shigella sonnei 44–5, 48–9; and children 49

skin cancer 6–7, 17, 36, 127, 218, 221–22, 226, 230, 237; age groups 239; and gender 240, 244;education 239; effect of ozone depletion 246; lifestyle 244, 245; media reports 236; professionals attitudes 247–48; socio-economic groups 239; sun and biological effects 245; tourist perception and target groups 237–40, 246
small group behaviour 169
social access to holidays 207–12; disability 208–11; elderly people 209–11; improving 211–12; positive benefits of 209; special needs 208;
socio-sexual interaction 279
Solomon Islands Tourism Development Plan 100–2
spa tourism 206; in Israel 206; development and marketing of 206–7
spillover leisure hypothesis 155
sun protection programmes 254; implementation 254; intervention 255–56; planning 255
sunbathing, history of 248
sunburn 115, 117, 142, 127, 136, 246; behaviour change, facilitating 251; individual assessment of risk 250–51; knowledge of 246; points of influence 252; role of lifestyle 251; tourist attitudes towards 128, 246, 250, 253
survey, composition of 161; methodology 159
syphilus 69–70

tetanus 33, 232
tour operators 3, 5, 10, 38, 51–2, 59, 101, 104, 215, 221
tourism; and destinations 91; benefits of 158; development 6; ethnographic studies of 156; for medical reasons 205; growth of 1, 15, 24–5, 235; health

implications 99–103; health threats affecting 3–5; social impacts 155; sociology of 14; special interest 15, 89–104; Tourism Council of the South Pacific 91, 100–2
tourists; alcohol consumption by 112, 115, 120, 129, 142, 157, 163, 270, 281; assumptions 8; definition of 154, 199; knowledge of 75, 163; studies of 75, 84, 108–9; transience of 280
Tourist Authority of Thailand 186
tourist behaviour 14–15, 77, 81, 83, 120, 158, 260; and age 122; effect of surroundings 169; positive experiences 116; presence of partner 122, 144; sexual 16 (see also *sexual behaviour*)
tourist drug use 112, 129, 136, 157, 163, 168
tourist health 23–43, 109; and age 109–10; and smoking 109; availability of information 256; health 109; history of 23–4; knowledge of 109; perception of health 126; scope of 157
tourist motivation 91, 111, 154–5, 183
tourist questionnaires 75–6, 78, 109, 112, 135, 160; and control groups 110; factor analysis 123; and gender 140; limitations of 110–11; response rate 139–40
tourist responses to holidays 125
tourist risk behaviour 8
tourists, alcohol and age 110; alcohol and gender 121, 165
transfusions 73
travel, growth of 67; health implications of 25–6
travel agents 10, 38, 41, 101, 104, 215, 221–22; and the provision of health advice 224
travel clinics, UK 220
travel health information 223–25; acquisition of 223; delivery of 223; variables influencing the provision of 223–24
travel health leaflets and posters 227
travel health promotion 215–32; challenges 216–17; definition 217
travel medicine 1–3, 13
travel restrictions 4
travel-related illness, extent of 93–99; information sources 93; surveys of 94
traveller; behaviour 67–9 types 112, 141; and sex 67–9
treatment 11
tropical diseases 24
tuberculosis 101, 202
typhoid 6–7, 11, 35, 58–9, 91, 93, 217

vaccines 11, 40
Vibrio cholerae 49
Vibrio fluvialis 49
Vibrio parahaemolyticus 49

water, potable 35, 49, 53, 58–60
water, sea 36
water quality 100–1
World Health Organisation 5, 32, 58–60, 62, 67, 70–3, 90, 94, 184, 219, 268
World Tourism Organisation 59, 67, 152, 199

yellow fever 24, 217
young persons socio-sexual lifestyles 163

Place index

Afghanistan 6
Albania 265
Albufeira 60
Algeria 265
American states 204
Amsterdam 269
Antilles, The 276
Arad 206
Armenia 265
Asia 1, 47, 49–50, 52, 67, 83, 98,
　103, 180, 220, 230
Asia-Pacific 95, 101, 194
Auckland 93–4, 100
Australasia 68, 71, 83
Australia 51, 90, 93–4, 97, 104,
　179–80, 188–94, 243–4, 252, 254,
　264, 273
Austria 206, 265
Azerbaijan 265

Balearics, The 55
Bali 92, 97
Bangkok 179, 194
Bangladesh 48, 98
Bath 153
Belarus 265
Belgium 6, 265
Benin 265
Berlin 266, 269
Birmingham 39
Black Sea 269
Bombay 4
Botswana 265
Brazil 71, 138, 146

Brighton 156
Bristol 153
Bristol Channel 153
Britain 7, 12, 57, 74, 202, 209,
　230, 252
Brixham 153, 160
Bulgaria 265
Burma 95

Cairns 97–8
California 249
Calcutta 32
Cambodia 95–6
Cameroon 7
Canada 244, 265
Canary Islands 55
Cardiff 153
Caribbean 50, 68, 71
Central Africa 67, 72, 78
Central Asia 68
Central Europe 260–61, 265–66
Channel, The 153
Chile 265
China 98
Cook Islands 104
Copenhagen 143–44, 156
Cornwall 153
Croatia 265
Cyprus 55
Czech Republic 265, 269

Dead Sea 206–7
Denmark 206, 244, 264
Devon 153

Place index

Dominican Republic 53, 55
Doncaster 139
Düsseldorf 275

East Africa 67, 72–3, 78, 261
East Asia 68, 73
Eastern Europe 28, 29, 32, 68, 152, 230, 260–61, 265–65, 269
Edinburgh 224, 269
Egypt 52, 265
England 16, 48–9, 158, 225, 243, 254
Estonia 6, 265
Europe 29, 51–2, 58, 83, 190, 210, 224, 235, 246, 260–61, 266–67, 269, 275
Exeter 228

Far East 52
Fiji 92, 97, 101
Finland 31, 265
Florida 38, 55
France 4, 74, 265, 276
French Polynesia 97

Gambia 8
Georgia 265, 269
Germany 4, 51, 191, 206, 265–66, 274
Ghana 265
Glasgow 26, 29, 30, 39, 224, 228, 275
Glasgow International Airport 228
Gloucestershire 229
Gozo 156
Greece 265, 268–69, 275
Greek Islands 271
Guadacanal 96, 100

Hackney 269
Harley Street 205
Hawaii 17, 201–4, 212
Heathrow Airport 4, 40
Honiara 96
Honduras 50
Hong Kong 98, 265
Hungary 265

Iceland 265
India 3–6, 67, 72, 98, 265, 276
Indonesia 92, 265
Irish Republic 205, 265
Israel 17, 201, 206–7, 212, 265
Italy 4, 265

Japan 190, 265

Kazakhstan 265
Kenya 5, 55–6, 155
Kirghizia 265
Korea 75, 182
Kuwait 265

Latvia 265
Lauvi Lagoon 106
Leuven 269
Liechtenstein 265
Lithuania 265
Liverpool 39
London 70, 75–8, 275
Luxembourg 265

Macedonia 265
Malta 15, 55, 108–32, 265
Malaysia 92, 97–8
Manchester 39
Mediterranean, The 15, 18, 29, 51
Mexico 47, 51–2, 265
Mexico City 51
Middle East 68, 73
Moldavia 265
Monaco 265
Moscow 6
Morocco 47–51, 265

Nepal 98, 265
Netherlands, The 244, 262, 265, 275–76
New Caledonia 97
New Dehli 4
Newquay 153
Newton Abbot 153
New Zealand 90, 93–4, 97, 99, 104, 190–92, 249
Nigeria 265
North Africa 28–9, 32, 68, 73
North America 51, 58, 67–8, 71, 83

Place index

North Carolina 111
Northern Europe 29, 52
Northern Ireland 225
Northern Queensland 97
Norway 265
Nottingham 77, 135–48

Paisley 8
Pacific 1, 16, 68, 73, 89–90, 103, 203
Paignton 160, 286
Pailin region 96
Panama 24
Papua New Guinea 96
Pattaya 80, 186
Penzance 153
Philippines, The 155, 180, 182, 265
Plymouth 153
Poland 6, 265–66, 269
Portugal 48, 55, 265
Prague 266
Pune 72

Qatar 265
Queensland 98, 243

Rajastan 5
Rarotonga 104
Rhodes 23
Rockhampton 98
Romania 27, 265–66, 269
Russia 33, 93, 265

St Petersburg 49
Sahulu Island 100
Salou 53, 59, 61
San Marino 265
Santorini 267
Scandinavia 57
Scotland 24, 26–7, 31, 39, 51, 110, 225, 244, 254
Sea of Galilee 206
Serbia 265
Siberia 6
Singapore 93, 97–8
Slovakia 265
Slovenia 265
Solomon Islands 92, 96, 98, 101
South Africa 78, 145, 265
South America 51, 98

South Asia 30, 67, 72, 179
South Pacific 15, 89–91, 99–100, 102
South-East Asia 1, 15–17, 49, 67, 72, 78, 89–91, 94, 97, 102, 179–88, 189
South-West England 152–75, 279–92
South-West Pacific 89
Southern Europe 29, 48, 52, 269
Soviet Union 6
Spain 27, 30, 55–6, 141, 219, 265
Strasbourg 269
Sub-Saharan Africa 67, 71–2
Sudan 265
Syria 265
Sweden 48, 191, 265
Switzerland 4, 51, 57, 265

Tadjikstan 265
Tanzania 265
Tarragona 53
Teignmouth 286
Thai-Burma border 96
Thailand 49–51, 67, 72, 78, 92, 95–6, 98, 155, 180, 182–88, 189–90, 265
Torbay 16, 18, 111, 152–75, 274, 279–92
Torquay 160
Totnes 153
Townsville 97
Trinidad 265
Tropical Africa 53
Truro 153
Tunisia 51, 55–6, 265
Turkey 52, 55, 265, 269
Turkmenistan 265

Ukraine 93, 265
United Kingdom 14, 17, 24–6, 30–1, 33, 37, 49, 52, 67, 69, 77, 134, 147, 218, 221, 224, 226, 229, 231–2, 235, 239, 244, 246, 264–5, 273–41, 276, 292

USSR 6, 32
United States of America 34, 71, 180, 190, 224, 265

Utrecht 261

Vanuatu 92, 96–7, 101
Venice 23

Wales 49, 153, 225
Weather Coast 100–1

West Africa 5, 7–8, 24, 276
Western Europe 68, 71, 180, 261, 269
Weymouth 153

Zambia 265

For Product Safety Concerns and Information please contact our EU representative GPSR@taylorandfrancis.com
Taylor & Francis Verlag GmbH, Kaufingerstraße 24, 80331 München, Germany

www.ingramcontent.com/pod-product-compliance
Lightning Source LLC
Chambersburg PA
CBHW050551170426
43201CB00011B/1659